WHISPERING
IN THE GIANT'S EAR

By the same author
Blue Clay People

WHISPERING IN THE GIANT'S EAR

A Frontline Chronicle from Bolivia's War on Globalization

William Powers

BLOOMSBURY

Photograph on p. vii by Barbara Riester

Published by Bloomsbury Publishing, New York and London
Distributed to the trade by Holtzbrinck Publishers

All papers used by Bloomsbury Publishing are natural, recyclable
products made from wood grown in well-managed forests. The
manufacturing processes conform to the environmental regulations of
the country of origin.

Library of Congress Cataloging-in-Publication Data

Powers, William, 1971–
Whispering in the giant's ear : a frontline chronicle from Bolivia's war
on globalization / William Powers.—1st U.S. ed.
p. cm.
Includes bibliographical references.
ISBN-13: 978-1-59691-103-1 (pbk. : alk. paper)
ISBN-10: 1-59691-103-4 (pbk. : alk. paper)
1. Sustainable development—Bolivia. 2. Indians of South
America—Bolivia—Government relations. 3. Globalization—
Economic aspects—Bolivia. 4. Globalization—Social aspects—
Bolivia. 5. Powers, William, 1971– I. Title.
HC185.E5P69 2006
984.05'2—dc22
2005032037

First U.S. Edition 2006

1 3 5 7 9 10 8 6 4 2

Typeset by Westchester Book Group
Printed in the United States of America
by Quebecor World Fairfield

CONTENTS

In memory of the Guarasug'wé people

Map 1: Bolivia

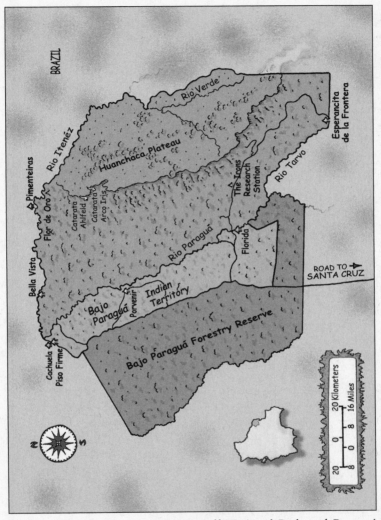

Map 2: The Amazon Project (Kempff National Park and Paraguá
Indian Territory)

AUTHOR'S NOTE

Bolivia has long been Oblivia. Dubbed the Tibet of South America, the landlocked South American nation has been on the radar of only the most intrepid of outsiders. A Cold War rumor had it that Bolivia was the ideal place to lie low in a nuclear war; since the country had no strategic importance, neither side would blow it to bits.

That's all changed. Over the past few years Bolivia has become a world flashpoint because of its Indian war on globalization. The mainstream media, from CNN to the *New York Times,* have headlined Aymara women in derbies and layer-cake skirts standing down tanks. Indigenous protests have ousted giant multinationals and two pro-globalization presidents and are on the verge, five centuries after conquest, of establishing the hemisphere's first Indian government.

I lived in Bolivia from 2001 to 2005, in the midst of these historic changes. This book, then, aims to bring to life our long-obscure and increasingly important South American neighbor through a blend of memoir, travel, history, and on-the-ground reportage.

Though I range landscapes, disciplines, and characters, central to the story is my unfolding relationship with a single Amazon Indian, Salvador, who rises from backwater obscurity to national leadership. Salvador links the book's three main narratives: an Amazon tribe struggling to survive; a nation overcoming oppression and constructing an identity; and a global community pioneering a new green globalization, through the world's largest Kyoto Protocol rainforest experiment.

Bolivia is one of the world's ten "megadiverse" countries, almost five times the size of Great Britain but with only nine million people under its snowcapped Andes and rainforest canopies. Its majority Quechua, Aymara, and Guarani cultures buck modern trends of monotony like single-use zoning and total quality management. The price of Bolivia's wholeness, if you will, rises in a fragmented world. For the first time in history, economically poor but ecologically rich countries such as Bolivia might thrive as what I call "natural nations" largely through producing certified timber, ecotourism, and carbon ranching, and cultural services such as alpaca and llama products, native weavings, and ethnotourism. At stake in Bolivia, then, is a healthy alternative to McWorld: a "green globalization" that provides flourishing nature and culture to a world that is in want of it.

While a work of nonfiction, this book takes the sort of poetic license inherent to such accounts. All places, events, and people are real. However, some of the folks you'll meet have experienced grafting either to reduce the number of people coming on and off stage (a particular community member may be a composite of two); telescope chronology (four years is a long time, and this no daily journal); or protect privacy.

Those desiring only the strictest adherence to data, statistics, and wickedly precise chronology might consult my analysis of the Amazon Project in the technical book *Biodiversity: The Richness of Bolivia* or one of my conference articles. No? Now how did I know that?

In the end, I seek as much to evoke as to explain. I've kept things rather personal so that readers might more enjoyably explore a country that is not located someplace else, but is rapidly becoming another place.

PART I
The Shimmering Forest

CHAPTER 1

I MET SALVADOR the day the dead jaguar rolled into town. The enormous cat lies in the hatch of the bus that passes weekly through this Amazonian village in northeast Bolivia. It's seven A.M., and the sun has just cracked the tips of the jungle canopy. Leaning over some children gathered around the bus, I reach out to stroke the jaguar but immediately recoil from its sleek, spotted coat. It feels *alive,* as if just dozing. A moment passes without a twitch, and I squeeze in among the children and take hold of a paw that overwhelms my palm. I part the cat's lips and slide my finger over its teeth. A scent rises up from the jaguar that's nothing like death; it exhales a fertile wildness, something like a decomposing log reborn as fern and fungus, grubs and grass.

This hamlet, no more than a hundred thatched houses surrounding a jungle clearing, takes the name Porvenir: the Future. The Chiquitano Indians who live here begin to gather in a second half-moon around the small children and me, and the grumbling begins. *The jaguar should stay here in Porvenir.*

One of the Indians confronts the bus driver, a light-skinned urbanite with a thick mustache. "You slammed the jaguar with your bus."

"It jumped in front of me!" the driver responds defensively.

Silence. The New Yorker in me awaits the inevitable counterpunch, but none comes, despite the fact that the Chiquitanos outnumber the driver fifty to one. There's Ximén and Sebastián and dozens of other villagers I've met on this, my first, visit to the Indian Territory. Smirking at the very back of the crowd is the tiny Gaspar, an older chief from the next village over, who's already nursing his first beer of the day; Gaspar has been tipsy since I arrived. Finally, one of the Indians mutters that "obviously" the jaguar was blinded by the bus headlights, and the driver whapped the big cat on purpose. Everyone gathered knows that a jaguar's fur is worth a small fortune upriver in Brazil.

"Speak up!" the driver demands of the Chiquitano.

"The jaguar was killed on our lands," he mutters even more quietly, staring at his feet.

The bus driver strokes his mustache as if considering this but then suddenly spits on the ground and says definitively, "The jaguar is *mine*." He slams his hatch shut, shoves the Indians aside, climbs behind the wheel, and maneuvers his machine across the grassy field. Everyone seems paralyzed. The bus is swallowed into a dark tunnel of rainforest, and the clearing is once again silent.

Over a breakfast of steaming *surubí,* a tasty river fish, I listen to the complaining of the villagers, minced with hints of what you might call anger, but these sentiments lapse into resignation: *That's just the way it is. Outsiders have always robbed us. And, besides, there are plenty of jaguars.*

I realize what I'm up against. The first step in my new job is to *concienciar* or raise consciousness among two thousand Indians living in seven isolated communities. The word *concienciar* involves both being aware of exploitation, which these folks certainly are, and gaining the confidence and power to do something about it—a thoroughly daunting task.

Salvador missed the jaguar incident. In his role as overall paramount chief of the seven chiefs representing each of the villages in which I'm to work, he was away in the municipal capital pleading the case for an Indian Territory. Back in his simple adobe home now, he's hunched over a bowl of *charque* and seems so exhausted I fear his round face could flop right into the food. When we arrived here at his house together— he'd tracked me down and invited me to dinner—three of his five young children bolted over and wrapped him in hugs. His wife, considered to be the most beautiful in Porvenir, kissed him, but she wasn't smiling. I detected annoyance; Salvador has been working so much recently that he's rarely home.

Dinner begins to perk him up. His posture straightens and he smiles, revealing a front incisor ringed in gold. The sun angles low through the window, and his eyes narrow as he looks at me: "You could use a bath."

Soap and towel in hand, we head toward the river together, but soon find ourselves in the midst of a pack of villagers. They accumulate in our wake, each trying to nudge closer to Salvador. He asks them about their families and health. We're walking toward the setting sun and are nearly into the jungle when we finally stop, weighed down with Salvador's fans. They're eager for him to speak. He throws his towel over his shoulder and obliges, beginning in a deep baritone: "We need a house to live in, not so?"

Everyone agrees, but in a puzzling way: their collective affirmation comes out as a sigh as lethargic as the dripping jungles around us.

"*This* is our home," Salvador says, the sweep of his hand taking in the rainforest, and traces in simple Spanish his progress marking the Indian Territory boundaries, securing free legal help, and lobbying officials. He says that they are advancing toward their goal: a permanent, indivisible Indian Territory for their children and children's children. "After so much slavery, we'll have a homeland."

Instead of watching Salvador, I focus on the reflective faces of his listeners. I know the statistics: fifty percent have malaria; eighty percent are unemployed. Was the person who named the village Porvenir joking? The hamlet is a human sore festering on a smooth rainforest skin. Allowing my gaze to drift

5

over the heads of the listeners—who are all shorter than me, matching Salvador's five feet ten inches at the very tallest—I take in the graffiti-covered billiard hall; the families crammed into mud huts; an old man winding strips of rubber he's harvested from the jungle into misshapen balls to sell to tourists—of which there are none. As weak as they are, these Indians have repeatedly been recruited into the grunt work of the global economy: tappers in the Rubber Era; mules in the Cocaine Era; and now the first rumors of loggers up the road.

By the time Salvador and I finally get into the river, the sun has set. We've lathered and rinsed in the warm water, and he's floating a few feet from me with only his large toes, chubby middle, and face breaking the water's surface. His appearance recalls the Marlon Brando character in *Apocalypse Now*—the fleshy body, almost imperceptibly stooped shoulders, strong nose, generous lips, a bit jowly. He's staring up at the tree canopy above and into broken patches of night sky, one of them cradling a harvest moon, and I'm thinking about his listeners' receptive faces; reactive, receiving information from Salvador. Has the landscape shaped them as victims? Above our heads is a sultry tangle of lianas, creepers, hemiepiphytes, and vines enfolding some of the highest diversity of life on earth—and an equal proportion of death. The place doesn't exactly lend itself to human ambition.

When I told a cynical acquaintance back in Santa Cruz, the Amazonian boomtown where I live, he likened my new job to "preaching heterosexuality in a gay bar." Mission: absurd. Probably get laughed out of the place. He went on to say that Bolivian Indians have been abused so long that "they see themselves as victims and have no idea how to resist." And their main oppressors, oddly enough, are other Bolivians.

You might say that Bolivia has colonized itself. When the Spanish Empire closed shop here in 1825, the Europeans who stayed on didn't seem to notice—and still don't. Even within Latin America, the world's most unequal region according to the World Bank, Bolivia is considered one of the most corrupt, per Transparency International's annual index of political dishonesty. It's also divided along a razor-sharp racial edge.

Highland and Amazon peoples compose almost two thirds of Bolivia's population, the highest proportion of Indians in the hemisphere. It's as if the United States had 160 million Apaches, Hopis, and Iroquois. And while native leaders like Salvador are no longer forcibly sprayed for lice with DDT before meetings with government officials and are today allowed into town squares, Bolivia's pigmentocracy continues. Indians are barred from some swimming pools; they are still *peónes*, or virtual slaves, on haciendas, such as the four hundred Guarani families reported as captive in Alto Parapetí and Wuacarteta. Their ancestral lands have been sold by corrupt officials to timber and mining companies. If North Americans enslaved people, South Americans enslaved the land—and its people in the bargain. Indians have historically been "organic" to the land, legalese for being no different from tree, vine, stone, and jaguar.

And the ruling whites governed with a singular mix of incompetence and buffoonery. Bolivia has never won a war. The oligarchy let Chile, Brazil, and Paraguay gobble up *half* of Bolivia's original territory. One particularly craven Liberal Party dictator, as Bolivians will resentfully tell you, in 1903 put down a map of his country on the ground and declared that he'd give Brazil the area under his horse's hoof. The horse stomped on Bolivia's Arce state, which was subsequently carved off and is to this day part of Brazil. And when the increasingly inbred oligarchs weren't busy handing over their *patria,* they liked nothing better than overthrowing one other. Indeed, from 1825 to its transition to democracy in 1982, Bolivia witnessed 188 coups.

"I heard about the jaguar," Salvador says in his baritone voice. He's rolled his paunchy body out of his float and has sunk his feet into the muddy riverbed, his upper half dissolved in a moon shadow. "That's the last jaguar anyone will take. Everything in this acre around us," he says, making a circle on the water with his finger, "is *ours*."

An urgent squawk of parrots punctuates this, breaking the persistent *riiiii-riiiii* of forest insects. "The *acres* are ours," he repeats, handling the word *acres* with care, as if it might break. Again he's forming circles with his fingers, and I feel uneasy, since my idea of an acre is square. Does Salvador imagine them elliptically, like stones dropped in pool? I'm wondering how many jaguars live in each circular acre, and whether they are owned or free. And I'm wondering whether little Gaspar is drunk again, and how Salvador made the decision not to drink himself into a cozy forgetfulness. How here, in the most languid of places on earth, did he decide to fight back?

CHAPTER 2

"I CAN'T BELIEVE all this is *ours*," says a representative from one of our corporate investing partners. We're looking down from a Cessna over high jungle, having just lifted off from Salvador's Porvenir.

"Actually, this is still the Indian Territory," I say, as diplomatically as I can muster. "On the other side of the river, that's . . . '*yours*.'"

He nods slightly, enraptured by the view as we cross the Paraguá into the marvelous Kempff National Park. Stretching out to the horizon below, trees bursting in pink or lavender intersperse with the forest's dozens of shades of green. We're flying fairly low, so I squint to spot some of the park's mammals: tapirs, red brocket deer, silvery marmosets, pumas, maned wolves, and giant anteaters. One tenth of the world's remaining thousand giant river otters live in the park's waterways, alongside capybaras, freshwater dolphins, and black and spectacled caiman. Kempff is one of the largest undisturbed wilderness areas in the neotropics—including the biggest piece of virgin cerrado habitat left on earth.

Off to our right fly two other Cessnas. All told, we're an eclectic delegation of twelve, including Nature Conservancy and local conservationists; Bolivian government officials; and VIPs from three energy firms: British Petroleum (BP), Pacific-Corps, and the largest supplier of electricity in the United States, American Electric Power (AEP). We've just finished our annual board meeting in a five-star-hotel conference room in Santa Cruz and are off for a little romp in the woods.

9

Behind the BP representative and me sits Frederico, a thirty-seven-year-old Bolivian forestry engineer and Kempff's director. He leans forward and exclaims over the engine, "These are your carbon credits!" Frederico is talking about the trees.

I translate it to the BP guy, who flashes me a look that says, "No shit, Sherlock." The companies know quite well they've invested millions to buy up several logging concessions below, doubling Kempff to an amazing three million acres, and launching it to United Nations World Heritage status. Instead of being bucked, corner-nipped, and slabbed, the trees will be left wild to absorb the greenhouse gases causing global warming. It's a writ-large version of the United States' 1980s cap-and-trade arrangement that successfully reduced chlorofluorocarbons and repaired part of the ozone hole. Under the much grander Kyoto Protocol on Climate Change, multinationals can earn "tradable credits" to offset their emissions reductions requirements. Bolivia, as host country, gets forty-nine percent of the credit value; the Indians receive investment through sustainable development projects and, hopefully, their ancestral lands; and the giant river otter narrowly averts extinction.

Perhaps most remarkably, traditional opponents—Amazon Indians and corporate energy titans—are protecting the area together. These perennial foes are now bedfellows. Well, almost.

Back in Porvenir before we'd departed, I saw Salvador bent over another villager seated in a rattan chair. Even from a distance the villager's face looked swollen, and I hustled over to a sight far worse than I anticipated. The young man's face was vaguely purple and paralyzed with an enormous, festering insect bite under the cheekbone.

"He needs to get to a hospital," I told Salvador, who asked me if I had any suggestions.

I sounded an idea off my Bolivian colleagues: What about an emergency evacuation with one of the Cessnas? Impossible,

they said. We feel for the guy, but the VIPs are on tight sched-
ules, and we need all three planes. The subtext: *the plane's not
for Indians.* The best I could do was take up a collection; I
tried to press a wad of Bolivian bills into the man's palm, but
he refused it, embarrassed. Salvador accepted the money and
promised to try to find him a spot in a cargo truck out of the
Territory.

I'm wading out toward Ahlfeld Falls. Our planes landed yesterday at Kempff's remote, luxurious Golden Flower Lodge,
and today we made it here via a six-hour motorized canoe ride
up a log-choked tributary of the Iténez River, which separates
Bolivia from Brazil.

With me are Rick and Julia, two fiftysomething executives
from the Arlington headquarters of the Nature Conservancy,
the world's largest conservation group. The three of us are
wading into a pool ringed with lush rainforest vegetation. A
deluge of water cascades over the fifty-five-meter headwall
into the basin, filling the amphitheater with wispy breezes.
Julia is the first to notice a particularly marvelous sight: yellow birds dip into a fissure behind the falls, where they nest
in crevices. From our angle, a good thirty meters away, they
seem to plunge straight through the block of water. But Rick
says it's an optical illusion; they actually thread themselves
through air pockets.

We've treaded out into the water, but are wary of the falls. A
Brazilian adventurer was recently swallowed by a rip here and
drowned. We keep our distance. Crisp wavelets lap against
our cheeks as Rick says, "When I first visited Kempff a decade
ago, there was nothing here. *Nada.* Can you believe what we've
built!"

I look around and see no handiwork of toolmaking bipeds.
It's God's country, the beating heart of an authentic wilderness; we are the only humans in a territory of *thousands* of

square miles. This waterfall is one of twenty cascading off one of Kempff's most impressive geographical features: the Huanchaca Plateau, a sandstone escarpment rising eighteen hundred feet above the surrounding plain. The plateau inspired Sir Arthur Conan Doyle's *The Lost World*, which he based on Percy Fawcett's 1910 Huanchaca expedition notes.

Rick continues, "Nope, there was nothing here. We created Golden Flower Lodge, put in the trails, purchased the boats that get you back here."

"It's spectacular," Julia says. She's a strikingly handsome woman who made millions in the Internet boom before joining the Conservancy. "I'm just thrilled to be out of the conference room. *This* is where it is all happening. You know, I think we've finally got the economics right."

What is a pristine rainforest worth? How about fresh air? Clean water? They are worth an infinite amount—and nothing. Infinite in the aesthetic, spiritual sense. I have as difficult a time, personally, putting a number value on a rainforest as I would putting a price tag on my mother. How much are your children worth to you? Some things have an intrinsic value that is priceless. But the free market alone, its invisible hand unbound, assigns no value to ecosystem services—phenomena like the ozone layer filtering cancer-causing ultraviolet rays; a forest spewing out oxygen; a healthy river acting as a watershed.

The grandest of all ecosystem services, regulation of our entire planet's climate, is broken. A broad scientific consensus that includes 153 Nobel Prize scientists says that human activity is causing dangerous global climate change. Many scientists believe that we have a twenty-year window to prevent widespread impacts on our lives. Rising temperatures allow invasive species and diseases to spread northward, much as dengue fever has spread to southern Texas and appears headed for Tucson. Polar-ice melt will cause a one- to three-foot rise in sea level by the end of the century—sufficient for a storm surge to flood low-lying coasts in Florida, Louisiana, and other U.S. states. As Columbia University geochemist Wallace Broecker put it, "Climate is an angry beast, and we are poking it with sticks."

The Kyoto agreement, signed in that Japanese city in 1998 and since ratified by 189 countries, seeks to incorporate climate maintenance into free market decisions. A series of pilot experiments have been set in motion to put Kyoto into practice, including the conservation of pristine rainforests to sponge carbon dioxide from the atmosphere. Ours is the largest such Kyoto experiment in the world.

The three energy companies we are with find themselves faced with a choice of two options under Kyoto: they can reduce their greenhouse-gas emissions (e.g., through cleaner technology, such as switching to solar) or they can increase the planet's capacity to absorb greenhouse gases (e.g., through conserving trees that would have been cut down or planting new ones). Some people feel a certain ambivalence about this idea, if not downright anger. After all, shouldn't these industrial giants have to reduce their emissions, rather than continuing to rampantly pollute while buying off swaths of the third world to sequester carbon dioxide? There is a surprisingly logical answer to this: they *do* have to reduce emissions as well. Under the Kyoto Protocol, only 25 percent of credits for greenhouse-gas reduction can be achieved through "green" activities (such as tree planting or reducing deforestation) while 75 percent must be earned through "brown" activities (such as switching coal power sources over to cleaner coal, or solar). These percentages correspond to the sources of climate change: 25 percent comes from deforestation ("green" sources) while 75 percent comes from emissions, as from cars and factories ("brown" sources). So, in the end, the proportions are right.

But then there's something even more important here: What would happen if the Amazon Project *did not* exist? What if the global community decided to address global warming only through brown activities? The existence value of this massive forest would plummet to nothing. Its value would be that of its clear-cut-timber and cattle-pasture potential. But with the project, it is worth millions of dollars a year simply to exist. And because the protocol requires not only global-warming mitigation, but makes two additional demands—sustainable development and biodiversity benefits—part of the funds are helping Salvador's people organize themselves, obtain ownership over their land, and develop ecologically sustainable business on it. If ever there was a win-win situation, this appears to be it.

Later that evening, back at our camp near the falls, the talk is euphoric. In time, I would come to look back on this trip as the early days of the revolution. There is a sense that we are ecological pioneers, at the vanguard of a radical green globalization. The multinational-company representatives are as genuinely fired up to make this work as the tree huggers. Phrases like "internalize externalities" and "prices reflect true environmental costs" are tossed back and forth over the campfire, as Che Guevara and Tamara Bunke once tossed their very different revolutionary terms over other Bolivian fires. An AEP representative says that because of this, her grandchildren may still have a chance to do what we're doing now: camp in a pristine tropical forest. "Rainforests are disappearing at an acre a minute around the world, but not here they're not," she says. "Not if I can do something about it!"

As the peace of the Amazonian night settles around us, the fires crackle out, and we are all in our sleeping bags listening to the jungle or slipping into dreams, I sense that the rainforests around us continue to work 24-7. They suck threatening carbon dioxide out of the air and spew forth the oxygen that could save the planet; they shelter endangered species; and they act as a bulwark between an ecocidal and genocidal globalization and Salvador's Chiquitano Indian people. As I drift off to sleep, the peace I feel seems like world peace.

But the next morning I'm having one of my postmodern moments.

We're halfway back along the river to Golden Flower Lodge and the airstrip, and we've cut the canoe engines to photograph an enormous black turtle sunning on the bank amid a flurry of yellow and red butterflies. Everyone's been so perky about the Amazon Project that I've instinctively gone on guard. At thirty-two, I'm the youngest in the group and have partly been shaped by my generation's peculiar skepticism. What if this experiment is just another throwback to the Enlightenment, that grand attempt to demystify and secularize, to subject natural forces to rational control and promote human happiness?

I'm fond of Goya's sketch of an Enlightenment social planner dozing off at his desk. A ghoul-studded extravaganza of cruelty swirls in his dreams, giving the lie to the well-ordered plans he's drafted. The illustration's caption reads, *The sleep of reason begets monsters*. Indeed, the Enlightenment is awash, and we needed neither Goya nor *de jour* postmodernists to tell us so. Utopianism was shattered, as Ruggie puts it, "By Nietzsche, Freud, Wittgenstein; Darwin, Einstein, Heisenberg; Braque, Picasso, Duchamp; Joyce, Proust, Beckett; Schoenberg, Berg, Bartók; two world wars, a Great Depression, Nazi death camps, Stalin's gulags, Hiroshima and Nagasaki" long before Lyotard, Foucault, and Derrida pronounced and relished in its demise.

But for now I shake off these doubts, reminding myself that I came here precisely *because* the Amazon Project is quintessentially anti-utopian. This enterprise uses reason only to adjust free market incentives and then gives human tinkering a backseat to nature. This is three million acres left to revert to the beautiful anarchy of wilderness. These are Goya's monsters unrepressed. It's enough to make even Nietzsche feel warm and fuzzy.

We've left the dizzying oxbows of the Ahlfeld tributary and

are motoring up the wide Iténez, turtles and butterflies long behind us. A thin fog has fallen over the river, but we do spot a family of capybaras, the world's largest rodent and found only in the Amazon, crossing in front of us, a line of five—the two parents and three little ones. They panic. Daddy dives under and swims to the Brazilian side, and mommy dog-paddles it back to Bolivia, her youngsters in tow. And the fog certainly can't shroud Kempff's colorful birdlife—harpy eagles, Amazonian umbrella birds, hoatzins, and parrots.

In one of the rare gaps in wildlife sightings, the AEP representative, Jim, muses aloud, "That guy back in the village with the face thing—was that contagious?"

"Isn't that a pink river dolphin?" asks Julia, and Jim's query passes quickly, but I catch it as the first time anyone has mentioned the Indians, though they are the key to the experiment's success. Sure, we've finally got the incentives right, but this Amazon reserve is woven into the fabric of a nation headed for a great social convulsion. Bolivia has been internally colonized for so long that it's impossible to know what it might become when pent-up Indian energy is unleashed. Bolivia's very identity as a nation is up for grabs. Waltzer got it right when he said that a nation is invisible and "must be personified before it can be seen, symbolized before it can be loved, imagined before it can be conceived." I grip the canoe's gunwale as we lean into a wide turn, eager to be here for the birth.

CHAPTER 3

Several months earlier, La Paz, Bolivia

T HERE'S A JOB in the Amazon," Anaí says, flopping onto my office sofa with her briefcase and throwing one bare leg on the cushion. "You'd be perfect for it."

Anaí (pronounced Ana-EE) has been acting like this lately. Gets right to the point. Neglects even the Bolivian *hola* and cheek kiss. And she's caught me red-handed with my chair swiveled toward the window. I'd been daydreaming, staring out at Bolivia's most famous Andean peak, Mount Illimani. But my view is actually a reflection of the mountain in the mirrored office tower across from mine. I find myself, disturbingly, twice removed from Illimani, neither climbing it nor looking at it, but rather gazing into its metallic blue image.

"I've already got a job," I say.

Anaí shakes her head. "Not like this one. It's the world's largest Kyoto experiment. If it works, it'll be replicated in dozens of countries. Everyone's watching."

Big deal. I'm certainly not job hunting. My employer, a large international aid agency, has transferred me from West Africa to Bolivia, where I've secured two promotions within a year, to deputy country director, a tenured notch on the managerial track. But Anaí gets up and paces my office, talking animatedly about Indians, rainforests, global warming, "new fibers grafted into the global economy," and "part of the revolution." Excitement begins to rise in me as she describes the job, but it's immediately dampened by doubt—Anaí wants to get rid of me. Or at least she doesn't seem to care if I leave La Paz to move to the polar opposite side of Bolivia.

Anaí and I met a year ago in a Latin-dance class in La Paz. She came with a mutual friend. After an hour of the awkward salsa turns, Anaí and I sat down and ordered *mojitos cubanos*. I learned that she was an overachiever, with both business and engineering degrees from the best university in Buenos Aires. Though barely thirty, she was a lead climate-change negotiator for the Bolivian government.

Then Anaí told me she was a turtle in her past life. She wanted to use her professional training to heal humanity's relationship with Pacha Mama, or mother earth, and that was why she'd gone against her father's wishes that she use her expensive skill set ("that *he* paid for, as he loves to remind me") to make a fortune in the private sector. Anaí told me that when she gazes up at La Paz's peaks—Illimani, Murorata, Huayna Potosi—she sees them in the Indian sense, as closer to the spiritual realm than lower points. Her sibilant Spanish sounded a bit Aymaran. Despite hailing from wealth, Anaí was proud to be mestiza. "I'm part Inca," she said to me once, winking. I smiled and reached over to touch her eyelid's extra fold, which, along with her thin, slightly squat figure, and *café con leche*-colored skin, revealed a splash of Indian blood.

We started having lunch together on workdays, and then came the evenings together in La Paz jazz bars and dim cafés, discussing economics and ecology and spirituality. Once she reached between two cappuccino cups, took my hand—and smelled it. And another time I caught her sneaking a sniff of my neck while kissing me. When I asked her about it, she shrugged and said she was getting to know me.

We began taking weekend jaunts to the Urmiri hot springs; to Sapahaqui Valley, which drops out of the llama-strewn altiplano into fields of wildflowers; to the Coroico cloud forests; to the Huayna Potosi base camp; and to intersections with the ancient Inca roads that crisscross the mountains around La Paz. On one of the Inca roads, Anaí first introduced me to chewing coca, the thumb-sized green leaves that Bolivians chew as a mild stimulant and to adjust to altitude. She pressed them one by one into my cheek.

Our favorite getaway was her family's two-century-old hacienda in a narrow valley outside La Paz. One weekend we had it to ourselves. After walking through the peach orchards in fragrant bloom along the river, we sat in her dining room, where servants ladled quinoa soup into our bowls in front of a fireplace. Then there were llama fillets with *chuño,* followed by chocolate cake. We talked about the near impossibility of sustaining lifetime love, particularly with international lives and careers. But as we delved deeply into our past relationships, I felt barriers dropping. After dinner we dragged blankets out into the orchard. Later, I would recall the evening only in pieces—the smell of turned earth and peaches, the warm breeze, a moon appearing over the canyon's lip, our bodies joined. As the first hints of morning light were breaking, Anaí said something to me in Spanish; I can still feel her breath in my ear: "Maybe this never has to end," she said. "Maybe two people can just go on feeling this way, exactly how we feel right now."

But a few days later she told me we could not return to the hacienda. We were cooking together in my kitchen at the time, and I stopped chopping a leek and asked her why. Anaí's straight, soft hair obscured most of her face as she said, "My father yelled at me last night: 'If you're so happy about an Indian revolution, then you might as well start giving up your privileges now!' I was furious with him until I realized he was absolutely right."

Our relationship became subsumed in the changes erupting around us. We stared less into one another's eyes, and more into gatherings of Indians: the marches, sit-ins, and hunger

strikes increased in number and intensity. Though the Aymara-
and Quechua-led 1952 social revolution had broken up many
of the country's enormous haciendas, strongholds of power
that had held the Indian majority as slaves, it was far from complete. As late as 2001, when Anaí and I met, the reforms had
barely touched Bolivia's eastern lowlands, and even in the relatively progressive east, de facto apartheid was alive and well.

The 2002 elections brought Indians into the halls of power
for the first time, as their political parties swept a remarkable
forty-two percent of congressional seats and fell just a smidge
shy of the presidency. The would-be president, the Quechua-
speaking Evo Morales, entered congress as the head of the opposition. Previously snow-white, the new congressional floor
burst into a rainbow of colorful shawls, lacy, wide pollera
skirts, and flamboyant head-feathers as Guaranis, Ayoreos,
Aymaras, and Quechuas took their seats. The Bolivian congress began to look like Bolivia.

But the Indians' euphoria soon hardened into a stark real-
ization: forty-two percent is still the opposition, not the government. The presidency was held by mining millionaire
Gonzalo Sánchez de Lozada, known simply as Goni, one of
the more corrupt leaders in recent memory—and an acquaintance of Anaí's father. Early in his tenure, frustration over
Goni's policies mounted, and the Indians took to the streets.

Even right now, as Anaí finishes telling me about the
wonderful opportunity in the Amazon, a group of Aymaras
streams beneath my office chanting slogans in their language,
their earnest faces reflected in the mirrored tower under the
image of Illimani. "Why should I leave?" I finally say to her.
"They want to make me director."

"*Really*, baby?" Anaí said, her eyelashes fluttering with
irony. "Then would you get a real penthouse?"

*   *   *

When I first arrived in La Paz, my personal assistant handed me three sets of keys: one to my corner office; the second to a shiny new Toyota Land Cruiser, to which I had unlimited personal use; and the third to my very own penthouse.

Well, it was almost the penthouse. Each day after work I'd pass a bronze plaque that heralded my residence as BUILDING OF THE YEAR, CITY OF LA PAZ and step into the elevator and press the PH button, rising above all twelve floors to my elegant pad. Though I lived alone, I had three bedrooms, four bathrooms, a Jacuzzi, and maid's chambers. Formerly a nineteenth-century Portuguese embassy, the twelve-story tower grew right out of the original Victorian structure. So impressive was his work that the architect christened his building Illimani after the Inca's most sacred of peaks. Each morning I unfurled my ceiling-to-floor bedroom curtains to a brand-new performance. My view of Illimani was never the same, her colors, her interplay with clouds, and the snow-line always in flux.

The place was so perfect that at first I thought it *was* the penthouse, until my second day when a Frenchman joined me in the elevator and did not press any of the buttons below PH. His inactions puzzled me, and I eyed him suspiciously once or twice on the way up. We both got off together, and as I was fishing out my keys, he introduced himself in a nasally accent, saying he worked with a mining company. "I live in zee penthouse," he said, "so we are neighbors I suppose." Mr. Frenchy then bounded up five steps to a door I hadn't noticed.

On one occasion, Anaí asked me as she looked through my window past La Paz's pastel-colored skyscrapers to its hardscrabble canyon-sides, packed tight with squatters, "Why do we live in two worlds instead of one?"

She asked it first, but I had subconsciously been toying with this question as my awareness of the Indian protests deepened. During my year in La Paz, I'd become much too comfy. Like several hundred other foreigners here, I'd come to Bolivia as an aid worker. Bolivia is the hemisphere's poorest country besides Haiti. Half of the population lacks access to freshwater; literacy rates are abysmal; chronic hunger plagues millions every year; thousands die each month of preventable illnesses like diarrhea. We expatriates bring skills—in economics, engineering, project management, agronomy, law—as well as hundreds of millions of dollars a year from our Western donor nations, to work with Bolivians to do battle with poverty. Aid workers' posh pads, company cars, and Western-level salaries are justified by simple labor economics: it's the only way, the argument goes, to attract good people to a third-world backwater like Bolivia.

But even if this were true, did it have to be true for me? It's not that I was unhappy with the progress in my work. Quite the contrary, I had learned an enormous amount about alleviating poverty during my years in Africa, particularly about how to ensure "community ownership" of projects so that they are "sustainable." And in Bolivia my microcredit programs had ninety-nine percent repayment rates. These small loans to poor women were helping small businesses take root and flourish. In our health program, we were reducing a deadly disease called Chagas'—caused by the bite of a beetle that crawls down out of thatched roofs each night—by investing several million dollars in the construction of houses with tin roofs. And to avoid the terrible "dependency syndrome" I'd seen in Liberia, we maintained a firm commitment to the requirement that families themselves provide the labor and all local materials for our projects, an approach called tough love. And, so as to build local capacity, we implemented nearly every project through local Bolivian counterpart organizations, rather than directly through our own offices.

There was a lot to feel good about, but also hitches. For one, since my project portfolio had grown into the millions of dollars, I was rarely able to leave my La Paz desk, where I was busy

with reports, budgets, and meetings. On the rare occasions I
got on the plane to Cochabamba or Trinidad or Sucre, I sensed
from the overwhelmingly Indian participants that they were ap-
preciative of our work but wanted more than microloans and
the end of Chagas'; they'd made such strides toward taking national political power that they thirsted for the whole shebang.

I receive an invitation to a party around the time Anaí barges
into my office and announces the Amazon job. The party is
thrown by Serge, a forty-year-old Swede of Somali descent,
who works for the Swedish government aid agency and takes
pride in a fashionably fluffed Afro. Anaí accompanies me to
Serge's lavish, two-story penthouse and trails me along the ap-
petizer table. We take our overflowing little plates into a corner,
nibble on crackers with Brie, and survey a living room of light
skin; Anaí is quite possibly the only Bolivian in the room. I run
my finger across the spines lining Serge's bookshelf and remove
Graham Hancock's *Lords of Poverty,* a critique of development
aid. I read part of the book's satirical epigram aloud to Anaí:

The Development Set is bright and noble,
Our thoughts are deep and our vision global;
Although we move with the better classes,
Our thoughts are always with the masses.

Development Set homes are extremely chic,
Full of carvings, curios, and draped with batik,
Eye-level photographs subtly assure
That your host is at home with the rich and the poor . . .

Enough of these verses—on with the mission!
Our task is as broad as the human condition.
Just pray to God the biblical promise is true:
The poor ye shall always have with you.

When I look up from the book, Anaí is gesturing at the wall behind me. Sure enough, through all that blond hair and good cheer hangs an "eye-level photograph," this one from UNICEF, of a bloated Horn-of-Africa child holding out an empty cup. "Can we get out of here?" Anaí whispers.

I edge my way through the crowd to thank Serge, who stands with another of my acquaintances from the Netherlands development agency. They're looking down over the lights of La Paz. The Dutchman points to the top of another tower and says, "*There!* That's my penthouse." As they compare penthouses, Serge asks me where I live; I point over to the top floor of Illimani.

"The penthouse?" the Dutchman asks.

In the distance, fires burn in the streets below my building, their primal glow striking a contrast with the electric lights of all the skyscrapers. From Serge's penthouse I can barely make out Indians dancing around the fires. These men are among thousands who today streamed into the city from all over Bolivia, part of the biggest national march to date. "No," I say, distracted by an idea forming in my head as I look down at the Indians. "It's not quite the penthouse."

I quickly excuse myself, but as I'm walking away Serge calls out with an audible smirk, "What *could* you mean? Either it says PH on the button or it doesn't." I take Anaí's arm. As we head for the door, I tell her there's something I want us to do the next morning.

"Almost there," I say to Anaí.

"About time," she responds, struggling with a canvas bag of blankets and canned food slung over her shoulder. I'm hoisting another. Nearly out of breath, we arrive at the high school, which has been transformed into impromptu living quarters for hundreds of lowlands Indians. We step inside. Balancing our heavy loads, we pass a room filled with particularly gaunt campesinos wrapped in blankets—some of the hunger strikers—and thread our way through the gaps between dozens of bodies in the hallways, mostly asleep. These are Bolivia's majority Indians, disparagingly labeled *indio, puro, t'ara, idiaco, cholango,* and *medio pelo.* They, like my Aymaran maid, Fatima, experience discrimination, an example of which I personally witnessed one day recently while walking with Fatima on errands. We were passing through La Paz's fashionable South Zone when a muscular Bolivian pushed past me and viciously shoved her off the sidewalk. Fatima's reaction was a revelation for me. Numb to the action itself, she was amazed that the man had been willing to touch her.

When we find the gym and go inside, Anaí and I are assaulted by the dank air and stifling odor of unwashed bodies. Several hundred people are splayed across the gym floor, at least half of them sleeping, the others sitting up talking in low voices or milling around. Spotting one of the volunteers on hand, we head in her direction, but as we step gingerly between bodies on our way to her, a small child on the ground wakes up, takes one look at us, and screams.

It's a piercing scream, sheer terror, that wakes up the people around her and startles me so much that I nearly drop my St. Nick's bag. In a flash, her mother is comforting the child, who's whimpering, *"Kharisiri! Kharisiri!"* and shielding her eyes from us. The volunteer takes my arm and ushers us across the gym.

"You can put the food in the kitchen," the young Bolivian volunteer says calmly, when we've established distance from the terrified child.

"What's *kharisiri?*" I ask her, but she's moved off. We follow her instructions, separating out the canned and boxed food and delivering it. The woman then returns and points to the clothes and blankets we've brought: "Put those in the middle of the room."

Anaí and I lug the loads to the area she is indicating. *It feels strange,* I reflect, *to be doing such tasks myself.* Like other expats—and Bolivians of Anaí's elite class—I have an Indian driver, doorman, housekeeper, and messenger. The role reversal comes as a relief.

I expect a mad rush for our goodies. Instead, people rise one by one from their blankets to inspect the alpaca sweaters, wool socks, and thick blankets. Each time, one or two things are lifted up and rejected with a frown before one, and only one, item is settled upon. In this way, everything is gradually distributed until there is nothing left. The little girl took one of the last things in the pile, a teddy bear Anaí had thrown into the bag.

I ask the volunteer again about that scream, and she says that the child thought we were *kharisiri, or predatory* ghouls. I do my homework later and find out that these monsters, also known as *pishtaco, lik'ichiri,* and *ñakaq,* have a long history in the Andes, dating back to the sixteenth century. The marauding ghouls troll Indian communities for victims, stealing their fat to use for medicines, creams, and to lubricate airplanes. Alternatively, they go after blood or body parts. *Kharisiri* today appear in the form of doctors, engineers, anthropologists, and "gringo" development workers; in the past, they were more likely to have been priests. In almost every case, Lesly Gill observes, "an outsider or powerful individual from a superior race, class, or nationality profits from the primitive accumulation of oppressed peoples' vital bodily substances." The ghouls reflect the Indians' deep insecurity about their own bodily integrity, certainly related to the threat to their cultural survival.

Back out on the street with Anaí, the echo of that girl's panic continues to haunt me, and yet at the same time I feel my load strangely lightened. When I tell Anaí, she thinks she knows why: "At least we're trying to reach across the chasm.

And if we feel at all relieved, it's because a people that oppresses another people cannot be free."

Moving on is not an unfamiliar feeling for me. The movers have packed up the last loose items in my apartment; as a final perk, my agency is picking up the tab. I've shipped some belongings to be stored in the States, but the bulk will go along with me to Santa Cruz, where I am to start the new job. Anaí shows up, waves, and disappears down the hall toward my bedroom. I hear the door close. The last boxes are taped shut, weighed, and carted to the elevator.

When the movers are gone, an enormous silence hangs over my empty apartment. I walk along the hardwood hallway to my bedroom, replaying my reasons for doing this. On the surface, it's because of the Amazon job. Trading my pay, perks, and pension for a salary typical of a Bolivian professional is not the soundest career move, but I know it's part of reaching across "the chasm" Anaí talked about. I'm also an adventurer by nature, and this job certainly promises to be an adventure. Beneath these motives, however, I can hear something even deeper; I know it's there but can't yet articulate it.

I open my bedroom door. Anaí is standing by the window with her back to me, gazing beyond the pastel high-rises of Sopocachi and Río Abajo *valle* at the jagged white peak of Illimani. The sky is indigo, one of Rilke's "intensified skies, hurled through with birds" racing in a flock toward Illimani.

We'd talked about "us" of course. We concluded that, for now at least, our relationship was with the world and not just one person. She said at one point, "What are our little emotions, however steamy, when the whole planet is overheating?" She said that she "feels dedicated to a calling beyond the archaic coupledom." Already the black sheep of her conservative family, she'd worsened matters when she'd announced that, no, marriage and kids were not on the way; instead she'll be heading off to my alma mater, Brown, as visiting scholar on global warming. Then, it'll be off to Europe for the next round of Kyoto. *The higher cause.*

This is our last moment together in my apartment. Anaí twists her light green dress between her fingers and fans it out to the sides the way little girls sometimes do. I slip my arms around her, and she laces her fingers into mine, pulling my hands to her belly. We look out at Illimani, glowing hot white, burning an afterimage on my soul.

CHAPTER 4

THE LLOYD AERO Boliviano jet passes dangerously close to Illimani. From my bedroom window the peak didn't appear so textured; striped with fissures, her gale-blown face looks angry. A huge chunk of her snowpack has cracked and appears set to avalanche. My mind drifts a bit south to Antarctica, where a hundred-mile-long iceberg is said to have just calved off the Ross Shelf. Avalanching and calving on the brain, I can't help but wonder if such events are linked to global warming and picture a deluge of ice-melt gushing down from Illimani into La Paz.

Beyond rooftop Illimani, I look out the window over a vast nation that contains nearly every world climate and terrain. Bolivia has been declared a "megadiverse" country out of appreciation for its dense mountains, compact valleys, yawning salt flats, and low-lying tropical forests—and the bountiful creatures inhabiting them. The only species in relatively low abundance is a certain largely hairless biped known as *Homo sapiens*. Bolivia has one of the lowest human population densities on earth.

Even so, we're not crossing some remote stretch of the country. Below us is the development axis of La Paz–Cochabamba–Santa Cruz, and yet I see nothing human-made. Sure, La Paz is a traffic jam, but from the plane it reminds me of the Italian wedding scene in the film *Easy Money*. The camera pans back from a backyard reception to reveal hundreds herded together in a fenced-in square, surrounded by dozens of other identical, empty backyards. One sixth of

Bolivians cram into La Paz, while an untouched landscape rolls out beyond.

Why doesn't somebody just build something? Six-lane highways and traffic cloverleafs for starters, and then why not line them with parking lots and box stores. Subdivisions! Haven't Bolivians heard of those? All I see below are enormous national parks like Carrasco, Amboró, and Pilón-Lajas, surrounded by other empty spaces that might just as well be parks.

Respectable economists like to stroke their facial hair and lecture about the Paradox of Development, utilizing a large number of complicated graphs to say that it takes money to make money. Bolivia doesn't have capital, so it can't build the stuff that would create the capital needed to produce more stuff.

I have two questions for our economist friend regarding the myth of growth for growth's sake, which incidentally is also the ideology of the cancer cell. First, is the end goal down there more capital, or is capital one of the *means* to another goal, namely human well-being? The king of Bhutan, one of the few nations as traditional and mysterious as Bolivia, put it best when he summed up, in his endearing accent, his country's economic policy as Gross National Happiness. Second, is more capital the only way to develop an economy? To this our bearded economist friend would give a resounding yes—as I too would have before I began Bolivia-gazing. But something rather counterintuitive has dawned on me. What about *less* capital as a tool for smashing poverty and growing an economy?

It's right out of Economics 101: as the supply of pristine nature goes down worldwide, and demand for its existence goes up, its value increases. Bolivia's development failure has paradoxically led to a success. It has something the world values now more than ever: a country-sized chunk of unspoiled wilderness. Through ecological tourism, green-trade, and payment for global environmental services, for the first time in history it pays for Mother Nature to stay.

Everyone knows that capital begets capital—and perhaps today nature begets capital—but there might be yet another positive-feedback cycle: How about nature begets nature? Modern marketing is virtually unknown here; nature in Bolivia is a gigantic infomercial for itself. Even a veteran travel-writer found himself bewildered when trying to write the *Culture Shock Bolivia* travel guide ten years ago, saying that "setting in most countries is like stage scenery, background for the plot of daily life," but Bolivia's stark, intrusive settings "function as protagonists and antagonists."

Philosopher David Abram writes that in the West "our attention is hypnotized by a host of human-made technologies that only reflect us back to ourselves, and it is all to easy for us to forget our carnal inherence in a more-than-human matrix." In Bolivia you can't forget your carnal inherence; Pacha Mama is sovereign. Amero-Indian animism—a spirituality that weaves nature and people into the same cloth—penetrates even the ideas of many urban mestizos. Bolivia is the living terrain of German and French philosophy, like Husserl's animist "life-world" (*Lebenswelt*) or Merleau-Ponty's concept of humans and nature forming a common "flesh of the world." As I gaze down at more variety of virgin space than I've ever seen, I feel the landscape itself shaping my thoughts. Perhaps nature still speaks clearly enough in this place to be heard. Maybe in this way it can rescue itself.

All at once I see it: interlaid circles mark an increasingly tropical landscape, the road rings circling the Amazon-basin city of Santa Cruz, where I am to live. Through the slightest hint of fog interacting with bright sunshine, the rings shimmer and waver as if someone had dropped a stone in the center and out they rippled.

When I arrive at the Santa Cruz headquarters of Fundación Amigos de la Naturaleza (FAN, or the Friends of Nature

Foundation) from the airport, I'm half-surprised the taxi driver accepts the same boliviano currency I'd been using on the altiplano. I had begun to think I deplaned in an altogether different country. Frosty La Paz seems a planet away from this steamy tropical city.

I'm about to meet my new colleagues and try to disguise the wet patches forming on my shirt underarms. As the taxi rolls away, I feel momentarily disappointed with my new employer. Since my interview took place in La Paz, I have not seen their facilities, which appear modest for the country's largest national conservation group: two decent-sized brick buildings set in a wide lawn, under mango trees. FAN doesn't even have an address; incoming mail says "kilometer seven and a half on the old road to Cochabamba."

But FAN's executive director, Gisela Solares, quickly changes my impression as we begin a tour. A Bolivian from Sucre, she's lived abroad for many years. Educated in business administration in Barcelona and Cartagena, she conveys a mix of Latin warmth and Western efficiency. In a Spanish textured with Iberian and Caribbean softness, she explains that besides the two main buildings, FAN also runs a pair of field offices, a plant-genetics lab, and an airstrip. Her minuscule nose ring takes on a glint of sun, and a dozen earrings trace the cartilage of her left ear. At one point she asks, "You're aware of the battle of the watermelons and the grapes?"

I am, naturally. Bolivia's lively constellation of environmental groups has broken down between these two fruits. "Watermelons" are green on the outside, red on the inside—eco-commies who consider capitalism to be intrinsically ecocidal. "Grapes" are green through and through, wanting to save the rainforest through tinkering with economic incentives within capitalism. FAN is a grape threatened to be mashed by watermelons, especially archrival Probioma, which has been smearing FAN in the Bolivian media as "a puppet of multinationals," in bed in the Amazon with polluters like BP. Gisela is vehement about this. FAN has not sold out! The foundation has rejected several potential contracts with other energy firms on principle, she says, accusing the watermelons of being jealous of FAN's success.

This real, live local NGO feuding is exciting to someone like me. Until now I've worked exclusively in international institutions such as the World Bank and Catholic Relief Services, but local groups like FAN are becoming increasingly important, as international organizations farm out frontline work to cut costs. Formerly mom-and-pop operations, local NGOs now attract stellar professionals like Gisela, who have helped turn Bolivia into a mecca of environmental innovation. Bolivia's track record is indeed remarkable: world's largest forest-based Kyoto experiment; world's first debt-for-nature swap; world's largest protected dry tropical forest; experimental Indian park management; rapidly growing protected-areas system; a National Environmental Fund; world leader in international efforts to protect the endangered vicuña; progressive forestry legislation; a national biodiversity conservation agency; a total ban on the trade in domestic species . . .

Hold on a minute! Ever since Prime Minister Indira Gandhi declared at the 1972 Stockholm conference that "the environment cannot be improved under conditions of poverty," the idea that third-world countries are too poor to be green has become so commonly encountered that it's trite—and yet completely at odds with the reality in Bolivia. Bolivia turns the famous Environmental Kuznets Curve—the theory that economic development is correlated with higher environmental quality—on its head. If nature appreciation is indeed a "full stomach" preoccupation, why is Bolivian policy so green? How is it that in the absence of two centuries of Bolivian Muirs, Thoreaus, and Audubons the country is so pro-wilderness?

I file such questions away as Gisela introduces me to my new colleagues, some of FAN's sixty full-time staff. I meet my deputy, a twenty-eight-year-old Chiquitano Indian with gelled hair and a Reebok sweatshirt, whom Gisela introduces by the curious name Esmeeters, and then a personal hero of mine, Dr. Rene Frank, an Austrian biologist and guru of Amazon conservation. Finally, we walk into the office of FAN's public relations guy, Len, who is thirty-seven years old and sports a vaguely 7-shaped rocker hairdo and eighties-era, plastic eye-wear. Unusually eccentric for a Bolivian man, he's clad in a garish lavender shirt with tiny white polka dots. Gisela asks him to tell me about what he does at FAN.

"What *I* do?" Len says. "This gringo doesn't even have a place to string up his hammock!"

Len volunteers to take me house hunting. We race through Santa Cruz in his old Soviet Lada, still in its original maroon. Seeing a red light ahead on the second ring, Len hits the gas and we shoot through it, an oncoming car brushing our bumper. Oblivious to the honking horns, he explains that Santa Cruz exploded from a town of just fifty thousand thirty years ago to its current 1.2 million through a boom in oil, soybeans, timber—and cocaine trafficking through Brazil and Colombia en route to the United States. Lots of new buildings went up as the economy soared. But a recession resulted from the fall of commodity prices, the classic third-world dilemma of not diversifying the economy beyond raw materials, and everything tanked. "Including real estate," Len says, "and because everyone's broke you don't even need to rent." He takes a corner much too fast and adds, "We've got *anticrético*."

There is no translation for this Bolivian word. This is a concept I've yet to see anywhere else, but it has become common in Bolivia. You put down a deposit in dollars and may live in the house or apartment as long as you want, receiving the full amount back when you leave. In the meantime, it's working capital for the landlord.

"With ten thousand dollars, you can live well," Len says. "If you deposit twenty thousand, we're talking five, six bedrooms, gardens, air-conditioning, the works." Here he pauses, adjusting his enormous glasses. "And with thirty thousand," he chuckles, trying to imagine such a sum, "you will live in the hacienda of your dreams."

"But what if the landlord spends the deposit and can't give it back when you want to move?" I ask.

"That only happens fifty percent of the time," Len says. "And when it does, the house is yours . . . as long as you don't leave the country or try to sell it."

I tell him I'll just rent. And one more thing: I want to live "like a normal Bolivian," no more quasi-penthouses. To this he responds, "You have two choices, amigo: wealth or poverty. There's nothing normal here."

Two percent of the population lives in luxurious walled-in homes mostly in one of three choice neighborhoods: Hammocks, Palms, and Equipetrol (yes, it's a neighborhood named after an oil company). Len takes me through each of these well-heeled hoods clustered around the second and third road rings. "Let's check out some other areas," I suggest.

Beyond the neighborhoods named after oil companies stretches the hinterland, a vast and sprawling slum reminiscent of third-world urban areas the world over. Finally, we come to one of the few slivers of middle-class-dom in Santa Cruz: Urbanización Lisboa—the Lisbon Urbanization—called Urby Lisboa for short. It's not a barrio, but a *barrito,* the seed of a neighborhood. It's just two parallel streets that look like an equal sign from above, a cacophonous mixture of fifty differently shaped stucco homes, their red-clay roofs the only common denominator. One two-story house has small windows with grilles and a pergola, but most are not so fancy. Hammocks drape across patios and living rooms. Tropical succulents, cacti, and leafy plants crowd any available space and migrate into an adjoining park with towering toborochi and tajibos over an assortment of old wooden benches, cracked brick footpaths, and raised iron garbage pails with the bottoms rusted out. A half dozen woolly donkeys herded by a Quechua woman in a derby and layer-cake pollera skirt act as lawn tractor. In this neighborhood, form follows funk.

One Urby Lisboa house has a little sign out front with a phone number. I call, and the landlady, hearing my foreign accent, comes immediately. She's blond, blue-eyed, and lives in Hammocks. "Are you sure you don't want to live in Hammocks or Palms? I can get you a house in either area, much nicer and *safer*." I don't. I feel relaxed in Urby Lisboa, and while the house is big—two stories with three bedrooms—it is also simple, with a tiny garden and two unmatched palm trees above an overgrown lawn.

She mentions the rent; I name a considerably lower amount that she immediately accepts. For a second I wish I'd gone even lower. There is no refrigerator or stove. I'll have to buy them, she says, but insists on installing an air conditioner into what will be my bedroom. "The humidity," she says, "makes it impossible to live in Santa Cruz without one." She starts talking about her yearly trips to Miami for medical checkups, and her husband's in the oil business and oh-those-*collyas*, the Indians from La Paz, they just don't want to work as maids anymore, they think they're too good for it, but their *ideas revolucionarias* will never spread to Santa Cruz. *Todo tranquilo*. We don't need a contract she says, and she seems in no hurry for the rent or a deposit. "I'm so glad to have a North American here," she says as she leaves.

Over the first weeks in Urby Lisboa its charms and quirks unfold. My neighbors and I chip in a dollar a week to pay a watchman to circle our two blocks all day long. He's a friendly, gray-haired chap who is immediately enamored with my dog, a shepherd mix that I carried on the plane with me from La Paz. Anaí and I adopted her as a puppy from La Paz's sole dog pound and named her Pacha Mama.

So all day the guard circles the two blocks with Pacha Mama, crossing paths with horse-drawn carts hawking melons, honey, milk, and cooking gas. You never have to go shopping since the supermarket aisles roll past your door, vendors advertising their particular product with a sound evoking it (an electric cow moo for milk or ice cream; a whoosh of pressurized gas for cooking fuel). One day I return from work and am chatting with the guard about his day circling the block hundreds of times with my dog when he mentions as an afterthought, "Oh, and one more small thing. Pacha Mama bit one of the neighbors. Lots of blood."

What! Pacha Mama has never bitten a soul in her life. Has the drop in altitude from the Andes to the tropics thrown off her equilibrium? The watchman points out the victim, a boy of thirteen or fourteen across the street, and I bolt over to him with the watchman ambling along behind.

"Are you okay?" I gasp. He's got a six-inch-wide bandage wrapped around his leg over the bite.

"Sí, bien," he says, his father emerging from a hammock, smiling.

"I'll pay the medical bills." *Please don't sue me!*

"The boy was teasing Pacha Mama," the watchman scolds.

"Just put him on a leash from now on," his dad says, smiling. "It happens. *Todo tranquilo.*"

From then on Pacha Mama circles the block with the guard—on a leash—and I realize I'm no longer in radicalized La Paz. If a vicious canine taking off half your child's leg doesn't stir up any emotion, what on earth will? I take a taxi to the city's central plaza, and the fare for the full ten-minute ride is just fifty-five cents. We're driving along, the taxi driver whistling, when I notice the fuel gauge is below empty. At the second ring juncture he says, "I'm so terribly sorry, but could you lend me the fifty-five cents now?"

Of course, I say, handing him the money. He gushes thanks on me and pulls up to a gas station. "Fifty-five cents!" He and the attendant discuss the day's soccer match as I watch the pump gauge rise from zero to fifty-five cents in less than one second. The bottom of his gas tank barely slicked with gas, we somehow make it to the plaza, where I join in Santa Cruz's favorite sport besides soccer: town-square sloth-gazing.

The Amazonian sloth. Indolence is the armadillo-sized mammal's only true habit, sleeping or resting, as it does, twenty hours each day. When motivated, it moves along the bough of a tree in its trademark upside-down position at four tenths of a kilometer an hour; unmotivated, a mere five meters an hour. Someone, no one is quite sure who—or maybe the sloths "have always been there"—released a family of sloths into the plaza's palm, paquío, tajibo, and almendrillo trees, where they have come to reside.

Below, the humans. It's a wide plaza, so full of foliage that it's a veritable jungle itself, surrounded by the stone cathedral and stucco-sided Spanish colonial buildings with quatrefoil windows: the national theater, municipal government, and Amazon cultural center. Squeezed in the middle is the Irish Pub, with its trademark green-and-orange leprechaun, run by the pudgy, befreckled Michael, a transplant from county Waterford. Beat-up taxis and Jeeps with tinted windows, good stereos, and eighteen-year-olds from Hammocks, Palms, and Equipetrol drive under these buildings, honking at friends. In the plaza's center, older *cruzeño* men play chess; shoeshine boys charge twelve cents for a fierce shine; and espresso salesmen with their shoulder-strapped aluminum thermos pour wickedly sweet shots of Brazilian *cafezinho*. I buy one, staring up into the trees as I sip and stroll, on the lookout for sloths.

I'm not the only one. Plenty of folks from Santa Cruz, or *cruzeños,* stroll in couples or families, glancing up into the tree canopy—to no avail. I've spent an hour at it. *Nada.* The sloths' hairs host an algae that is green during the rainy season and brown during the dry season, so that the animal is camouflaged with the surrounding foliage and moss. This near invisibility is enhanced by sheer slowness, and it dawns on me that this is what they do for a living, these sloths. They move so darn little that predators such as jaguars, harpy eagles, anacondas, and ocelots can't see them. They live a *tranquilo,* vegetarian life in absolute harmony with nature, or in this case with Santa Cruz.

Finally, I cheat. Up ahead is a family with several small children gawking at something above. Fired up by my espresso, I maneuver my way across the plaza at a clip until I reach them. Squinting, I don't see a thing until, finally, my eyes settle on a lump that looks like the shape of a termite nest, or, no . . . It's moving! Or rather it moved a millimeter. *The revolution will never come east.* My landlady is certainly right. This sweltering Amazon city is populated by 1.2 million *tranquilo* sloths.

CHAPTER 5

I T'S DAWN IN the Jesuit mission town of Concepción, ten
hours up the road from Santa Cruz in the middle of the
Grand Chiquitania's undulating, dry forests. I've snuck away
from the Indian leader, Salvador, and the rest of our group,
lured by the sound of violins emanating from the corner of the
plaza. In the slanting, pink-hued light the church emerges
from between a cluster of palms—and I suck air. I'd seen photos of the famous Jesuit missions, but never expected such
a combination of grandeur and simplicity. The shape of the
church is almost barnlike, a triangular *teja* roof over white
adobe. But the mission's façade is a delicate array of swirling
wood-carvings and muted pastel painting.

The balance of the wide silence of this remote corner of
Bolivia and the melodious violins leans in favor of the
latter as I enter a side courtyard in search of an entrance into
the eighteenth-century cathedral. This church, and indeed
the hundreds of square miles around us, have changed little
since the Jesuits were expelled from South America in 1767.
The Chiquitania is but loosely controlled by government;
here the Church holds sway. Though the Jesuits resided here
for a mere thirty years before their expulsion for the crime
of getting too cozy with the Indians, they did more to affect
architecture and norms in those three decades than in the
twenty-four decades since.

I find the entrance and see five adolescents sitting in a crescent
around sheet music balanced on wooden stands, letting loose
a hypnotic Bach concerto. Their coppery skin and straight

black hair tell me they are Chiquitano, the same tribe as Salvador. They're practicing, even at this ungodly hour of six A.M., for the biannual Baroque Festival.

This festival tries to capitalize on the mystique surrounding the classic film *The Mission*, in which Robert De Niro and Jeremy Irons play colonial-era Jesuit priests teaching and defending the Chiquitanos, as well as the coveted United Nations Educational, Scientific, and Cultural Organization (UNESCO) World Patrimony status bestowed on Concepción, San Ignacio, Santa Ana, San Javier, San Miguel, and the other towns comprising the Jesuit Mission Circuit. For ten days, dozens of famed classical musicians from around the globe play concerts with locals, including these teenagers, in picturesque churches throughout the region. Despite the marvel of the event, it is in its infancy, as undiscovered as the rest of Bolivia. At different times I have been to all of the Jesuit mission towns and have yet to spot a single foreign visitor, except during the festival itself.

In his famous PBS interview with Bill Moyers, *The Power of Myth*, Joseph Campbell draws a distinction between the beautiful and the sublime. The sublime transcends mere beauty in merging with eternal forms. That's the feeling I have now. The sunrise in the windows; these Indian youths expertly manipulating their bows; the carvings blending native and Christian spirituality around the altar; and the Indian-painted frescoes on the walls. A fragile membrane between a respectful European and receptive native cultures, certainly sublime.

Honk-honk, comes a grating car horn from outside. *HONK!*

The music comes to halt as Len, clad in a metallic blue polyester shirt, appears in the side doorway and announces, "The Green Wagonette is off!"

For the first hour in the car I'm grumpy. Not just because of my measly five minutes of sightseeing; we only got two hours of sleep. I'd had a hard time grasping Len's logic last night when we'd arrived in Concepción at four A.M. and he'd announced we'd stop for a "siesta" before continuing on to Kempff Park and the Indian Territory.

"Let's just roll on through," Salvador said rather sensibly.

"I need my beauty sleep," Len said, steering toward a cinder-block flophouse cum karaoke bar where we all crashed on foam mattresses. Now we've got ten hours behind us, fourteen more ahead, the first leg of a two-week orientation trip where I'm to visit the Indian Territory villages and lead trainings. The journey is already wearing on me. In my La Paz job, I always flew to project sites, and I started a comfy precedent when I flew on my first trip to Kempff, accompanying the corporate donors. This time I'm shoulder-to-shoulder with my colleagues—Salvador and three other Chiquitanos, two park guards, and the flamboyant Len—sandwiched into a Nissan Patrol 4×4 we've affectionately dubbed the Illustrious Green Wagonette.

The Wagonette is a time machine. It began yesterday, when Len picked me up at my Urby Lisboa home, and we crossed the Santa Cruz rings through Equipetrol, where strapping Bolivian guys in muscle shirts swaggered beside thin, young women in brightly colored miniskirts. Among the Miami-gazing upper classes plastic surgery is cheap and common, and Western men fly in to find brides among Santa Cruz famed *camba* beauties, the elite of whom walk runways as Italian-Bolivian designer Pablo Manzoni's *Magníficas Bolivianas*.

As the rings petered out, we found ourselves amid boxy cinder-block houses that gave way to cattle and soy farms. We crossed a bridge over a wide river and entered the moonlit beginning of the Grand Chiquitania. One hour, then two. The large industrial soy farms gave way to ranches, and then the electricity ended, with just occasional pockets of light, including one hacienda far off to our left: "Hitler's personal photographer," Len said.

Bolivia has been a haven for former Nazis, including the

notorious "Butcher of Lyon" Klaus Barbie, who arrived in Bolivia in 1955 and resided in La Paz under the alias Klaus Altmann. Barbie earned his living as a narcotrafficker and assisted in a Bolivian coup, but was discovered in 1971 by Nazi hunter Serge Klarsfeld, a Jew whose father died in Auschwitz. Not until a moderate Bolivian government came to power in 1983 was Barbie arrested and deported to France, where he would die in prison. The butcher of Lyon, yes, but Hitler's personal photographer? Len: "He's got hundreds of his photos of Hitler all around the house. An incredible collection."

At midnight we stopped in a village roadside joint for *cafezinho* coffee and some tasty *cuñape,* a rudimentary crumpet popular in eastern Bolivia. All the way to the Concepción hotel it was moonlit hills punctuated by enormous egg-shaped rock fissures jutting out of the rolling landscape.

Now we're driving once again through yet more expansive dry forest, and I wonder to myself how we can possibly go further back in time. We've already traversed contemporary Miami, Nazi Germany, and eighteenth-century colonial Spain. Suddenly, with a spine-jolting thud the Illustrious Green Wagonette drops off pavement onto dirt—and we are in Indian country.

The dusty Chiquitania transforms into high forests, and we no longer see any modern structures, just the occasional thatched hut. I'm getting antsy. The seats feel hard and we're squished in. I've got an Are-we-there-yet? grimace on my face. But there's plenty of good humor being traded around me as the sun traces a higher arc. Salvador produces a light green plastic bag bursting with coca leaves. He and the others stuff the leaves into their cheeks. Len politely refuses; the bag comes to me.

Just say no is my first reaction, straight out of high school health class. But I dismiss this as silly; sucking on coca leaves isn't doing drugs—as I'd learned from Anaí in the Andes during my virgin chew. The thumb-sized leaf's relation to cocaine is that of a Shirley Temple to a sidecar. Bring your cheek to a fine bulge and you'll feel little more than the buzz of an espresso. It takes a hundred pounds of coca to make a single gram of cocaine. The leaves get smashed into a liquid pulp, bathed in chemicals and petroleum, boiled into a thick paste, and finally transformed into the powder so coveted in my own country.

No, the tension in the car has nothing to do with spiking one's veins with smack or turning into a coke-addled moll; it's all about race and social class. Salvador and the other Indians dip in; the professional, light-skinned Len does not. Coca is a campesino thing, *de los indios,* similar to the way Salvador and company sit directly on the ground sometimes, right on Pacha Mama—even when chairs are readily at hand. Or how millions of darker-skinned Bolivians offer the first sip of their drinks to Pacha Mama by pouring a splash onto the ground. Coca is entwined with Inca cosmology and has social, medicinal, and spiritual qualities, as I witnessed among La Paz Aymaras scattering the leaves on a colorful weaving to tell fortunes.

I palm the green bag, all eyes on me. The forest races by outside the car. I decide to take the plunge and dip in, pulling a dozen or so leaves out of the bag. They smell like dry leaves in the fall. When I stuff them into my cheek, the stems poke my gum and the taste is mildly acidic, causing my glands to secrete a gush of saliva. I force a pleasant expression, and slowly the stems moisten and settle into a mushy ball in my cheek.

The Bolivians' reactions to my coca dip is complicated. Len, who has an opinion about everything, is uncharacteristically mute at first and then teases me for being the *cocalero norteamericano.* The Indians silently tongue their coca wads, striking an ambivalent pose. Salvador joins Len in a bit of good-hearted teasing and seems to warm up to me a fraction. But I feel more alienated from white and Indian Bolivians alike.

While the campesinos are pleased to have me on their side of the chewing chasm, they are not chipper. When you hear for centuries that your race is inferior, you begin to believe it. By chewing I'm "slumming it" and also acting *muy indio*—very Indian—vernacular for "very low." They expect their "betters," seen through the distorted lens of self-loathing, to be aloof from such peasant habits, and their appraisal of me plummets along with their own self-esteem about the enlightened company they thought they'd been keeping.

The landscape outside deepens to ever-thicker jungle. Along with pavement, electricity, and piped water, we've nearly left behind Government and Church. San Ignacio was the last municipal outpost, and even the Holy Roman Empire hasn't made it yet. If the United States has a "meat-loaf line," which separates distant suburbs where they allegedly no longer eat meat loaf from the real rural America where they still do, Bolivia has a "mythology line"—and we've crossed it. We've entered a storied landscape similar to Australia's aboriginal songlines, in which nature evokes dreamtime myth. When an angular mammal darts across the road, vanishing into the bush, Salvador asks the park ranger at the wheel to stop and backtrack; sure enough, a fox lurks just beyond the lip of jungle, her unblinking eyes watching us. As we drive forward, Salvador explains the three souls: Serata, Sea, and Muo, or the fire soul, shadow soul, and free soul. Muo is first to leave your body when you die and inhabits the body of a particular fox. That fox is one of his ancestors and cannot be harmed.

We arrive at one last trace of humanity: a crude government checkpoint to control timber pirates going after mahogany. It's no more than a poorly screened hut and a woody liana strung across the road. We stop and cut the engine, and a bearded man in a rumpled green uniform steps out and nods once. "Where to?"

"Indian Territory."

I struggle to suppress a chuckle. It just seems too Wild West to be real. The grizzly fellow pokes his head into the Wagonette and asks, "And him?" He's talking about me.

"Strategic planning training," I utter. My attempt at curt coinage falls flat. The bearded man doesn't extract his head from the car as I'd hoped. Instead, he continues to breathe on the driver's neck and screws up his face, evidently trying to understand at least one of the words I've just said. I suppress an urge to explain, which proves wise. The man removes his head from the Wagonette, evidently satisfied, and without wasting further words lets down the liana.

Trees seem to lurk ever taller. We're not far from the Indian Territory now. Len and the guards have dozed off, but Salvador, who never seems to sleep, asks me, "Do you know about the seven skies over the Amazon?"

I shake my head and look at Salvador's profile next to me; he's staring toward a late-afternoon sun rapidly sinking to a harder angle against the trees and throwing into relief his strong, aquiline nose. In his deep, lyrical voice he talks about the Amazon's seven skies, each alive with mesas, waterfalls, borochi wolves, and lush forests "just like this one." He tells me about the "tree of the world," which holds up the seven skies, saying, "We don't know which one it is, so we have to be careful and ask permission of the tree's *amo* [spirit owner] before taking it down."

A small wooden sign announces the Indian Territory—and two hours later we narrow in on Porvenir. This is not the same Porvenir I visited in the Cessna. This time I can feel the jungle in my tight lower back and taste it in the coca between my teeth.

I'm not thinking straight as I take a three A.M. river bath with Salvador. He's floating faceup, and I imitate him, rolling onto my back and inflating my lungs for buoyancy. Looking into a dark, moonless sky—or is it *skies?*—I think of the previous time I bathed here with Salvador, and how he traced out

46

circular acres with his finger. It strikes me that he didn't mean circles at all, but rather cylinders. I'd been thinking in two dimensions; Salvador, in three. These cylindrical acres stretch up like redwood trunks encompassing the Amazon's seven skies, enfolding troposphere and stratosphere: the earth's surface and its interaction with swirling gases.

Mythology moves, and I wonder how Salvador and these two thousand Chiquitanos are coming to understand our brave, new Amazon Project. Maybe beneath all the scientific talk of "forest carbon" and "sequestering greenhouse gases" and "mitigating dangerous planetary climate change" there's a deeper truth: a tree holds up the world.

CHAPTER 6

M Y PRIMARY GOAL for this two-week trip to the Indian Territory is to listen. This is my orientation, a chance to get the lay of the jungle before launching into the harder work ahead. That should be enough for my first trip, but Salvador has other ideas. He insisted back in Santa Cruz that I teach "strategic planning" in each of the villages along the way.

So here I am at nine A.M. on Porvenir's grassy knoll, Magic Marker in hand, surrounded by a half circle of several dozen community members who volunteered to attend when the event was announced the previous day. I launch in with logical frameworks, institutional missions, and concrete intermediate-term objectives. I lay it all out with flip charts, interspersing examples relevant to their rural reality. But it doesn't take long before I notice the antsiness. Those gathered shift on their rough-hewn wooden benches. *It's just the tropical morning heat,* I tell myself, prattling onward: "You can concretize long-term goals with results and activities." More shifting and blank faces. A mango plummets from a nearby tree, and all heads pivot toward the fruit.

Len, dressed in a clash of green pants and a purple shirt, comes over and whispers in my ear the Spanish equivalent of KISS, or keep it simple, stupid. I take down my color-coded strategic-planning matrix and put up a fresh, blank sheet. I ask the group in the most simple terms, "Why . . . plan?"

Their interest immediately percolates. *"Para vivir!"*—to live—the village chief calls out. Other responses rapidly follow: "To eat!" And then, building on that idea, "To sleep!"

Other responses: "To have bread and life" and "For our children." Soon, a familiar baritone voice booms out, "Now we plan for subsistence. We need to start to plan for the future."

It's Salvador, of course, his gold-edged tooth glinting in the sun. That gets us going on something I took for obvious: What exactly is *the future*? Here in the Amazon where everything is day-to-day and hand-to-mouth, the glorious present reigns. There appears to be no word in their native language for future.

But Salvador has an inkling of the future and tries to make the others feel it through decreasing its distance from the now: "*They,*" he says in Spanish, nodding in the direction of the long road back toward Santa Cruz, "will take our forest from us if we're not organized. If we don't plan our future, others will plan it for us."

There's a hush when Salvador finishes. Everyone is rapt, and I seize their attention to ask them to dream a little. "You *plan* toward your dreams," I say slowly, "so they'll come true."

Complete silence until the chief suggests, "What about tractors?"

Guffaws and chuckles, as the others mutter "tractors." The chief looks somewhat wounded. They're laughing because the idea sounds outrageous in a place without oxen and plows, not to mention electricity, piped water, or phones.

"I dream of taking my cattle into the park!" another says. I can tell from his smirk that he's a wise guy, the class clown, but Salvador takes his comment seriously. Just over the river in Kempff is prime pastureland, now off-limits. "That isn't a dream," Salvador says. "It's a nightmare."

The next day I'm across the river that separates the Indian Territory from the 1.5-million-acre chunk of forest added to Kempff to sequestor carbon and control global warming. Salvador, Len, and a FAN forester look on as I squint for a reading on the tape measure I've got wrapped around a tree trunk. "One hundred thirty-eight . . . and a half."

The forester takes a GPS reading and records the circumference. "A damn good year for oxygen," he says.

"A bumper crop," says Len.

We've covered several of Kempff's sixty testing parcels, slogging through swamps and thick forest to get biomass readings. Heavy rains have produced one third more growth than the previous year, sponging up a whole lot of globe-heating CO_2. "We're sucking millions of *tons* of greenhouse gases out of the atmosphere."

"So British Petroleum can keep polluting," says Len.

Salvador is measuring the next tree in the parcel, and I ask him if he really gets what we're doing.

Salvador reads off the number, stands from a squat, and says, "We say our forest is Pacha Mama's lung."

"And we're doing a routine checkup," the forester says with a chuckle.

Pacha Mama's lung. Again, metaphors. *The seven skies; the tree that holds up the world.* I've got so many questions to ask Salvador. This part of Bolivia is not only off the map for Church and Government, but even for the yet more intrepid institution of Anthropology. The Amazonian cultures in this area are little researched, so I'm relying on parallels from other parts of the country and world—and on Salvador himself. Later that day I try to question him: "Salvador, when you say 'Pacha Mama's lung' do you mean . . ."

I fade out midsentence. He's looking at me as if I've got a pocket protector and taped glasses. "Amigo Bill," he says in a patient voice, as if teaching a child, "you need to get into the rhythm of the Paraguá."

We leave his hobbit's cottage of a home, with its thick thatch over a rectangle of adobe, and head into the heart of his farm, where he grabs hold of a ripe pineapple, snaps its spiny stem, and skins it with his machete. He hacks off a chunk and hands it to me, the warm juices gushing over my lips and onto my shirt as I try to eat. We both laugh over the sloppy go I'm making of it. He's got a supermarket of food bursting from the rich, riverside soils: coffee, corn, tomatoes, and an array of fruit trees including banana and cashew, both of which we sample. The bananas come off the tree a blazing yellow. We bite into tart cashew apples, and Salvador says, "I love the country. You don't have to do much work back here, in the rainforest, unless you want to. Everything just springs up from the ground!

"In the city it's all about money. But here I just walk into my farm, pick pineapples or grapefruits, or into the jungle for *maracuyá. Es un paraíso.*"

Several pairs of the area's ubiquitous parrots fly overhead, emitting their anxious cries, little flashes of green and yellow. The bitter taste of cashew apples is still in my mouth. My wet shirt sticks to my chest and stomach. We stroll into high-growth cambará forest, mostly in silence now; a familiar feeling of slowing down enters me, a marvelous ease.

As we wind our way through contoured crop lines and orchard rows back toward Porvenir, Salvador says, "You don't spend any money here. Everywhere you go someone invites you for a drink, a bowl of turtle soup, *cualquier cosa.* Everything's shared."

When I lived in Washington, D.C., for graduate school, I became enamored with the idea of voluntary simplicity. I was not alone. Other Americans, disillusioned with what materialism had wrought, were reading Vicki Robin and Joe Dominguez's *Your Money or Your Life,* which argues that we trade our precious hours of life for money, then use that money for things that bring little satisfaction. Their idea was to ratchet down your expenses to a level of "enough"—since both *too little,* as well as *too much,* are recipes for unhappiness. As expenses are ratcheted down, and savings grow, we have less need to work for money and, thus, more free time to focus on what we really love.

This new voluntary-simplicity movement was dubbed *post-capitalist*. People from modern, industrial societies were for the first time consciously scaling back consumption, instead of trying to increase it. One PBS documentary showed professional couples in Holland, a hotbed of postcapitalism, selling their cars and riding only bikes. They also scaled back to the bare minimal amount of household products. As one Dutchman explained, "With shampoo, I start by using half my normal amount. If that still lathers, I use half of that half. I keep halving it each time until it has no effect, and then I increase the amount slightly every day until I find the perfect quantity."

But voluntary simplicity has always been confined to a few rebels, never taking root in the mainstream. When Thoreau said that most people lead lives of quiet desperation, he meant they are in a rut, trapped in a system of beliefs that includes the seductive accumulation of stuff, along with its illusion of immortality. He went off to Walden Pond to demonstrate how little you need to thrive—$61.99¾ for eight months, including the cost of his cabin. But viewed from Salvador's Amazon village, such conscious efforts at simplicity seem absurd. Here there are no halves to split. It's an authentic, precapitalist simplicity.

Our Chiquitano world-tour continues as Len, Salvador, and I roll from one village to the next. I find my rhythm with the strategic-planning gig, largely by replacing my entire curriculum with one single question: *What's the future?*

This question begs many others, and our Socratic discussions in Cachuela, Piso Firme, Florida, and the other Kempff-bordering villages are lively and long. Maybe this open-ended pedagogy works so well here because it's circular, the shape of people's thoughts. Time is cyclical. "Indian time," my Hopi, Navajo, and Pueblo students used to call it when I worked after college as a teacher at a New Mexico middle school for gifted and talented reservation youth. Neither teachers nor students at the Santa Fe Indian School wore watches. Sure, classes were run by the bell—they had to be—but everyone seemed to think and move on instinct. Indian time strikes a sharp contrast with our own Newtonian-Kantian "absolute time," which is unidirectional and points like an arrow toward the future.

I first began to understand the concept of cyclical rather than absolute time during an Outward Bound–style camping trip into New Mexico's Wheeler Peak Wilderness. A social worker and I mixed six of her "high risk" students with six of my "gifted" kids for three days of challenging mental and physical exercises. We'd asked the students, all of them Native American, to bring along something to share with the group, and one of my thirteen-year-olds read something from Black Elk of the Oglala Sioux:

Everything the Power of the World does is done in a circle . . . The wind, in its greatest power, whirls. Birds make their nests in circles, for theirs is the same religion as ours. The sun comes forth and goes down again in a circle. The moon does the same and both are round . . . Even the seasons form a neat circle in their changing, and always come back again to where they were. The life of a man is a circle from childhood to childhood and so it is in everything where power moves.

For planning to make sense there must be a future. But for these Chiquitano people, as for many First Nations peoples, there is no finish line in life—not even this year. Love, marriage, parenthood, old age, death—none of your rites of passage belong to you. Oral peoples believe that your life has already happened thousands of times. You reenact the *urmyth,* a kind of archetypal story. You may play your part timidly or with gusto, but when you choose a spouse, build a dwelling, or have your first baby, you are repeating something rather than creating it afresh; you do not forge time's arrow, you join time's cycle.

The irony does not escape me: Salvador asked me to teach planning, and at every turn I'm being taught not to. Certainly not to overplan, overprepare. That's what I did when I packed for this trip, and it's turning into an increasing burden. In each village, lowering my bag from the Illustrious Green Wagonette's roof rack practically requires a forklift. It's one of those enormous army-style duffel bags, but with reinforced sides and wheels, and positively loaded with "just in case" sorts of things. It's so unwieldy that two park guards have to climb up on the roof to lift it down to me, and I drag it along dirt or grass, the wheels sinking under its weight and hopelessly clogging.

Salvador, for the exact same fifteen-day journey, has a single navy-blue schoolbag, half full of air.

The first time I unload my bag, a small crowd circles me. I fish out my Sierra Designs tent, my PUR water filter; as I shuffle past my foul-weather gear and piles of clothing, I present in a flourish a mini-stove, a camera, my North Face sleeping bag, and an orange Therm-a-Rest air mattress.

Later that evening, after sitting around the fire playing guitars, singing, and chatting with the caciques, Salvador and I head off to our neighboring sleeping quarters. I have everything just right: the self-inflating mattress laid out, my camping pillow nestled into the top of my mummy sleeping bag, a headlamp strapped around my forehead for easy visibility of everything. Finally, I whip out my sleeping mask and earplugs.

Meanwhile Salvador has strung a cotton hammock between two trees, nestled in, and fallen asleep, using one of his fleshy arms as a pillow.

My magical bag of stuff starts to drive a wedge between the villagers and me. Sometimes, while bathing together in rivers in the evenings, one of them would ask how much my high-end tent or sleeping mattress cost; I'd give a vague answer, and they would never push me for a price.

How much does it cost? The question comes to take on undertones; as in, not just the cost in dollars, but the cost to my soul. I try to explain to Salvador that I wear the sleeping mask so that I don't wake at first light and use the earplugs because, frankly, he and the other chiefs snore. Salvador laughs and suggests that I wake with the sunlight and sleep with the jungle sounds, of whatever variety.

I'm tempted to brush all of this aside. After all, I'm just doing what any good Boy Scout would. *Materialism?* That's what I left behind in La Paz: the almost-penthouse, the Jacuzzi, and the SUV. But even so my bag feels heavier each time I lug it from the Nissan's roof rack. I start to feel out of the groove. Salvador, Ximén, and the other caciques and villagers are not weighed down by possessions, carrying around their easy spirits the way Salvador carries his feather-light bag. What's more, I suspect that the fact that they live as simply as the animals in the forest has led to the *continued existence of that forest*. There are no soulless strip malls here, because these people neither own, nor seem to desire, anything you might buy in one. There is no pollution because they own no cars. The villagers move by foot or canoe, breathing forest-filtered air, maintaining fit bodies without dieting or running on a treadmill. And those healthy bodies are certainly connected with their buoyant spirits and easy laughter. And deep sleep.

"Get into the rhythm of the Paraguá," Salvador told me that first day. As we circle back to Santa Cruz, I feel vigorous and enlivened—if somewhat naïvely so. You need to look at things for a while before their deeper nature unfolds, and I would come to see a murky future already slipping into the fibers of Porvenir. And FAN itself is partly to blame.

CHAPTER 7

O N ONE OF our road trips, Salvador shares a parable with me: A nearly naked Indian man is whistling his way through the Amazon jungle around his village, when he comes upon a development official with a clipboard who asks him what he's doing. "Walking in the forest," the Indian says, prompting the other to lecture him on why he should be working instead, suggesting the Indian cut down the forest for a five-hundred-head cattle ranch. When the Indian man asks him why, the development expert says, "To earn money."

"Why do I need money?" the Indian asks.

"So that you can pay for your children's college."

"Why do they need to go to college?"

"So they can support you in your old age."

"Why do they need to support me?"

Exasperated, the official blurts out, "So that you can retire and stroll happily through the forest!"

"That's what I'm doing right now," the Indian says, continuing on his way.

This story becomes a little too real on my next trip to the Indian Territory village of Piso Firme to visit Mike's cows. The Kyoto Protocol on Climate Change requires experiments like ours to include "sustainable development" activities that improve the livelihoods of local communities while protecting carbon-inhaling forest reserves. Fair enough. But when the Amazon Project was launched a couple of years before I arrived, our corporate partners suddenly dumped over a million dollars on the Indian Territory's subsistence communities—and things went awry. Among other projects, the money was invested in an "eco-cattle" initiative, under which only a tiny part of the rainforest was to be used for intensive cattle production and the rest left virgin. To carry out this plan, FAN sent a newly minted Santa Cruz agronomist named Mike to the Indian Territory.

When FAN's director, Gisela, and I arrive in Piso Firme, we find Mike, hairy arms across his chest, blocking the front door to FAN's guesthouse. The two-bedroom house is intended to remain empty to host visitors from neighboring villages, but Mike has taken over the place for himself and his wife. As we approach the door, his stern expression melts into a smile, and he offers us chicha, the traditional Bolivian drink made from fermented corn.

We pass through the FAN "guesthouse" to the back patio and relax in wooden chairs as Mike's young wife silently serves us cold chicha.

"Welcome to my home," Mike says when we lift our cups.

Don't you mean FAN's guesthouse? I want to point out, but don't. The handsome Mike continually jumps up to refill our chicha cups, asking Gisela and me our opinions of various topics. Looking out at Mike's neat lawn, I remember my briefing back in Santa Cruz; FAN is paying to cut Mike's grass. After all, it still *is* technically the guesthouse. Mike is good at playing both sides of things. For example, while preaching the gospel of ecologically sound cattle ranching, Salvador told me Mike has his own large personal herd and has been hiring villagers to cut down rainforest for extensive pasture.

But with Gisela and me around, Mike never mentions his own cattle, of course. Instead he pours us more chicha and croons about his ecologically sound model pastures. "I'm implementing the Costa Rica model," he boasts. "The farmers get up to five times as many cows on an acre and save lots of rainforest."

I ask him how many head of cattle he personally owns, but

he is vague and then smoothly deflects the subject back to ecological ranching, offering to show us an example. Piling into
the truck, we head through cornfields and bush for a few kilometers, stopping along the way to pick up an old man; Mike
lays a hard look on him, passing an unspoken message. At the
site Mike escorts us into a gently forested area and explains,
"This is ecological cattle ranching! We're implementing the
Costa Rica model." He goes on to detail a good model I know
well from my work in other countries. Simply put, it's intensive ranching rather than extensive. Instead of normal pastures in which you need five acres to nourish one cow, you can
use those same five acres to feed five cows. This is done
through making each acre supply five times as much nour-
ishment, through planting nitrogen-fixing trees every ten
meters (the cows eat the leaves and tender branches) and sow-
ing especially nutritious grasses beneath them. Now the five
cows need only five instead of twenty-five acres to roam and
feed—and the extra twenty acres can be kept as unspoiled
rainforest.

To simplify the idea, Mike mock-munches a few times, as if
chewing cud, and says, pointing to some nitrogen-fixing trees,
"The trees are the cows' *meat*. And the three varieties of fast-
growing grasses I've planted are their *vegetables*. Strong cows,
strong people!" He throws his arm around the old man's
shoulder, a perfect photo op. The old man, on cue, forces out
a toothless smile.

Gisela beams at this magician Mike, who is helping people
and the environment with his hard-won agricultural skills. I
even start finding myself impressed by Mike's worldly use of
the phrase "Costa Rica model," though he seems to say it a
bit too often.

I try talking to the farmer directly, but each time I ask him a
question, Mike jumps in with a quick answer. I finally ask if
he would kindly let the old man answer for himself. I lick my
lips and ask again about how he set up this five-acre pasture.

But the old man just keeps repeating in a Godfather-like rasp, "I wanted to leave something for my grandchildren."

Gisela mutters, "*Verdad,*" nodding at the man, then looks at me as if to say, "Can we go now?" Mike too is eager to leave.

But I press on: "*What* do you want to leave for them?"

"The ecological cattle ranch," Mike says.

"I'm asking *him,*" I say, and look back at the old man, who exclaims, "This!"

"What is *this*?" I press on in Spanish.

"This will be my grandchildren's inheritance," the farmer says, his arm taking in the sweep of the model pasture.

"Right, but what exactly will their inheritance be?"

He considers this and gazes into the nitrogen-fixing trees. A pregnant moment ensues, as everyone shifts nervously, most of all Mike. The man squirms and weakly offers, "*Esta . . . cosita*"—This little thing.

The man has no clue. I charge along the path into the supposed five acres of model pasture. Mike shouts for me to stop, saying that the whole five acres looks the same as this part and that lunch is waiting back in Piso Firme. But I march forward, and sure enough, within a minute what had been a lush and beautiful ecological pasture is now a barren field.

Stumps. Intermittent shrubs jut out of the gently rolling landscape, but mostly it is a typical Amazon clear-cut, rainforest denuded for extensive pasture. When the others catch up to me, also out of breath, I lash out at Mike, "Where's your ecological pasture?"

Mike is equipped with a pat answer: "A fire took it out."

"This is slash-and-burn, not natural fire damage," I say, and Mike knows he cannot deny it. I turn to the old man: "Did you get a cow from FAN?"

"Three cows," he says proudly. From the reports I'd read, dozens of cows had been distributed by FAN to community members like the old man, one cow for each hectare of ecological pasture planted, as an incentive. He'd received the cows from Mike but had not done the labor-intensive work of setting up the ecological pasture, instead razing the place with ax and flame. Mike does not, evidently, believe in his professed "Costa Rica model," instead promoting quick but ecologically unsound scorched-earth ranching.

The absurdity of the situation covers me like the sweat from the midday Amazon heat. I open my mouth to say something more, but nothing comes out of my dry throat but a kind of croak. This is enough to set off the old man giggling and then into a howl of laughter, his toothless mouth wide-open, his frail body shaking. Mike is certainly not laughing. He knows that misusing project funds and lying about it to superiors is grounds for dismissal.

The old man's laughter eventually dies down to a wheezing snicker, and then even he goes silent, the four of us sweating away in the middle of a deforested cow field in paradise.

I fire Mike, but it's not easy. Gisela's on my side, but I find myself entangled in a mess of loyalty and nepotism, leading right up to the park director, who insists I do a full report and then tries to filibuster the issue through a three-hour meeting in his office, going over every little bit of the report.

As the weeks turned to months, I uncovered dozens of examples of a classic development sin: promoting dependency. Mike's free cows turn out to be part of a pattern. I come across a half-million-dollar satellite Internet setup in Porvenir—blanketed in dust. Before I arrived, FAN introduced the Internet to "connect the Indian Territory with the world," but there was no community contribution that might have promoted ownership of the equipment. It was used for several months, mostly for gawking over porn, until the satellite system failed. The computers were then used for word processing until the solar-powered batteries ran down and the keyboards became jammed with dust.

It didn't end there. A high school scholarship program FAN started was perfect in one way: every single student dropped out. This was because there were no entrance exams, and everything was paid for, down to erasers and junk food, giving neither parent nor student a sense of ownership. Next, a health clinic was started and never completed because the community, accustomed now to free handouts, failed to come up with their in-kind contribution. Finally, a microcredit program loaned out well over a hundred thousand dollars, but had an abysmal repayment rate of fifteen percent.

"It wasn't our way," says Salvador. Beneath the failure of these projects is a philosophical divide: industrial thinking versus indigenous thinking. It turns out that when the university-educated Bolivian Mike wasn't posturing for visitors, he was chastising the Indians for their primitive backwardness, and encouraging them to follow Brazil's example and "put the land to work for them." As Westerners this makes perfect sense; the land should work for us as efficiently as possible. Industrial thinking is based on man's domination of nature. "Progress" means wild lands need taming and primitive people need civilizing in the quest for economic growth. Indigenous thinking is different. Life cycles back again, so the idea is to harvest with care and engage in "reciprocity" or giving back into the cycle. This is why Bolivians give regular offerings to Pacha Mama and, when hunting, often ask permission of the animal's *amo* before taking its life.

Now it's easier to see why that screaming girl in the La Paz shelter saw me as a *kharisiri*, or ghoul, come to steal her body parts; or why, when referring to Westerners, the Lakota use the term *washeeshu* ("he who steals the fat"), and the Yupik Eskimos, as Barry Lopez reports, refer to whites "with incredulity and apprehension as 'the people who change nature.'"

I begin to realize that the Chiquitanos and I must take a few steps back and develop a common language before we can move forward to achieve legal title to the Indian Territory and develop a sustainable economy on it. Luckily, such a new linguistics is already in the works in the realm of global ecology, where the "primitive" and "advanced" fuse. So Pacha Mama becomes Gaia; the seven skies are now biosphere; and the tree of the world is carbon sequestration. Fine. But where to start? These terms are still too abstract to bridge the gap with Salvador and the crew, so I decide to begin with a single word: *nature*.

I know it will be tough going. I'd been through linguistics boot camp as an eighteen-year-old at Brown University. Each of Brown's "units" of forty first-year students had six upper-class counselors including a gay and lesbian peer counselor, third-world peer counselor, and women's peer counselor. Their main job was to join late-night hallway chats and patrol our vocabulary. Here's one Tuesday night at Brown, a group of us procrastinating in the hall with Lanie, our women's peer counselor:

One guy starts to say, "This chick I knew in high school—"

"Squak! Squak!" Lanie jumps up and flaps her arms like wings.

"Whatever. Anyway, like I was saying this one chick—"

"Did she have wings?"

"Girl!" I whisper to him. "It's *girl* not *chick*."

"*Girl?*" one of the first-years (we'd been drilled not to say fresh*men*) says, looking at me in horror. "Was she five?"

"Gal?" a Texan in the group drawls.

Here Lanie sheds her wings and sits back down: "Look. There's a nice neutral term between *boy* and *man*. What is it?"

"*Guy,*" someone says.

"Right. But unfortunately we have no such word between *girl* and *woman*. *Gal* is degrading. So until somebody comes up with one, all females are women."

"Over what age?" the Texan asks.

We eventually settle on seventh grade.

With time I came to see such discussions as vital rather than absurd. Throughout our first year of college, the forty of us began to treat each other more sensitively and finally to engage the world in new ways. It's much more than semantics; it's "generative language" used to imagine and construct things like race, class, gender, and ecology.

But my attempts at communicating the idea of "nature" to two thousand Chiquitanos prove even more difficult than eradicating *chick* from young American minds. Whereas we "civilized" Westerners have externalized nature, to the Amazonians it is a part of themselves that cannot be sliced out. I am told the closest phrase they have for what we call nature is "the shimmering forest."

But they simply *must* understand—even if they do not accept—the idea of nature as an abstraction. That's the way the rest of the world sees it, and it is the basis of the project. I flail around with mixing curricula, from Freire's *Pedagogy of the Oppressed* to interactive games to participatory-learning and action exercises, but the discussions always come down to one thing: giving more free stuff as FAN has always done.

Gisela and I try to tag-team at one gathering. "The era of free handouts is over," I say in Spanish, hoping I'm getting the sense across correctly. "Mike's free cows, the loans that never got paid back. All of that is history."

Gisela grabs a marker and draws a pyramid on the white board. "*Miren* . . . There are three stages of development. The lowest stage is *emergency*," she says, scribbling that word at the bottom of the pyramid. "At this level we're talking about free food distributions, medicines. Like in Africa.

"At the top of the pyramid is *development*. That's where you take charge of your own livelihoods. FAN and other outside groups become like coaches. But *in between* emergency and development, on the pyramid, is a stage which contains parts of each. Now . . . where are you now on this pyramid?"

Expressionless faces stare back at us. Finally one cacique says we are at the bottom of the pyramid, in the emergency stage. As I take the Magic Marker from Gisela, I ask, "Is there an *emergency* in the Indian Territory?"

Some snickering here. Everyone knows that there is neither war nor famine in their idyllic part of the world, where food springs from the ground and leaps out of rivers. Still, a strong tension permeates the room; some of the caciques don't want the FAN gravy train to end. "Our bridges are down!" one of them says. "Can FAN come and rebuild our bridges?"

I suggest that they organize together and fix it themselves as they did before FAN came into the picture. Or else they might convince the municipal government to assist. *Impossible! Only FAN can do it!* Here Salvador jumps in: "FAN has been like the father giving everything to his sons. Spoiling them! When will the father let his sons stand on their own feet?"

Knowing nods all around. The general consensus is that Salvador has a damn good point. One of the chiefs extends the metaphor, saying that only when you have strong, independent sons can they help you in your old age. Everyone agrees that this is also an excellent point. But, nevertheless, ever so subtly the chiefs loop back to their demand for a free bridge from FAN.

CHAPTER 8

I END UP learning something from an unlikely source: *Apis mellifera* or the Amazonian honeybee. I'm traveling with three of the caciques downriver to the village of Piso Firme when our motorboat crosses paths with that of a colleague, Arnildo, who's FAN's park-protection manager, accompanied by a forester and a park ranger. We cut engines and allow our boats to bob together. Amid jovial backslapping and uttering *"Qué tal che?"* a silence grows. I take in the sights of our random stopping-point along the wide river: a gleaming bay off to the left where freshwater dolphins surface, snorting, not ten meters away.

"Vámanos!" someone shouts, and engine cords are yanked. Before heading along, Arnildo tells me he's left an Isuzu pickup truck for me in Piso Firme along with "some chains, machetes, and axes." I smile, finding it quaintly adventuresome that he would mention such tools, and also wondering why he was telling me and not the driver.

When we finally arrive in Piso Firme, I climb into the shotgun seat ready for the seven-hour drive across the Indian Territory to our workshop in the hamlet of Florida. But the chiefs remain outside the vehicle, shifting from one foot to the other. Looking at the trio in the rearview mirror, I realize that I no longer see the seven caciques as a single entity. At first they were just "the seven chiefs." They do dress alike—old jeans and T-shirts, with sneakers or cowboy boots—and are uniformly friendly, though not gushing with warmth. Tough country men, they laugh hard and seem full of a near infinite patience. But of course each one is distinct. Of the three with me now, Ximén is barrel-chested and slightly cocky, while Sebastián is as phlegmatic as his plump face and middle suggest. The third, Gaspar, is by far the smallest of the chiefs and represents the smallest of the Indian Territory's villages— Cachuela, population eighteen: Gaspar and his family. He's also the oldest, his face brown and withered like gingerroot, and he's usually smirking as if over a private joke, and sneaking the occasional pull on his whiskey flask.

I'm about to get out of the car and hurry things up when Gaspar comes over, jingles the car keys, and drops them into my lap. The obvious finally dawns on me: none of the chiefs knows how to drive.

But neither am I prepared for such a long haul along treacherous mud roads. In years of international aid work in both Africa and Latin America, I'd always had drivers. Now that I work for a local Bolivian NGO, skeletal budgets mean professional staffers often have to drive themselves—a reality that proves unfortunate in this case, since within two hours I plant the Isuzu in an enormous mud-hole. The wheels spin as if through butter.

The four of us climb out and study the problem. The caciques come up with a plan: we will shove logs under the chassis and then use a long felled tree as a lever to lift the truck up and insert other logs under the wheel. They start into the jungle with axes and machetes to collect the materials.

"Whoa!" I exclaim. They stop in their tracks. "Before launching into such an . . . overly complicated plan, let's first try a simpler solution," I say in boundless gringo wisdom. I suggest that simply placing logs under the four wheels will give us enough traction.

Polite nods. And then they continue to follow through on *their* plan. I beg and grovel, and they finally, grudgingly, give my idea a shot. I ensure them it is bound to work. After all,

I figure, if it worked in Long Island ice storms it will certainly do the job in an Amazon jungle.

The plan fails miserably, and the now chuckling chiefs go back to implementing their original plan. But the delay in trying my idea has cost us. Not only have I dug us deeper into the hole, but dozens of bees have now located us. A half dozen swarm around my face, and scores more begin to fill the truck cabin and explore our backpacks and gear in the open bed.

I help chop and haul wood to the car, all the while swatting bees away from my face. When I mention to the diminutive Gaspar that the bees have certainly found us, he replies, "Not yet."

"They sure have found us!" I say, shooing a few away.

The chief, cryptically: "They will come."

We've got the materials ready. One tree pole, felled and skinned of its branches, acts as a giant lever, perched on several fat logs. Other logs are standing by to be shoved under the back wheels once we've pried the truck up high enough with the lever. Just as things are ready, I notice a change in the air. A ubiquitous drone, a growing static; what were mere dozens of bees had become hundreds, and now certainly thousands. "*Now* the bees have come," the chief says, smiling, gap-toothed.

I yelp with the first sting, and the caciques tell me to get into the truck.

"I'm not getting into that hive," I say, staring at the bees covering the dashboard, seat, and wheel.

They tell me there is no other choice, that more bees will come, and it will only get worse. They know, as I do not, that whenever you stop in this part of the Amazon, within twenty minutes the area bees have found you, searching your vehicle and bodies for salt. Go slowly, they say, nudging me into the driver's seat.

The buzz! My insides are clenched into a nervous knot and I'm ready to explode with the first sting. The bees move away as I sit down, but as I touch the immobilizer alarm button, one stings my pointer finger. I spring up, yelping and swatting bees, receiving a few more stings under my shirt and on my scalp. I run fifty meters from the truck, swatting all the while. The stocky Ximén eventually catches up to me, laughing and saying that I screamed like a woman.

I ask, "How far are we from the nearest house?"

He ponders a moment, then says, "Fifty kilometers."

"How often do vehicles pass by?"

"Once in a week, *con suerte*. Some weeks nothing passes."

Gaspar catches up with us and says the emergency lights are on, and they don't know where the button is. "The battery will die!" he exclaims.

They both insist I need to get back into the hive, turn off the emergency lights, and most importantly get the pickup out of the mud.

Gaspar now changes tack. He puts a tiny hand on my shoulder and says, "You are a bee."

I momentarily forget the pain of my stings and look down at Gaspar's slight, finely wrought face. He continues, "Just relax. If you don't get nervous, *no pasa nada*." By tensing up, he explains, I was going against the "bee energy" and causing them to react against me. I needed to go with the flow.

With fresh resolve, I turn and walk back—toward the dreaded pickup. As the buzzing sound builds, I repeat to myself, "You are a bee. You are a bee." I slide into the front seat, remarkably calm, repeating my mantra, gently shooing a bee off the alarm button and pressing it, putting the key into the ignition, turning it.

The Indians are in position. I feel the back chassis rising, shouts ring out, and logs are shoved under the wheels. Meanwhile, bees are in both my ears and one is headed up my nose. They perch on my eyelashes and eyebrows, burrow in my hair, explore my leg hairs. "You are a bee." I *was* a bee! Not a single sting, and their little legs, which had felt so creepy-crawly, are now just a light tickle. That they are not stinging further builds my confidence. I am fully relaxed, the communal buzz a gigantic om.

On command I press down on the gas, and slowly, beautifully the pickup rises up out of the hole, traverses those few precious meters. The caciques slide in and we begin to move forward into the next six hours across the Indian Territory to Porvenir, bees finding their way one by one out the windows.

I've drawn a sun, bursting with color, rising over a horizon. I say to the group before me, "A *vision* is like heading toward the horizon. If you walk toward the horizon, do you ever get to it?"

Fourteen pairs of eyes stare back at me and soon begin looking at each other. There's a change in the room that is creating a nervous tension. In addition to the usual seven chiefs, seven Chiquitano women are present. When I suggested the idea at the last meeting, the resistance was incredible: "Women?! Women have never come to the meetings!" Me: "Are women different from men?" Them: "Of course!" "Are they less able to participate in meetings?" "They've *never* been at the meetings." "Could they?" And so on. It was the tiny Gaspar who finally convinced the other chiefs: "He's saying we can bring our women with us."

But the nervousness is not about "bringing their women with them" but having women in the conference room for the first time. And we're about to make decisions that will affect the shape of the program. This is also the first time the communities will have direct voice in planning the next five years of the project. Until now, it's always been handed down from on high.

Salvador finally takes a stab at my question: "You walk toward the horizon but never get to it."

"Exactly," I say. "Before we set up our five-year plan, it's time to think big about your vision for your Indian Territory *twenty* years from now. If you look out toward the horizon, what do you see?"

"No more malaria," someone says. "Schools with trained teachers." The gender differences become evident: women speak up for health care, as the men argue for better roads. Both men and women talk of a healthy forest full of borochi, jaguar, howler monkeys, and painted hochis. The scores of visitors who pay good money to experience their Amazonian wonder. Harvesting timber in a way that does not hurt the forest. I record their phrases on the poster paper as rays shooting out from the colorful sun.

Smiles all around now at what they've imagined. "Now," I say, "what are some *specific actions* we can take over the next five years that point us toward this vision?"

Here a real democratic process kicks in, which lasts two full days. This is like learning to swim for them. There are lots of circular, meandering anecdotes, completely unrelated to the topic, about the tangible stuff of subsistence. As facilitator, I allow us to tread water, but always gingerly, along with Salvador, point out that others—logging companies, white government bureaucrats, and missionaries—will plan out their future if they do not.

Now and then, we also slip and slide back into dependency. One cacique hints again toward the need for FAN to pay for a fallen bridge.

Here, one of the women jumps in: *"Quieres que Mikecito regrese con sus vaqitas y pollitos?"*—You want little Mike to come back with his little cows and little chickens?

A lone voice booms forward, echoing through the conference room: *"Sí, quiero vaquitas!"*—Yes, I want little cows. It's Gaspar, flashing a gap-toothed grin.

Here the women take charge. They know this is definitely the wrong answer. One uses a biblical image. "FAN has been giving us fish rather than teaching us to fish." Others just plain dig into him, saying that he should buy his own damn little cows and chickens. Pretty soon the group, led by the women, have poor Gaspar in a corner. I, of course, am thrilled that they have internalized the root-out-paternalism concept. Finally, even Gaspar shrugs his shoulders and admits with a rascal's grin that, yes, he can raise little cows himself.

These small, significant victories aside, the meetings are mostly numbing hours of repetition. The same points being made in different ways. At these times I ask myself if I lack the patience for frontline community work. I should have stuck to check-signing in La Paz. But then I remind myself, *You are a bee*.

I let their dynamics drive the process. I try to let the strategic plan grow out of their reality. Nobody's throwing around vocabulary like *climate change, biosphere,* or even *nature*. But I sense they are slowly absorbing the connection between their activities and the world's well-being. As the hours turn to days, we produce a notable result: a coherent plan that everybody appears to both understand and feel passionately about. The two main objectives they come up with are the ones I would have prioritized had I designed the plan alone. They also make a clean break from paternalism. First, they decide to focus on nailing down legal title for their Indian Territory: "We need a house to live in," one cacique says. Second, they wish to increase their incomes through ecologically benign business, such as certified timber and heart-of-palm export. "With the money, we can improve health and education," Salvador says.

During our postworkshop chicha, a positive energy ripples through our group. Laughter and jokes bubble up (Gaspar's "Yes, I want little cows!" is oft-repeated). While I know that implementation will be even harder than planning, I'm just flowing for now with the magic of our worlds coming a bit closer together.

CHAPTER 9

L OST TRIBES ARE not part of the plan," one FAN colleague tells me.

"But Salvador says there are people back in Kempff," I say.

"Salvador! He needs to forget about the past." I look out the window at the palm trees on the edge of FAN's Santa Cruz property. Not even the slightest breeze ruffles the green fronds. He continues, *"Mira,* let's say there are a few. Is there any point in trying to save them? You've got momentum with the program now and you'd be wasting your time trying to track them down."

I see his point. The two thousand Chiquitano people that we *know exist* are increasingly energized; we've got trainings to organize, campaigns for territory to spearhead, and organic heart of palm to harvest and export. But I'm still intrigued. Salvador said he's visited "the other tribe" or the Guarasug'wé (pronounced Wa-ra-soo-WAY)—several times in their remote hamlet within the park. Linguistically they are as distinct from his Chiquitano tribe as Bantu is from Swahili, and also much more isolated from modernity, existing somewhere between hunter-gatherer and small agriculturist.

"They're back there," Len says. He inches forward on his chair, and I catch a slight whiff of what can't be anything other than Old Spice aftershave. "It's no myth. Salvador wants you to go to see pure Indians, living in perfect harmony with nature." Like most of what Len says, I take this with a grain of salt and pay a visit to German anthropologist Dr. Jürgen

Riester, a septuagenarian who lives in Santa Cruz and has been studying Bolivian culture for decades.

"The Guarasug'wé? I pronounced them dead ages ago." Riester has a face of soft wrinkles, a tangled white beard, and a kind look in his eyes. He lived with this "lost tribe" in the late sixties, doing research. "I saw the last wedding between two Guarasug'wé, before their gene pool dried up." When I tell him others have seen Guarasug'wé, he shrugs and says, "We're anthropologists, not Gods; sometimes we get it wrong."

The meeting with the anthropologist does it; I decide to go to Guarasug'wé country. I stay up late in my Santa Cruz balcony hammock, pouring over everything ever written about the Guarasug'wé—a grand total of one book, Riester's *Guarasug'wé: Chronicles of Their Last Days*. Candles and incense ablaze, and Andean music on my stereo—charangos and walaychos strummed to the rhythm of wancara drums, overlaid with zampoña cane panpipes—my imagination follows Riester's account into the Indian Territory under the Amazon's seven skies, heading toward the Guarasug'wé *Ivirehi Ahae*, or "the land without evil."

I'm with the skinny park ranger, Misael, in a motorized canoe, racing up the Iténez River to the remote Guarasug'wé hamlet of Bella Vista. Light shimmers on a river beautiful and barren. I lucked out and got that last spot on a FAN ecotourism charter to Golden Flower Lodge and am going by boat from there. We slice through the water, into a candy store of birds: wading in the shallows, soaring above, fleeing just ahead of us. The muddy riverbanks are swallowed by a shock of deep green jungle.

We stop for the night in a park ranger encampment, Tacural, where five Bolivian soldiers in fatigues meet us at the boat.

The captain, a horse-faced man with a .44 strapped to his belt, shakes my hand. The four enlisted men, all dark-skinned, stand shyly behind him. They can't be more than eighteen. "Routine patrols," the captain says. When they are out of earshot, Misael tells me they're after drug *traficantes* smuggling into Brazil.

That night, the bugs attack. Hundreds of bees surround me as I wash my dish under the wooden piranha-shaped COCINA sign (I breathe deeply, letting them land on me); spiders and flies also abound. Craving comfort food, I pull out a large yellow bag of peanut M&M's from my backpack. I dive under my bed net with my candy, an armada of malarial mosquitoes soon ramming against it. Spotting the bright yellow package, Misael's children, three and five, who live in this camp along with his wife, sit below my bed and stare at me. I slip them M&M's until the bag is empty.

The next morning it's raining hard. Misael and I head off anyway in the motorized canoe, the rain stinging our faces; the riverbanks, misty blurs. Dr. Riester told me that for the Guarasug'wé, a canoe carries a person to the next world after death. Your soul travels up an Amazon River tributary like this one toward a hole in the sky and slips into the seven skies. For a couple of hours it's an oppressive sameness of jungle wall. I pull my green park-ranger-issue rain jacket tight around me and close my eyes, imagining the fish, caimans, and eels below and the jaguars and foxes lurking just out of sight. And then finally we pass a structure. Then another. They're made of thatch, with the roofs caved in, and Misael tells me that these are the places where Guarasug'wé used to live.

Within five minutes of climbing the embankment in Bella Vista, I meet a Guarasug'wé woman, wrinkled, with high cheekbones and small eyes. She approaches me, a four-year-old boy clinging to her skirts, and says she's Flora.

"Is he your son?" I ask. The rain has lessened to a fine mist, and I sense the sun might break through.

WILLIAM POWERS

"No, his mother—my daughter—died. Of hepatitis," she says in an unusual singsong Spanish that I would soon come to associate with the Guarasug'wé tongue. "We took her across into Brazil, but she died."

A silence shrouds the moment. Misael is in the park-ranger hut to my left, pulling *charque,* or dried meat, off the vigas. I hear and smell frying onions. Eventually, I ask Flora if she speaks Guarasug'wé. She doesn't understand my question.

I repeat the question in another way, and when it finally dawns on her what this strange white man is getting at, she breaks into a huge smile. The emotion, it appears to me, is embarrassment.

"Noooo . . . !" she says.

I gently press her on it, and she does dredge a single word out of her memory: she points to a bird on a limb over the river and names it in Guarasug'wé. I repeat the word after she says it, prompting hysterical laughter from both her and the boy.

After a lull, she says, "Indians came from Brazil. I was small. They said, 'Speak to us in Indian!' but they spoke a different language! Not ours."

She plays with her grandson's hair and repeats softly, "Not ours . . . They went into the bush and died."

My few days in Bella Vista feel like fragments. From that disjointed first conversation with Flora (*They went into the bush and died*) until I leave, the only continuity is a tragic history ramming into the present.

For centuries the Guarasug'wé lived in communal longhouses where everything was shared. Their simple houses were easily abandoned as they migrated through the Chiquitania into the Amazon on the parallel trail of good hunting grounds and "the land without evil" (*Ivirehi Ahae*). The Guarasug'wé believed our physical life formed part of a reenactment of the

75

archetypal journey to *Ivirehi Ahae*. The prominence of *Ivirehi Ahae* in the Guarasug'wé worldview was magnified as Portuguese and Spanish colonists—and later the Brazilian and Bolivian governments—penned them into an ever narrower area. Remarkably, the Guarasug'wé eluded these opponents right into very recent times, as they continued their search now against the clock, their search for the land without evil.

But the global economy dealt the final blow. In the mid-twentieth century massive quantities of rubber were needed for a growing fleet of motor vehicles in the United States and Europe, and some of that rubber was found in Guarasug'wé lands. Bolivian and Brazilian rubber tapers on the payroll of wealthy barons invaded, enslaving the Guarasug'wé they could capture and killing those who resisted.

A few held on, abandoning one shelter after the next as they fled deeper into what is today Kempff National Park. But soon there was nowhere else to go. The rubber tapers were everywhere, and all that was left was to surrender or fight. The last Guarasug'wé cacique died in a standoff with well-armed and rubber-hungry invaders; their final shaman fell in a pool of blood soon after. The spine of their political and spiritual leadership cracked, and the last fifty or so Guarasug'wé disbanded and settled in the homes Misael and I saw along the banks of the river.

And they might have faded into extinction in those thatched homes but for the murder of a Brazilian policeman by narcotraffickers a few years ago. With the culprit at large and pressure to make arrests, the Guarasug'wé were scapegoated. Several were rounded up and beaten, and the rest of the terrified Indians abandoned their riverside homes to huddle together here in the hamlet of Bella Vista.

"Yo soy Guarasug'wé!"—I am Guarasug'wé!—an old woman named Kusasu exclaims in Spanish at a meeting I organize with Misael in the tiny schoolhouse, to brainstorm strategies for cultural rebirth. She then repeats the same thing

in Guarasug'wé, which causes the dozen teenagers present to break into embarrassed giggling.

"Why do you laugh?" Kusasu says. "How can you remember your language if you do not speak it?" She then shifts her gaze to me, "You can call me *sarí*—grandmother."

With this, the giggles become full-fledged laughter. The Guarasug'wé teens, in their shorts and T-shirts, have adopted the style of their adolescent counterparts in neighboring Brazil. Misael and I continue this ruse of a meeting, ours revealing itself for what it is: a fool's errand. Kusasu is the only one who speaks a decent smattering of the language. We adjourn and Kusasu invites us to her home. As we're leaving the schoolhouse, two men appear from the edge of the forest, their backs doubled over with canvas sacks dripping with bloody flesh. It's anta, or tapir, the half-horse, half-pig mammal found in South American jungles. Kusasu leads the burdened men and the rest of us back to her mud hut. The sacks are untied, revealing macheted chunks of tapir. The hunters' backs are covered with bright red blood.

Two young women get down to work. As they slice the meat into grillable chunks, their brown forearms are wet with blood. Meanwhile, others stoke the fire and skewer the meat with thin poles. As it grizzles and hisses on the fire, the smell makes me hungry.

For the rest of the afternoon, the night, and all through the next day, they would eat. Not three meals a day but a slow, consistent eating, the fire going, the meat sizzling, the gristle dripping onto cheeks and shirts. It's been two weeks since the last kill, and they're hungry. While eating with Kusasu and several relatives in the open-air kitchen next to their hut, I quiz the old woman about *Ivirehi Ahae,* the Amazon's seven skies, and the canoe ride to the hole in the first sky.

She tells me that's what "the ancestors believed," but real emotion only breaks out when she says, "Sometimes I miss my mother."

She chews a piece of tapir, staring off toward the river and the forest beyond. "It's nice to have a mother," she finally continues. "We would work all day, talking Guarasug'wé." Her eyes close, the rounded lids like moons, imagining the past. "Who can I speak *the dialect* with now?

"My children don't want to speak it, and my aunts and cousins are dead. Dead! *Sí, estamos perdiendo la cultura un poco*"—Yes, we're losing a little bit of our culture. With this understatement I completely lose my appetite. I excuse myself and walk down to the river and sit there in silence until well after sunset. That night I sleep fitfully, getting up at dawn to a sunrise over the river and marshlands, a few freshwater dolphins surfacing, and a hawk flapping to the other side of the river with a large fish in its claws. Why had Salvador encouraged me to come here to Bella Vista? My FAN colleague in Santa Cruz was right; this is a hospice of full-blown AIDS patients on their last T cells.

The case of the Guarasug'wé is not unusual. Of the sixty-eight hundred languages spoken now, half will be dead in fifty years—about a tongue per week. Next on the wait list for oblivion are the Udege of Siberia and the Amungme of Indonesia; Paraguay's Enxet and Kenya's Ogiek. Within Bolivia, the Guarasug'wé are to be followed by tribes like the Pacahuara, Araona, Uru-Chipaya, and Weenhayek. The villain most often cited is the spread of global capitalism to all corners of the earth, including the impact of television.

A common response to the extinction of languages is "So what?" Jonathon Keats argues in a *Prospect* piece "Viva Spanglish!" that we should let the old ones die and embrace hybrid tongues that adapt to the present, such as Spanglish, which "flourishes for all the reasons that minority languages are threatened. Capitalism, tourism, and television have eroded the linguistic authority of Spanish and English, encouraging their casual intermixtures." Keats seems to like words such as *amigoization* as "the process of Mexicanization of the U.S. Southwest" and *stationario* for writing stationery.

What he and others miss is that our planet's thousands of languages form an ecosystem. Just as in nature the ecosystem with the greatest diversity is the most robust, so too does human linguistic diversity provide a richer range of expression of how to thrive. The Guarasug'wé take with them over the chasm of extinction their own unique knowledge and cosmology.

It's time to leave Bella Vista, but Kusasu won't let me go. She points to a leafy plant that she says cures rheumatism; she presses my palm against a tree and says their mattresses used to be made of this bark. Like the few words of Guarasug'wé she still speaks, Kusasu offers these things up to me proudly, knowing that they're really not much at all. Misael has everything loaded and the motor roars to life. Walking down to the river with Kusasu, I ask her about Salvador. Her eyes come to life as she explains that he's been here many times.

"What does he come to do?"

"Just to be with us," she says.

Before I get on the boat, Kusasu takes my lightly freckled Irish hand in her wrinkled, bony one. What do I say to her now that I know who she is: the very last Guarasug'wé. The sound of the motor overpowers the swish of the river's eddies, and Misael nods to me, and I know as Kusasu does that there's really nothing to say, so I just keep her hand in mine for a very long moment and then let it go.

CHAPTER 10

"CRISIS IN THE Indian Territory," Len says, bursting into my office back in Santa Cruz. He briefs me as we hustle together to the new extension on the back of FAN's main building. The sign out front reads AMAZONA, short-hand for the fledgling Indian federation headed by Salvador that represents the Chiquitano communities around Kempff Park.

Salvador is just hanging up the phone as we enter. Lila is working at AMAZONA's sole computer—it's the first time I've seen a female included on Salvador's administrative team. This new office is a step up from the cramped cubicle in FAN's office that previously housed AMAZONA. *"Muy grave"*—Very troubling—Salvador says. He leans forward in his swivel chair, his paunchy midsection falling over his belt, and launches into the whole story.

The Bolivian government has proposed cutting an enormous two-hundred-thousand-acre chunk out of the proposed (very nearly approved, or so we thought) Indian Territory to appease two logging companies: Paraguá and Tarumá. Salvador shows us on a map exactly what this would mean: annexing the town of Cachuela, taking more than half of the portion allotted for Piso Firme, and pushing Porvenir practically flush with the river. "We won't have room to breathe," Salvador says.

We get into the legal issues. The logging companies do indeed have concessions overlapping with the Indian Territory, but they were dubiously obtained piecemeal from corrupt

Bolivian bureaucrats between 1985 and 1997. The concessions are not in use; the companies have not paid the required taxes. Most significant, Salvador adds, the government signed over something that "was not theirs to give"— Chiquitano lands. His voice grows in tenor and beads of sweat accumulate on his forehead as he says, "According to Article Six of the Forestry Law, in overlapping claims, 'original inhabitants' have priority. Our Indian Territory is 740,000 acres. It is indivisible and unalterable, and we will not give up a millimeter."

Salvador notices me reddening and says something that makes the blood catch inside my chest: "It used to be rubber, now it's timber. What happened to the Guarasug'wé is about to happen to us, the Chiquitanos."

Disparate images merge: a little girl screaming *"Kharisiri! Kharisiri!"* when she looked at me in La Paz and saw a marauding ghoul; the veins bulging from Kusasu's hands that felt like the roots of a cambará tree; and a haunting image of an Indian man long ago shedding a single tear. I find myself standing not only in AMAZONA's office in eastern Bolivia but in another space entirely, my feet tiptoeing along the edge of conquest. History and present collapse into one, and I feel what is for me a rare sense of moral clarity. I know that I will do everything I can to help Salvador and the Chiquitanos get their territory.

A long silence is finally broken by Len: "Salvador, you do realize who you are up against?" He says that the Paraguá company is run by the infamous Guillermo Roy, a Santa Cruz millionaire whose relatives' drug-trafficking activities are linked to the Medellín Cartel in Colombia. "Roy has the whole government in his pocket."

"Let them come," Salvador says, showing two large, fleshy palms. "Let them try to cut down even one tree."

* * *

Paraguá Indian Territory, far eastern Bolivia. Emergency meeting of the caciques

Salvador begins softly, gazing into the campfire more than at those of us gathered around it: "Are these 740,000 acres our home?"

"*Yes,*" the other caciques murmur.

"Do our wives live here?" *Yes.* "Our children?" *Yes!* "Yes? Are you sure?"

The other caciques appear off-balance. Salvador says, "Because my wife and children don't live here."

He pauses, and at the very moment one of the chiefs is about to correct him, Salvador stands up and hurls a log into the fire, causing sparks to fly, and booms, "Of course they live here! But Guillermo Roy's children don't live here. Will we let a stranger into our home to rape our wives?"

The caciques shout out "No!" in unison as Salvador turns the volume way down. "No, we will not," he practically whispers. "Nor will we allow the Paraguá and Taruma companies to rape our forests.

"*Compañeros,*" he continues, "can they hunt our last jaguars?" *No!* "Raise fences?" *No!* "Pen us in against the river like savages? *No!*" he joins in with the rest, his gold tooth flashing.

Salvador's words motivate the other chiefs to speak one by one. *Not one millimeter given up. Let them come to try to take our forests. We will hijack their tractors, their backhoes. They will never work in the Indian Territory. It is indivisible, sacred, whole, ours.* The deliberations stretch into the night. The coals glow orange and mustard yellow, the scent of smoke thick in the humid air.

Len, who has been punching away at a laptop computer, says, "*Ahora!* This is the first draft of the Declaration of the Paraguá. Tomorrow we *all* sign it—AMAZONA, the park, FAN, the municipality—demanding that the Bolivian government immediately title the full 740,000 acres of the Indian Territory forever!"

A cheer goes up. Little do we know, sitting around that remote campfire, what reverberations the declaration will have up to the highest levels of national government. For now we are swept up in solidarity; I sense sincere and heartfelt goodwill. Despite our varied backgrounds, we agree that this Indian homeland must exist. And in this moment we share a sense that we have some control over its destiny.

But the threat is much closer than we had thought.

The ink still wet on the declaration, we motor toward Santa Cruz in the Illustrious Green Wagonette but stumble across something alarming. Salvador spots it first: dozens of human bodies, shirtless and sweat-soaked.

When I look at the slippery mass eating hunted meat off sheets of slightly rusting metal, I think of maggots rather than men. It evokes a kind of hive, a gathering of worms. In actuality, these are several dozen workers squatting on a spongy, brown forest bed, eating after a day of timbering. We slow down to a crawl. Len is driving, with Gaspar sitting shotgun. I'm in the back with Salvador, a municipal official, and two rangers. We're all gaping at the camp of sweaty bodies, avoiding the thought of the rainforest destruction beyond the camp. The workers feast on Amazon wildlife: tatu, hochi, and jaguar. The hunting rifles now slung over branches were used to shoot their daily ration of meat.

These are colonists, *campesinos* from elsewhere in Bolivia who work for an industrial logging firm. While not yet in the Indian Territory, they log literally meters away, with nothing but the dirt road we are driving on separating their logging from the Chiquitano traditional lands.

I see the tension growing in Salvador's face. "Let's go," he finally mutters.

We drive in silence for a long while. The guards eventually fall asleep, but Salvador quietly stews, absorbed in thought. A bag of coca comes out and is passed around. Chewing the leaves into mushy wads energizes us a bit. Salvador asks the director if he will stop the vehicle, saying, "There's something I need to do."

My cheek still stuffed with coca leaves, I scramble up a steep rock escarpment right behind Salvador. The vehicle disappears from sight on the road below, and the sounds of insects, birds, and monkeys surround us. Finally, I stop beside a panting Salvador and follow his gaze into the expanse below.

Though I've walked and driven beneath the Indian Territory canopy many times, this rock overhang is a rare point where you can look out over its full green reach. The awe I felt flying over it for the first time returns, greatly multiplied by the matrix of soft breeze, animal calls, and the scent of wild fruit and flowers. Len and two rangers now come panting up toward our perch above the Territory. "*Jesus!*" one of the rangers says when he sees it. Gaspar finally joins us, his hands on his tiny hips, sweat dripping down his cheeks; he lets out a long whistle, then fishes his silver flask out of a pocket and takes a slow swig.

Salvador says to me in voice so small that the others can't hear, "Our Guarasug'wé friends are gone, and we can't save them." I survey the bulge of forest toward the horizon where Kusasu and the others in Bella Vista dead-end into the Paucerna River. Salvador continues, "We Chiquitanos are now the only ones left between this and a wasteland."

Salvador's face has hardened. Whereas for me it was enough to hear about the logging plans, Salvador had to smell the tart scent of felled mahogany and see the jaguar carcasses to fully feel his own potential extinction. I understand the parable of the tree that holds up the seven skies, but Salvador still lives in that world. Yet if he is to join the battle to save his forest home, he'll need to trade in his feather-light bag for a hard-shelled airplane carry-on; swap his tranquil papaya farm for conflict.

Salvador is looking down over a landscape that once was free, then enslaved, and has now become "unbundled territory," as Ruggie aptly terms such postmodern spaces. This land is embedded in a global *social imaginaire* that wants to free it once again—but according to a peculiar new logic. It is no longer cowboys versus Indians, but the two shoulder to shoulder. It is a place where multinationals wrestle one another, the one wanting to preserve it for global oxygen and the other desiring to chop it down for plywood. If the Chiquitanos want to protect their acres, they must do so on a battlefield of abstractions.

We've lapsed into silence. Len stands to my right; Gaspar, a few feet behind us with one foot raised on a chunk of rock; the park guards sit on the ridge with their feet dangling. The wind whipping in our hair, we all look toward the horizon over this carpet of rainforest where Bolivia's still-wild acres nudge into a denuded Brazil, and Salvador starts talking, and he's telling us a story.

It's such a beautiful story and so forcefully told that I start to believe it must come true. Salvador says they'll have their home forever. His five children and their children will live and prosper here in this place, Pacha Mama's womb. They'll win because they are not only right but are now also prepared. The wind takes hold of his phrases and carries them away, and I'm lulled into the tale until one word rips out of the story's fabric. It's a word I've never heard Salvador utter—a puff of breath that hits me like a cyclone. Salvador sees the shimmering forest and says *nature*.

PART II
Civilized Barbarians

CHAPTER 11

H IS NAME IS Daniel Irons," FAN's director, Gisela, tells me back at Santa Cruz headquarters. "He's an Australian millionaire. A bit . . . eccentric, but when I met him at that cocktail party, he kept talking about 'helping indigenous people.' " She jots down a phone number on a Post-it.

I call him several times but on each occasion am thwarted by his secretary. Finally, he answers the phone himself. I introduce myself and launch right into a pitch: I've heard he is interested in helping indigenous people. The lands of the tribe we work in the Amazon are under threat by a large logging company, and one key way they can achieve the economic power—and therefore political power—to fight that threat is by developing their own sustainable timber business on their land.

"Wait a bloody minute! You got me in the first sentence when you said *help indigenous people.* You see, my wife told me . . . Oh, never mind."

The next day Daniel shows up at FAN along with a man named Hart, director of a consultancy that provides technical assistance on forestry issues. After handshakes, a half dozen of us sit down around FAN's conference table, the air conditioner cooling the room. Hart translates for Daniel. After introductions Daniel gets to the point: "What you need are *aserraderos portátiles,* portable sawmills. Have you read the information I sent over? *La in-for-ma-ci-ón?*"

Hart translates. No one has seen it. Everyone listens respectfully as Daniel and Hart talk about huge markets for tropical timber in Australasia. Daniel: "I've got Singapore. Okay? I've got Hong Kong. I've got New Zealand, and I've got Australia! *Mucha madera!*" He twitches like an excited little boy as he speaks. I study his features—cropped gray beard covering his pinched cheeks and crawling well down his neck; teeth tinted slightly mustard yellow; bright blue eyes. Early fifties, maybe. Though wiry and erratic in his movements, an inner confidence is evident to everyone in the room; the assurance of the very rich.

Daniel's cell phone keeps going off. He takes the calls, jogging out of the room to talk and then apologizing loudly in English each time he comes back. I imagine a stable of stockbrokers on the line, but when the meeting ends, he says to me, "*Muchachas!* These Santa Cruz girls just keep calling me. And this one beautiful Brazilian. A little advice for you: the trick with women here is . . . Oh, another time. Bloody hell, I can't stand this conference-room shit, sitting around chewing pencils."

The veins in his thin neck now bulging out, he continues, "What do these people do? Anyway, let's put this deal together between two people: *you* and *me*. I don't understand a word they're saying."

I meet him at his place that evening. Suite 101 of Hotel Los Tajibos where he tells me he always stays while in Santa Cruz. We get into his permanently on-call taxi and head across the city.

"Speed up," he tells his driver, "we've got business to do."

The taxi driver steps on it, and we fly past thousands of souls carrying loads on their backs or pushing wheelbarrows, past the façades of cheaply constructed cinder-block buildings that went up during the city's 1980s boom. Daniel is saying, "I just want to stop and visit one of the girls who called earlier. The Brazilian, she's maybe twenty-two."

We stop, get out of the cab, and take a look at our destination: "Ah, shit," Daniel says. "It's a strip joint!"

90

Reluctantly, I follow him in, and the Brazilian meets us at the entrance, ushering us to a table in the front where another stripper in her early twenties joins me. Daniel's initial annoyance that his date turned out to be a stripper has evaporated. He orders cocktails for the four of us and, perhaps noticing my discomfort, asks me if I've ever been to a strip club. I tell him it's my first time. "Ahh! You'll love it, mate. I'll get the big show for you," he pays, and heads off to the bar, gesticulating wildly to the manager, explaining what he wants and slapping cash onto the bar. Meanwhile the girl next to me, wearing a bikini top and miniskirt, takes my hand and tells me I'm handsome.

Daniel returns rubbing his hands together saying, "All four of 'em," and then adds, "Okay, let's get the business out of the way. Here's the deal. I am retired, okay? I just want to go fishing. But my wife tells me, 'Go and help indigenous people.' So here I am."

He drains his drink and signals the waiter for another round. "I have absolutely no personal interest in this at all. None! My wife has three companies. I have had several—an export firm in Brazil, big hotels in the South Pacific. I'll tell you all about it some other time, yeah?"

Daniel is distracted by the Brazilian girl, who is tickling him. Meanwhile, a hand inches up my forearm and clasps my biceps. Daniel turns to me and says, "Translate this to her for me: *five-star hotel*." He holds up five fingers for her. "This Sunday, all day, pool, lobster, champagne." Both strippers nod excitedly when I translate *five-star hotel*.

"Okay," Daniel says, back to the business at hand. "So, I just want to be fishing, but I'm here to help *your* indigenous people. I have the markets."

He talks about the huge "pent-up demand" for tropical hardwoods in Australasia, especially as the forests in that region are being wiped out. While the tree species here are not the same, there are close substitutes. Daniel produces a ruler-shaped gadget that has inlaid chips of Bolivian species next to Asian species, the names engraved below. To my uninitiated eyes they look identical.

Then the plot thickens. Environmental activists in New Zealand have convinced their government to pass progressive laws that ban logging in all old-growth forests. Moreover, that country can import *only* certified ecological timber. "Picture it," he says, downing his second drink. "Bolivia could be *the* supplier of certified timber. This whole country is goddamn virgin rainforest and loaded with Indians. That's *both* environmentally *and* socially sustainable shit. If your Indians can get their act together—stop chewing pencils and get into the bush—they can make a killing."

"When do we start?" I ask.

Daniel squares himself to me. Smiling through his beard, he takes a slow drag on a cigarette. "I can deliver you the portable sawmills within sixty days. We're going to help indigenous people together!"

CHAPTER 12

RATIONALIZE IT as creative destruction: we'll take down the forest slowly enough to save it. The conservation code words: *sustainable logging.*

Bolivia has one of the most progressive forestry laws in the world. Anyone who wishes to log the Bolivian Amazon must to do so within a legally designated "annual use area" (*área de aprovechamiento anual,* or AAA) corresponding to just three percent of one's total concession; in other words, ninety-seven percent must be left alone. A full thirty years later, one returns to the original spot. And even within the tiny portion logged each year, strict guidelines apply: the area is thoroughly censused, and only trees above a certain diameter may be cut.

The law looks great on paper but is often ignored in practice—witness the chain-saw job we saw right beside the Chiquitano territory. Big logging firms are apt to bribe government officials to circumvent these rules. So how does a consumer know that the wood she buys is really from a sustainable forest? Through a SmartWood certification. This nonprofit uses international experts to ensure that forests are well managed and give their seal only to those that are. The organization applies not only strict ecological standards—for everything from how roads are created to which logs are felled—but also tracks the "social" side such as profit-sharing and gender equity.

Salvador and the Chiquitanos know that a SmartWood seal can bring a premium price in the world market and wish to get certified, but they face both demand and supply problems. On the demand side, while prices for certified wood are higher in most European countries, Canada, Australia, Japan, and New Zealand, in the closer U.S. market there is still little demand; American consumers are not yet convinced it's worth paying more for it. As for supply, the Indians are new to the business and lack start-up capital and market connections. Hence our reliance on Daniel's sawmills and expertise.

When not thinking about eco-wood, I find myself involved in a media campaign. Len and I help Salvador blast out a press release on the threat industrial logging poses for the Indian Territory. Salvador is invited onto a popular Santa Cruz radio program where he exposes a corrupt alliance between the Paraguá and Taruma logging firms and the national government that threatens to rob his people of their traditional lands and destroy wilderness. The next day the city's biggest paper, *El Deber*, runs the story under the headline KEMPFF NATIONAL PARK UNDER THREAT, accompanied by an image as dear to Bolivians as the Grand Canyon is to Americans: Kempff's spectacular Ahlfeld Falls crashing into the jungle.

But our media blitz fizzles. Guillermo Roy of Paraguá phones his buddy Pedro Mercado, director of *El Deber,* and he squashes the story. Len says bitterly that the major newspapers and TV stations in Bolivia are controlled by a tiny clique of elites going back to the colonial aristocrats. "Journalists get a bit of free rein to give the illusion of a free press," he tells Salvador and me, "but controversial stories are quickly buried."

Silenced in the press, we use other tactics. Salvador flies to La Paz to meet with representatives of INRA, the national agency charged with titling the nation's Indian lands, but comes back dejected, telling me INRA's rules are "longer than the Bible." He instead begins talking with members of a national network of Indians fighting similar battles. Meanwhile, we dispatch teams to cut a three-meter wide swath to demarcate the limits of the Indian Territory, which is all the more vulnerable for being a seamless blend into the forest around it.

But even as I notice a growing commitment in Salvador, obstacles arise from *within* the Chiquitano community. It begins with a curious question, aimed at me: "Why did you fire Mike?"

I say that Mike lied about his activities, and this alone means dismissal. But to top it off, he was cutting down rainforests for extensive cattle ranching, the exact opposite of FAN's goals.

Nods of agreement all around. *Sí, de acuerdo.* But then I'm asked again, and *again,* at every meeting with the seven chiefs and in many encounters with community members, "Why is Mike no longer among us?" I take a deep breath and calmly go over it again, until someone suggests, "Could we not just create a *trabajito* for *Mikecito*?"

I start to slowly go bonkers as, over the months, they try to wear down my defenses. Perhaps the worst part, since I'm an in-your-face New Yorker, is their indirect communication style. Their desire ("We want Mike back.") is stated in the form of a question ("Why is it that Mike isn't here anymore?"). It becomes a kind of water torture, the small drops penetrating my skin.

Their questioning is so persistent that I begin to suspect Mike is pulling the strings, cajoling or outright bribing the Indians to advocate for his job. But I finally realize that their feelings for the former FAN agronomist are genuine; solidarity is to blame. Regardless of his crimes, Salvador and the others feel emotionally attached to Mike and want him back in our circle. He had become part of *nosotros,* the Spanish for "we," whose three lovely syllables join the opposing ideas of "us" (*nos*) and "them" (*otros*) into one.

This sense of *nosotros* emerges in other moments, such as the time when a Chiquitano man originally from the Indian Territory (but now living in the regional capital) came to one of our quarterly meetings with an off-the-wall request: he wanted us to give him money for an expensive imported hearing aid for his daughter. I sat there, beside Salvador, feeling sorry for the guy. There was no way this would be approved. All of FAN's and AMAZONA's carefully crafted criteria lined up against it: our program priorities were titling the land and creating an economy on it—not hearing aids for urban Chiquitanos. Other nonprofits out there could assist with such a request, but not us.

But to my surprise, one by one the caciques voted, seven of seven hands in the air, to approve the expensive request. Procedures aside, this man and his daughter were part of *nosotros*.

Irked as I am by such rule-flaunting Chiquitano tendencies, I also understand. After all, I've felt firsthand the warmth of *nosotros*: those long, coca-chewing hauls to the Indian Territory; jokes and chicha; "becoming a bee" with the caciques. I've gradually become part of their whole.

When I first arrived in Santa Cruz and started working with my deputy, the twenty-eight-year-old Chiquitano man who called himself Esmeeters, I was dying to ask what his name meant in his native language. But I didn't want to pry without knowing him better, so I asked the flamboyant Len.

"It's Smithers," he said drily.

"Smithers?"

"Yes, but pronounced with a Latino accent."

I told him the only Smithers I knew of was from the television show *The Simpsons*.

"That's right," Len said. "The ingratiating assistant to Homer's ugly boss, Mr. Burns."

I knew the satirical cartoon *Los Simpsons* to be a hit program among the minority of Bolivians who actually owned TVs, including nearly everyone at FAN, but however did my deputy end up with that name?

"I don't even know his real name," Len said. "Nobody does. He's always been Smithers. It's no secret that he's the biggest schmoozer at FAN. I'm sure he's been kissing your ass . . . Mr. Burns."

The next time I saw him, I couldn't suppress a smile. "Why did you accept the nickname Smithers?"

He looked at me a bit puzzled, wearing a fake Rolex and imitation Nike shoes and said, "Because it's American."

But now Smithers has burst into my office with a concerned look on his face. "Someone from Indian Territory had a stroke! Can I please be excused?"

I agree, of course, and he rushes to the hospital. But a few days later when I'm doing a routine spot-check on my project budgets, my eyes pause on an unusually large expense for transport and medical care for someone with Smithers's last name. A little alarm bell goes off, and when I check it out, sure enough, the stroke victim is his uncle.

I call Smithers into my office and ask him about it. A bit defensively, he mumbles something about a line item flexible enough to be used for health care.

"For *relatives*?"

He looks at his lap. I decide to view this as an unconscious goof-up. We talk about conflict of interest for a while, and then I ask him to please send any such approvals to me in the future. He agrees enthusiastically, promising over and over that it will never happen again.

I dig a bit deeper, however, and find other check requests signed by Smithers for his sister and cousins. Although these were for tiny items such as per diems and travel, he is headed down a slippery slope.

Our quarterly review rolls around, and all of us huddle around a conference table: park and FAN staff, the seven chiefs, seven community women, and the grand pooh-bah himself, Salvador. A passionate moment ensues when Lila, AMAZONA's volunteer secretary, stands up and launches into a speech about how she has children and needs money and couldn't the Amazon Project budget come up with *"una ayudita"*—a little help—each month to the tune of eight hundred bolivianos?

On cue, Salvador stands up and supports her. "Lila helps hold AMAZONA together and deserves this *ayudita.*"

The other chiefs all weigh in supporting Lila. They are ready to move on to the next issue, but I stand up. *"Colegas,"* I say, "we need to discuss this more, but . . . *ay caramba!* . . . it's time for the chicha break."

I'm buying time. Over chicha, I corner Salvador and blurt out, "Salvador, what the hell was going on in there?"

He stiffens at my Anglo-Saxon directness, and I do a retake: "Don Salvador, this is a fine day indeed, and we've made an enormous amount of progress. You made so many beautiful points."

"Gracias," he says, flashing a gold-toothed grin.

"Just one tiny little thing, Salvador. Oh, it's really nothing."

"No, tell me, amigo Bill. What is it?"

I tell him again that it's nothing—and why don't we get some more chicha?—but he insists.

"It's just the itsy-bitsy issue of paying Lila a salary . . ." The diplomatic foreplay eventually blends into the problem: Lila is not only Smithers's sister but also sister of Smithers's brother, one of chiefs at the table. It would be a serious conflict of interest to vote her a stipend, even a small one.

Salvador listens intently, looking at me respectfully and nodding. I calmly explain that it would also set a disastrous precedent; next, the caciques would want a payment, which would be swept to a vigorous approval in the warm glow of *nosotros.* "I think we need to show some spine and stop this in its tracks," I say, wrapping things up. "Don't you think so, Salvador?"

"So it is," he says.

Success, I think to myself, convinced that my firm grasp of

Western ethics has persuaded the Chiquitano leader. As soon as we regroup, Salvador stands and says, "During the break amigo Bill made some fine points about the *ayudita* for Lila, and I think we need to reconsider." I'm doing cartwheels inside, as Salvador continues, "Yes, considering the amigo's fine points, I propose that we do not pay Lila the eight hundred bolivianos a month." He looks around the silent room and adds, "Let's just make it seven hundred and fifty!"

Salvador sits back down. I look over at Smithers and the park director. They avert my glance. I slowly rise, shoulders stooped.

"Compañeros," I begin, "I love the sister Lila as a friend and colleague. I know that she contributes so much to AMAZONA . . ." After several minutes of separating what-I'm-about-to-say from the person of Lila, I present the conflict-of-interest and budgetary-limits case. The park director remains silent, seeing exactly where this is going and not wanting to expend political capital with the caciques.

The Indians patiently support *la hermana Lila* (who in this case is *literally* their sister). They'll stay as long as it takes. The speeches in support of Lila drone on.

Though we've made strides toward understanding "the future," Salvador and company have been weaned on subsistence. Hunt to hunt and harvest to harvest, there is seldom a surplus with which to save, to invest, to plan. To them our program budget continues to look like a meaty tapir, blow-gunned down in the forest. Let's eat it before it spoils! We'll spend into the glorious solidarity of the now, where all is tangible and heartfelt. I've seen this dilemma recur during a decade of working with poor communities in Latin America, Africa, and Native North America: an overwhelming preference for present consumption. It goes something like this: there is a person sitting in our circle with a need; we have money; we must connect the money with that need. The twin tentacles of nepotism and presentism intertwine in a deadly grip. *These* people in *this* moment; all that is here and now.

There's Lila across the table, a frown etched in her fore-head. She does have kids to feed. But the donors demand we follow a code of ethics, and this is a clear breach: voting to pay a salary to a relative without a competitive interview process. I know I could stall, say it has to be approved at higher levels, but I instead sit back down, enter into the now, and let the money slide. Lila's face lights up, and I'm back in *nosotros*.

CHAPTER 13

B P ON THE line," FAN's receptionist says to me.
My first thought: *I've been caught.* Our investing partner knows I've been letting little nepotisms slide. But it's nothing of the sort, of course. "I'm worried about our buffer zone," he says, perhaps from the thirty-eighth floor of a glass tower in Dallas.

It takes a moment to get what he means. The Indian Territory, to him, is "buffering" Kempff Park from human impacts that might affect the millions of trees sucking carbon out of earth's atmosphere for BP. I tell him about the two logging firms, but he interrupts, saying, "We're not indemnifying the fuckers. They've got plenty of money. The solution is simple: Whip the Indians into a frenzy. Get them to fight for their lands and the companies will back down."

I move the phone away from my ear for a quick second, feeling disoriented. I bring it back to my ear but don't say anything. I look beyond the clutter of my desk, through the window to the palm trees in the middle distance. Before we hang up, he reminds me that "ours is the biggest rainforest-carbon project in the world" and that "people want to replicate it globally up the wazoo" and "there's a damn lot riding on it," but I'm catching only snatches. I'm too focused on what he said earlier: "The solution is simple."

It's not. New complications surface when I travel once again to the Indian Territory, to the village of Porvenir, and meet with the slight-framed Chiquitano Indian man named Apollonius, whom everyone has begun calling "the sultan." He pulls up in a Toyota pickup, its chrome fiercely shined.

"Nice truck," I say to Apollonius, drumming my fingers on the roof of what may well be the first privately owned motor vehicle in the Indian Territory.

"Thanks to you," the tiny man says in a fluty voice. "The heart-of-palm profits!"

It seemed straightforward several months back when I decided to assist Apollonius with his floundering heart-of-palm business. He was eager to expand, so I contracted a German business consultant through the Amazon Project budget to help him with production and marketing, and in record time containers left Bolivia, bound for a supermarket chain in neighboring Chile. The Chileans were happy with the order and sent Apollonius a big check, which he used to purchase his Toyota.

We drive together from the village clearing to his beautifully revamped factory. The place is silent, but he explains how it looked a few weeks ago. In preparation for the big Chile shipment, the entire village had been working: men in the forest collecting the tender cabbage from the assai palm; two dozen women in hairnets and protective gloves cutting, canning, and labeling. He lavishes thanks on me for sending the consultant to help streamline his production platform and locate markets.

As we drive from Apollonius's factory to his home, his vehicle's glass and steel, and the motor's roar, separate us from the strolling Chiquitanos outside, one of whom scowls in our direction. Oblivious to the scowl, Apollonius smiles, his tiny foot stretching for the gas pedal. Proud as a maharaja on an elephant, he waves at the people walking outside, as we take the long way around the town. "I've been telling my people not to hunt jaguars," he says, turning onto another dirt road. "Sure, I used to hunt, sell the furs, but it's not right! You know, it was my kids convinced me to stop killing jaguars."

This interests me. "So they haven't forgotten about Mou, the free soul," I say, unable to suppress a smile. Like Salvador, it seems these kids haven't lost respect for wild animals as the reincarnation of one's ancestors.

But Apollonius is shaking his head vigorously: "What's Mou? They've been watching Animal Planet. 'Jaguars are *endangered species*,' they told me."

A gleaming satellite dish greets us as we pull into Apollonius's driveway, the advent of global television programming in the Indian Territory, beamed in from neighboring Brazil. Carpenters are busy hammering together a new extension on Apollonius's house. Inside, his long combination living and dining room has a beautiful hardwood floor, shined so much it hurts to look at it. Screens fortify the ranch-style home against malaria-carrying anopheles mosquitoes. Both the bathroom and kitchen smell of bleach and are remarkably hygienic in contrast with the Indian Territory's typical chicken-pecked homes; even Salvador's house, despite his role as president of the entire Indian Territory, has a rough-hewn wood floor.

Apollonius's daughters, eight and ten, serve us Nescafé instead of traditional chicha. My host crosses his legs and lifts the coffee cup off the saucer with two fingers, his pinky idling in midair. "The whole house is made of *mara*," he says. Mahogany. Grows like a weed around here. His daughters head out the screen door, dressed in T-shirts and pure white sneakers probably purchased in Brazil. "I'm sending them to high school and college over in Brazil," he tells me. "They're going to be doctors."

I spend several hours chatting with the opinionated Apollonius. The seven chiefs: "They're like bureaucrats everywhere—they do squat! That's why I stay out of politics. Salvador is the only one doing anything." Books: "I only have one, Ayn Rand's *The Fountainhead*. I've read it nineteen times. That and the Bible." Lifestyle: "I get up every day at five A.M. and exercise. Lots of jumping jacks!" He stands up and demonstrates, his tiny body bouncing, a huge smile on his mustached face.

It turns out his taste for Ayn Rand and the exercise regime came from the same place as his capitalist spirit: Protestant missionaries. Priests haven't made it here, but preachers have. Though they have now left, Iowa evangelicals spent the better part of two decades in Porvenir nurturing a flock—and Apollonius became their star. Not only does he eschew alcohol and tobacco, but he's a poster child for the Protestant work ethic. "After jumping jacks I work," he tells me. "Every day except the Lord's day, and right until dark. How do you think I'm building my fortune?"

Here his usually cheery face becomes drawn. "The others are lazy," he says, frowning over steepled fingers. "Why do you think the Indian Territory is still just a jungle?"

Apollonius's question lingers with me, and several days later, back in Santa Cruz, I bring it up with Len.

"The little sultan picked up a deadly disease from the missionaries," says Len. We're cruising to a meeting across town in Len's Lada, having just navigated a second ring choked with pedestrians, motorbikes, and street stalls. "The disease is called *nature disdain*. It was passed into the human population by the Hebraic God's injunction from Genesis: 'Be fertile and increase, fill the earth and master it; and rule the fish of the sea, the birds of the sky, and all the living things that creep on earth.'"

I talk with Salvador about it too, over lunch. He's about to head back out to the Territory. "Amigo Bill," he says in his resonant voice, "there are two ways of looking at a tree." Here, an enormous pause. We're eating seventy-five-cent plates of the spicy chicken *majadito* dish with plantains and rice at the patio-restaurant next to FAN. I put down my fork and look at him.

"A modern man sees a tree different from an Indian. The modern man sees something to convert into money. But the

Indian sees it *de una manera integral*. He sees a house, a way to improve his health, he sees shade, he sees the fruits and nuts it gives, and he sees the animals that live in the tree, that he hunts. Do you understand what I mean?"

I look up for a moment at the flowering tajibo shading us, then back at him. "Sure, but Apollonius is as much Chiquitano Indian as you."

"Apollonius," Salvador says, "sees land and not territory."

Salvador recently explained this distinction for me. Land (*tierra*) is like a machine, a privately owned productive area from which to extract as much as you can. Territory (*territorio*) is an Indian concept: communally shared, indivisible, and based on a reciprocal relationship of taking and giving back.

After meeting Apollonius I begin to eye Smithers differently, and not because of his accounting slip-ups. He now dutifully brings all check requests connected to his family members to me for approval. In fact, he does everything perfectly. Smithers is more than a loyal yes-man. He soaks up the ideas like generative language and planning for the future and is on a steep learning curve managerially, taking a large part of the burden of day-to-day Amazon Project management off my shoulders. And I've found myself boasting to others that not only is he a joy to work with, but he's *from* the area. In fact, Smithers is the first and only Chiquitano from the Indian Territory with a college degree.

But other details sprout like minuscule weeds. He's upgraded his generic jeans to real Levi's. He's got a cell phone on his belt. While he's always used hair gel, hasn't Smithers turned up the volume to extrafirm hold? His black hair is slicked back into a helmet. I overhear my department secretary commenting on his noticeable new cologne: "It's Urban Decay." His brother, the chief of Piso Firme, has two hundred cattle, and his sister Lila is now on FAN's payroll. Smithers and his siblings, when I look more closely, have just a hint of

inbred genes. Smithers, for example, though considered handsome by FAN's female staff, has eyes that are just a bit too far
apart and a forehead a smidge flatter than it should be.
And his skin, isn't it lighter than Salvador's and Gaspar's, perhaps more akin to the complexion of the tiny, mustached
Apollonius?

CHAPTER 14

S IX O'CLOCK, HOTEL Los Tajibos. We've got business to discuss," Daniel says to me before abruptly hanging up the phone. He's back from Hong Kong, Malaysia, Singapore, New Zealand, Australia, Europe, Brazil.

I meet him at six sharp in the hotel. We each drain a Scotch in the gardens and then shuttle over to the city's best Japanese restaurant, using Daniel's on-the-spot taxi. It waits for us outside as we dig into sushi and sake. Everything, as always, goes on his credit card, which he shows me, asking if I notice anything strange about it.

"There's no name," I say, looking at the card. "Just a number."

"If there's a *name,* you have to pay something called *taxes*! All my shit's offshore." He shovels a yellowtail roll into his mouth with chopsticks and says, "Do you believe in evolution?"

I give him a blank look.

"ESP," he says, looking at me through the top of his wire-rimmed glasses, fingering his close-cropped beard. "I have it, but I'm a monkey."

That particular tidbit of Dada leads nowhere, as Daniel segues into other themes. His Australian accent makes such non sequiturs especially humorous. At other times his accent smoothes out into something nearly British, as in "Oh, but there's lots of staff all over the world," referring to his numerous companies. "I just don't know who they are." Or another time: "I've got the whole top floor of the tallest building in Sydney. I just never use it."

Heaps of sushi later, just as we are ready to leave, he finally says, "Oh, right, the indigenous people thing. My wife tells me, 'Help indigenous people.' Like I told you, *I'm retired*. I just want to go fishing. I have no interest in this personally, okay? But I need a business plan on that ecological timber thing. Something I can sink my teeth into. Can your boys come up with a b-plan?"

I'm with Salvador and Smithers first thing the next morning and we get the business plan rolling. We finish it in just a few days, and a FAN messenger drops it off at Hotel Los Tajibos, Suite 101.

On the phone later that same day Daniel says, "Get your bloody ass over here. And bring your bathing suit."

When I ring the bell to 101, a woman in her late twenties in shorts and a bikini top answers. She ushers us in, eyeing Silvana, a Bolivian colleague from FAN who insisted on coming along with me to meet the odd Australian millionaire. The television is tuned to CNN in the suite's living room. A maid clears the remains of a shellfish dinner and wineglasses from the table.

A bare-chested Daniel comes leaping down the carpeted stairs in his bathing suit. He has our business plan in hand, and a huge grin covers his face. "Your business plan is bloody brilliant!" He pumps the bound document in the air several times, then *throws* it toward Silvana and me. It misses us and collides with a wall. "I'm so bloody excited. I already FedExed five copies to Australasia."

After Silvana and I change into our bathing suits, the four of us walk across the hotel compound toward the sauna. As we walk, Daniel puts his arm around my shoulder and says, "Just to get this out of the way: I'd bonk yours and you'd bonk mine . . . *Now,* with that b-plan we are officially in business. I'll have those sawmills here in a jiff."

We do dry sauna, and then Daniel pays for massages for everyone, followed by steam sauna. As Silvana and Daniel's girlfriend get acquainted, Daniel says to me slowly, "I am respected in certain parts of the world for different things." His face and his body drip with sweat. "I've been around a long time . . . had thousands of lives."

Later, poolside, Daniel shares more about his past with me. It's a stream-of-consciousness ramble, but I gather that he worked as a secret agent in Central and South America in the eighties. Before that, he was a physicist and made his first million via a nebulous invention that he patented. He plowed that money into an export company in Brazil; then came several hotels in the South Pacific and various businesses in Australasia, especially in Australia, where he now lives with his wife in a coastal mansion outside Sydney.

I look at the fifty-five-year-old, handsomely graying man beside me and picture him in his different incarnations: as James Bond, 007; as the brilliant physicist; as the hotelier and business tycoon. A thought surfaces: *This whole thing is a big joke at my expense. Or is it? There's no denying he's rich.*

In the end I decide it doesn't matter. I feel sufficiently absorbed by the mystery of Daniel. With him there is always—and this is the best way to describe it—a sense of anticipation. Something big is always just about to happen. As for my original goal of "landing him" for the Indian Territory, I feel increasingly ambivalent. I've begun to see the effect of money: dividing the Indians, creating conflict. I also continue to be slightly suspicious of Daniel's motives: Why would this mega-capitalist be interested in small fry like Salvador's AMAZONA?

Everyone relaxed from our evening of sauna, massage, and swimming, Silvana and I shake hands with Daniel in his foyer. "This is stimulating me," Daniel says, referring to the business plan.

"Good," I say, trying to force a genuine smile out of my dwindling enthusiasm for the project. "I hope it happens."

"It *will* happen. And *I* am the one who will make it happen. Nobody else. I'll just keep stimulating you, and you stimulate me back, and pretty soon it'll be a big bloody orgasm."

When I'd caved on the *ayudita* or "little help" of 750 bolivianos a month for Smithers's sister, Lila, I knew I was on a slippery slope. Sure enough, the seven chiefs begin to eye the project budget, and they come up with an angle for dipping in themselves: per diem.

"We only get fifty bolivianos!" one cries out. "How can we survive in the city?"

Per diem—a daily sum to cover expenses during trainings or other events—is a perennial point of contention in community work. Per diem is never enough. So over the years I've developed an activity to nip this complaint at the bud: I have the group add up their own daily expenses, which are inevitably less than the per diem; after which the complaint usually wilts and dies.

They call out what they need for food, lodging, transport, and other expenses, and I write each figure on the board. Everyone agrees the total is the maximum they could reasonably spend per day: forty bolivianos, or just over five U.S. dollars.

"And how much is the per diem now?"

"Fifty bolivianos," one chief calls out earnestly.

"Exactly. As we see, you are actually receiving ten bolivianos more than you need. So you owe FAN a refund." I quickly add, "It's a joke. The extra ten is a kind of a cushion. All in favor of moving on to the next agenda item, the Indian Territory's dispute with Big Timber?"

No one is in favor. "How can we survive on fifty bolivianos?" one cacique calls out.

"Pretty well if you can survive on forty. We just did the math. Did we miss anything?"

"Chicha!" one calls out. *Included.* "A couple of beers in the evening!" *Included, under miscellaneous.* "Taxi!" *Included.* A dozen needs are called out, all of which are already on the list. Exasperated, one cacique circles back to "We need chicha!"

I respond that FAN pays for that. "Remember the two complimentary chicha breaks we had today?"

An hour passes. Two hours. Salvador is irkingly silent; I wish he would jump in on the side of logic. But an unspoken assumption lurks below the surface of the discussion: "We're sacrificing days of labor by being here. So we should be paid for it." Finally, someone raises this directly.

"But that's not per diem, it's a daily wage," I say, explaining that the trainings and workshops are voluntary, for their own benefit. Len gets up and buttresses this, as does Smithers.

Finally, Salvador intervenes: "*Compañeros!* Let's look for a Solomonic truce. We'll raise the per diem from fifty to eighty bolivianos. It's not a wage, just"—here Salvador drops the dreaded word pioneered by Lila—"an *ayudita.*"

"That's a wage," I say, noting that the forty boliviano surplus above their expenses amounts to an average daily wage in Bolivia. Vehement words in favor of Salvador's proposal! Len and Smithers have backed down now that Salvador has intervened. No one but me wants to ruffle feathers with the chiefs. An hour passes, and I realize this is an intractable filibuster. I give in. The per diem will be raised.

"*Bueno,*" Salvador says, "we're here to talk about my payment."

Four of us are seated in FAN's cramped finance office, a window-mounted air conditioner whirring. FAN's thirty-year-old administrator, Rosa, sits to my left, with Smithers and Salvador across the table. Despite the AC, Salvador is sweating hard, perhaps from the walk across from the AMAZONA extension in an adjoining building. A bead of sweat has accumulated on his upper lip and looks as if it might to-boggan right down his gold front tooth and into his mouth. The lighter-skinned Smithers's face is guarded.

Rosa shifts in her seat. The issue is delicate. FAN pays Salvador a monthly stipend of nearly five hundred dollars, a fortune in Bolivia, particularly for someone like him who does not hold even a high school diploma. Salvador negotiated his pay—and perks that include two additional monthly salaries, a year-end bonus, and nearly unlimited travel expenses—before I arrived. Originally negotiated as a temporary *ayudita,* Salvador's salary has become untouchable.

I answer Salvador's question with another: "Have you opened AMAZONA's bank account?"

He has not. I tightened the procedures several months back, and Salvador's payment has to go through AMAZONA instead of directly to him in cash each month. Salvador and the rest of AMAZONA knew perfectly well that they had to open this account, but only now, two months behind on Salvador's salary, is this really hitting home.

"Let's look for a *salida Solomónica,*" Salvador says, faintly smiling. "Why don't you just pay me right now, in cash, and for the *next time* we will have the bank account opened."

"Salvador, I'm sorry, but you know what the auditors said. Open the account and we'll deposit the money."

"I have responsibilities," Salvador says, his face tightening. He's sweating even more now.

I talk about donor procedures and insist that Salvador open the bank account first. It would take only a few days to get AMAZONA's legal documents together and do it.

"A man must fulfill his obligations," Salvador says, his voice now rising. Rosa looks increasingly anxious. Salvador's face darkens and I think, *We do have skulls under our faces.* But looking more closely, I perceive a touch of vulnerability mixed in with his determination to get his money and quick. Salvador has become dependent on us.

Civilized barbarian. That's what Salvador had called him-self. I hadn't fully understood his mysterious oxymoron at the time, but now it makes more sense. He'd used the term several weeks ago, out in Piso Firme for a meeting about Kempff Park, and the park director was saying to a group of the chiefs, "We've done a lot to help you get the Indian Territory. And we're almost at the finish line."

The director then paused, weighing his next, extremely delicate thought. "But what would stop you . . . once it's yours . . . from just cutting it down and selling it?"

Here the caciques launched into alternatingly impassioned and soothing diatribes about the importance of the park, of not clear-cutting or overhunting *los bichos.* As they spoke, the director, a forestry engineer, nodded enthusiastically. But all the while Salvador was strangely silent, his face drawn. He listened from the edge a school bench, his button-down shirt tucked into his jeans, belly hanging over his belt. When he finally did speak, his words were few: *"No le preocupe, Inge-niero, ya somos barbaros civilazados."*—Don't worry, Engi-neer, now we're civilized barbarians.

To borrow from Kissinger, Salvador has become a paradox within a contradiction wrapped up in a Pandora's box. By joining the conservationists, he had to pay a city rent, take buses, and buy groceries. In Santa Cruz, liaising with govern-ment officials and Indian leaders, he can no longer go into his back forty and hack into a pineapple, spear a tapir, or gather yucca. We'd taken him out of the delicate subsistence and barter economy, brought him into the cash economy, and be-gun to pay him.

And now he's in debt and feeling the pressure. From what I've heard, now that Salvador has a salary, his relatives knock at the door, and he's generous with loans he knows will not be repaid.

"I don't want to do this," Salvador eventually says, his face loosening up a bit, though he's still leaning forward, with his chest, shoulders, and neck muscles tense. He shifts to look toward the door, as if to make sure no one is watching, then says to me, "Can we talk in private?"

Rosa and Smithers step out, and the normally confident, resolute Salvador mumbles rapidly, "I'm begging you. I know I shouldn't need to, but I do because I need the money right now."

I shift in my chair, "Salvador, are you—"

"Yes or no?" he says, a completely uncharacteristic pleading look in his eyes. "Can you help me?"

"Yes." *If I can help you, I will.*

I ask Rosa to make the payment immediately available, and I drive him personally in one of FAN's pickups to the bank to start opening AMAZONA's account.

CHAPTER 15

F AN DOES NOT provide me with a car for personal use; instead of buying one I opt for the bus like the ninety-eight percent of others in Santa Cruz who own no car.

Luckily, since private cars are scarce, the *micros*—two-decade-old rectangles, about half the length of a yellow school bus—are plentiful. Each line comes by every seven minutes, passes within a block or two of any point in the city, and stops wherever you want. And like most things in Bolivia, which has the lowest cost of living in South America, bus fare is cheap: one and a half bolivianos (eighteen cents) will get you anywhere in the city. I hail one on the way to FAN each morning and back each afternoon, pressing coins into the driver's palm and squeezing into a seat between *cholitas* in polleras and schoolchildren in their white uniforms. The bus is filled with smells: sweat, stale tobacco, chewing coca, and of the occasional farm animal along for the ride.

Santa Cruz's *tranquilo* friendliness continues unchanged as the months pass, and the bus is no exception. One day, I'm headed for a destination downtown and ask the bus driver to let me know when we arrive. Ten minutes later a dozen of my fellow passengers spring into action. *"Ya estamos!"* and *"Acá se puede bajar!"* they call out, gently nudging me to the door, and pointing toward a corner one block away where I'm to turn left. I thank the driver and everyone else. The group, a random assortment of Quechua transplants, urban mestizos, and modern-looking youth, wave in unison, three quarters of the folks smiling. It takes me a minute or so to reach the far corner, but when I do, I steal a glance back toward where I'd stepped off the bus, and it is *still there*. The driver has the door open and smiles at me, gesturing that I should go left now. Three or four other hands emerge from windows, indicating the same direction.

Jogging too, I'm bombarded by good cheer. Two or three times a week I jog out of my sliver of middle-classdom, Urby Lisboa, and into the great slums around it. At the beginning I leash up Pacha Mama and jog beside her for protection, now that I know what a pit bull my shepherd can be. But after a few times I leave the dog at home. According to UN statistics, Bolivia has the lowest crime rate in South America. Rather than knifing me for my wallet, the hordes of tire-tread-sandaled urban Indians and ragamuffin children gently tease me, saying, "You lazy?" and "Is that as fast as you can go?"

"I don't see you running!" I rejoin, to which most call out something like "In this heat?" as they swing in their hammocks. Occasionally someone responds by mock-jogging beside me—but for no more than a few steps before downshifting to sloth speed and easing onto a shady stoop.

I puzzle over the small-town friendliness in a city of a million people. Sure, the city's motto is "Hospitality: The law of Santa Cruz" (and that may be the *only* law of this freewheeling place), but how is it that bus drivers earning two dollars a day wait patiently to see if I've looked both ways before crossing the street? And I'm jogging, after all, through poverty. These are the third world's "ruined peasants," displaced from the land by dramatic shifts in global capitalism, spreading into urban peripheries around the globe. Most of the homes I jog past along the dirt roads beyond the fourth ring have piped water and electricity but inadequate sewerage. The houses are made of mud or exposed cinder block topped with rusty zinc roofs and surrounded by a noisy assortment of pigs, chickens, and ducks, the people's rural pasts transplanted into ten-by-twenty-meter lots. Livestock and human feces are disease vectors, contributing to a high under-five mortality rate. And then there's mosquito-borne dengue and the occasional outbreak of cholera.

One day I'm feeling rather dismayed with the backdrop of my jog, my spirits only slightly buoyed by the jaunty comments. Why so much apathy and resignation amid such squalor? And I'm also, let's face it, feeling a touch of homesickness. It's one of those Bolivian holidays where everyone is gathered with their humongous families; I'm usually invited to join in with friends' or colleagues' clans, but it's not the same. All of a sudden—splash!—a freezing bucket of water is hurled my way. My face, hair, T-shirt, and shorts drenched, I see a grinning Bolivian mom in her late twenties with an empty bucket. She'd been in a water fight with her two kids, who are now looking at me with a trace of horror, not knowing how to react.

Neither do I. "Why did you do that?" I stammer. I've stopped short and am a soggy mess.

"You looked hot," the young woman says. The tropical sun belting down on us, I realize it is hot as hell, and now I feel refreshed. She goes back into her water fight, and I jog forward with mixed emotions. I feel slightly less lonely, charmed by her playful gesture. Yet part of me wants to tell her she's being too kind, that she lacks a proper sense of the tragic in life. If she had read the social science literature, she'd know she is embedded in a web of poverty, unemployment, malnourishment, and chronic disease, sleepwalking in the nightmare of the *social imaginaire,* a ruined peasant whose freedom is increasingly circumscribed by worsening inequality along an expanding urban perimeter, steadily pulsing against its own boundaries from legions of new immigrants—economic refugees like herself—evoking the image of a permanent stain.

Does she realize her nation is internally colonized?

Still soaked, I cross the fourth ring into the exclusive Palms neighborhood, the slums giving way to wide, paved streets with sidewalks; a vast golf course cut by rider-mowers instead of trimmed by donkey teeth; and near total silence. The only people around are the private security guards in front of tall, white walls partially concealing a variety of spectacular three-story mansions, some classically dove-colored, epicurean; others brightly shellacked, new-money kitsch. I'm tempted to say, "It's a different world," but, as Paul Farmer quipped of Paris versus Haiti, "That would have the distinct disadvantage of being wrong."

Not only is it the same world, but the same nation and the same square kilometer that includes mud-and-zinc shacks and my own house and hammock. It's Latin America, the most unequal region in the world, according to the World Bank, worse than Asia and Africa. Inequality is as Latin American as salsa music and magical-realist fiction; the richest tenth among Latin Americans earn 48 percent of total income, while the poorest tenth earn a mere 1.6 percent. (The equivalents for first-world countries are 29.1 percent and 2.5 percent.)

In Bolivia, this inequality cuts along a razor-sharp racial edge. Logging magnate Guillermo Roy, the man after the Indian Territory, lives in one of these mansions, as do many other of the several hundred non-Indian businessmen handed the lion's share of Bolivia's tropical forest, the sixth largest in the world. But, still wet from the bucket of water, I feel no moral clarity about it all; how does one square the spontaneous humanity of the have-nots with the unhappy exteriors of the haves?

The proposed Chiquitano Indian Territory contains within its boundaries six private properties, legally known as *terceros,* or third parties. These are small hacienda-type ranches, usually owned by non-Indians. The national law establishing Indian Territories (known as ITs) states that such titled properties cannot be confiscated by the Indians—so they become subsumed as islands of private property within the vast communal indigenous lands. And that's not always a bad thing. In the case of the Kempff-bordering territory, these six *tercero* islands take up only five percent of the total, and the white folks living there have come to peacefully coexist with the Indians after up to a century of residence. In fact, these six *tercero* families have been fighting alongside Salvador to nail down the IT once and for all because this will also seal their own properties as permanent. But there were just six. It became a reflexive phrase in our discussions: *los seis terceros.* Always six, not one more or less.

"Now there are seven," Smithers says to me one day in my office. "Seven *terceros.*"

"Six," I correct him.

"Seven," he says spitefully. "*Salvador* has declared himself the seventh."

I let the words sink in. "Impossible."

"Six thousand acres of prime land right outside Porvenir! Other *comunarios* are complaining that they can't even graze their cattle there anymore." Smithers spins out the story: Salvador has used his insider knowledge of the whole Indian Territory titling process—gained through countless meetings with lawyers and government officials—to resurrect some old property documents arguably linked to his grandfather and incarnate them in the name of his father to avoid direct conflict of interest. Quietly, the papers have been approved granting Salvador's family *tercero* status, their personal slice of the jungle pie. Salvador has evidently wiggled out of caste, emerging as the Indian Territory's seventh noble landlord.

"This is an abuse of power," I say, my chest tightening. Tattletale Smithers, his hair gelled firmly in place, gives me a told-you-so look. Smithers's smug grin upsets me as much as the news about Salvador.

I tell him I need to be alone to think. More than anything else I want to talk directly with Salvador, but he's off in Porvenir, so

I meet with two of the other caciques in town. They confirm Smithers's story, but shrug the whole thing off: "It's already been done. Nothing we can do!" I'm outraged, looking at these two caciques and thinking of some of the incestuous horse-trading that may have led to this. The *ayudita* for Lila and the caciques' inflated per diems. Was Salvador's support there the price of cacique acquiescence over the *tercero* land grab? Or were they simply resigned that the Big Boss, in this case Salvador, would capture personal gain from public office?

Not long thereafter I travel back to Porvenir and find the perfect moment to confront Salvador—in his home. I know it's delicate. This is an internal matter for AMAZONA, and the caciques are behind the new *hacendado* Salvador. Outwardly, nothing about Salvador's home has changed. It's the same humble adobe-and-thatch affair he's had since we first met. We exchange some pleasantries and his wife serves chicha to Salvador, myself, and the "sultan," Apollonius.

I've got it all rehearsed, the perfect diplomatic foreplay to segue into his six-thousand-acre bonanza. I clear my throat to speak, but Salvador turns the tables around completely and says, "I'm worried about Smithers." Apollonius nods in agreement. "We feel he is young. Inexperienced. He's making mistakes." Salvador ticks off some supposed procedural goof-ups, but the core issue seems to be that Smithers "can't work with people."

I'm about to jump up to defend my loyal deputy but hold my tongue to reflect. It seems Salvador is angered by a younger man stepping on his toes. Smithers's university credentials—a degree in business administration—have helped him see beyond the holy now and join me in imposing imperfect but better fiscal discipline on the project budget. For instance, he stood firm against Salvador's request for a salary raise.

But there's something even deeper at play: intervillage and interfamily rivalry. The cleavage is becoming clear. Porvenir (the Future) and Piso Firme (Firm Ground) are the largest of the Indian Territory's seven villages and have a healthy archrivalry akin to Yankees–Red Sox. Salvador and Apollonius hail from Porvenir; Smithers and his siblings from Piso Firme. There's bound to be tension between them, but not the type I imagined.

Salvador lowers his voice and says, "There are sultans in the Indian Territory."

Apollonius nods and repeats the word, "Sultans."

"*Sultans?*" I ask, my forehead wrinkling, and before I can help myself, look at Apollonius and add, "But I thought *you* were the sultan."

Apollonius smiles, liking the sound of that. But his face quickly snaps into seriousness. "That's a vicious rumor spread by the House of Smithers."

"Smithers and his family," Salvador says, "are the sultans of Piso Firme!"

"Who controls all the goods that come in from Brazil? Who has all that cattle?" Apollonius asks. "I'll tell you who: Smithers's brother, the cacique of Piso Firme! They've got everyone's bellies in hand." Salvador remains silent as Apollonius does the hatchet job on Smithers. Not only is Smithers's brother village headman, and his sister Lila now on our project payroll, but another of his brothers controls the movement of life-supporting goods from Brazil. Moreover, Smithers's father had enough cash on hand to put his son through private high school and college. Finally, Smithers's uncle, the son of the former *patrón* of the entire village of Piso Firme, continues to bankroll a small cattle and trading empire.

"So there it is, amigo Bill," Salvador says, neatly wrapping up our conversation. "Thank God that everything is clear about the true identity of the sultans."

When I arrive back in Santa Cruz, I immediately raise this issue with Smithers. He's livid. "The sultans are in Porvenir, not Piso Firme! Look at Apollonius. He runs his heart-of-palm operation like a *patrón*."

"He does give jobs," I say.

"He controls everyone's bellies. He gives, and he takes away. Apollonius is the real sultan!" He then adds, *"Y Salvador es el sultáncito."*—And Salvador is the mini-sultan.

I slump back in my chair, totally exhausted from watching the spears hurled between the House of Apollonius and the House of Smithers. The Indian Territory is turning into a burlesque of my first visits—what happened to the material simplicity and lingering river baths? Now Porvenir's sultan, fueled by a workaholism learned from Protestant missionaries, is using his heart-of-palm revenues to challenge Smithers's Piso Firme dynasty. And I don't even want to think about Salvador.

CHAPTER 16

D ANIEL IS LATE for the photo shoot. We've been waiting for him outside FAN's Santa Cruz office. I'm standing under some fruit trees and talking with Len as we both pick and eat overripe cherimoya, wiping the streaky juice off our cheeks. Salvador stands ten meters away, beside one of the brick buildings. He sips a chicha and chats in relaxed tones with Lila.

I'm updating Len on the increasingly divided Indian Territory, and lamenting about my disillusionment with Salvador. Len, who's wearing a seventies-style, Day-Glo green shirt that forms a confused retro combo with his eighties eyewear, says to me, "Salvador has become two people. He's torn between his heart and his desire for power." Daniel's taxi finally pulls up, and he and the forester, Hart, get out and walk briskly toward us. Len says, "Let's hope his heart wins."

"Sorry I'm late, but my ex, the *camba* . . . My divorce lawyer has been telling me . . . another time. Right." Daniel seems to get his bearings and adds, "The indigenous people?"

While Hart fidgets with a high-end digital camera, I introduce Daniel to Salvador. It is the first time the two have come face-to-face. They shake hands—and go on shaking for a long moment, in silence. Daniel stands two inches taller but is considerably skinnier than Salvador. In fact, the two of them are a study in contrast. Salvador's gaze is deep, sensual; Daniel's is pointed, laser-sharp. Salvador has smooth, round cheeks, while Daniel's are gaunt and concealed under a cropped gray beard.

Daniel is uncharacteristically mute during the handshake, and it is Salvador who finally drawls, *"Gracias por tu ayuda con el territorio indígena."*

Daniel understands *gracias* and *indígena* and says, *"De nada!* It's my wife who wants me to help *indígenas,* and I need photos for the marketing people."

I translate, and Salvador nods and smiles, though a bit thinly. I tell Daniel about the two logging firms who want to annex an enormous chunk of the Indian Territory, and how the Bolivian government is taking the loggers' side.

"I know these people!" Daniel says. "They're the same ones who threw indigenous people down the volcanoes in Guatemala in the eighties when I was a secret agent. *Volcánes! Helicóptero!"* He mimes this to Salvador as I hurriedly translate. "Those Nazis think indigenous people are shit!" Daniel's face is reddening. "Send me details, and I will blacklist those companies. They won't export a single board when I finish with them."

Salvador's smile is now both amused and warmer. He thanks Daniel.

"Don't thank me, thank them! Now I have an excuse to hijack their markets."

Hart is casting an exaggerated glance at his watch, and Daniel says, "Right, now, can you stand in the middle of those bushes? We're trying to do a kind of a jungle thing."

Hart mumbles in English that it "would be even better with a bow and arrow." First Lila stands in the bushes, then one of the caciques. Finally, it's Salvador's turn, but he refuses to step into the bush. "That'll work," Daniel says, as Hart snaps Salvador on the lawn from several angles. Salvador is not smiling. He looks somehow far away. "That's perfect," Daniel says, running his finger through his beard. "This, mate, is environmentally *and* culturally responsible shit!"

* * *

It is not until the next time I'm in the Indian Territory that I get to confront Salvador about his unethical land grab. We're both on Porvenir's riverbank, having just toweled off and dressed after a bath. I decide to get right to the point, and I ask him point-blank about the six thousand acres he annexed from the Indian Territory.

He looks at me, pulls on a sandal, and motions for me to follow him. We cross the now fully grown-over landing strip on our way to Porvenir's plaza: a few cows grazing, the adobe-and-thatch houses, and the big old ceibo tree, flowering bright red. We stand under the ceibo, and Salvador runs his fingers over the bark, frowning a little. "We've always been *peones.* Always. Do you know what that's like?

"My grandparents are from *más allá,* and they spoke Chiquitano, a lot of people were dying of malaria. Anyway, they came here during the rubber boom. There was a *patrón* here, an ugly mestizo man, and he used to whip us under this tree. Twenty-five lashes, thirty lashes. Even forty.

"*Ay caramba,* that *patrón* was so mistaken. The indignity."

Salvador is picking away slivers of the tree's bark with his too long fingernails as if chipping off dried blood. The jungle has encroached since my last visit, gaining ground against the cleared plaza. There's no wind. Salvador finally says, "Whenever the *patrón* came through this plaza, on his horse, we had to stop what we were doing and take off our hats. And when he returned from a trip, someone rang that bell"—Salvador indicates the one hanging from a tree branch that I'd heard so many times when we called community gatherings—"and we all had to come and welcome him back.

"All across the Amazon we, *los indigenas,* were part of the land. Whoever owned the land owned us and owned our labor. We had no existence, amigo Bill, apart from the land we were on. We were part of the acres."

What is the shape of an acre? I used to think acres were squared, fenced, and sold. Then Salvador suggested they are round as coins, or cylindrical like a stack of coins rising up into the seven skies. I've heard too that each one of us has an emotional acre inside. It's a space no one else can divide or control. We are sovereign there and can cultivate, leave wild, or smother our acre with asphalt; what we do with that acre is who we are.

My eyes, which have blurred out on the encroaching jungle border, snap back on Salvador, who is wearing the clothes of a free person. He's leaning against the tree now and telling me earnestly that he's worried the government will in the end side with the loggers, and they'll lose the Indian Territory, "and I want my children to at least have something."

"What happened to your lawn?" Len asks. We're cradling glasses of caipirinha up on my fourth-ring Santa Cruz balcony. I've invited him over after my trip back from the Indian Territory. He sits in the hammock, and I on a plastic chair, and I follow his gaze down into my garden: the two mismatched palm trees; a bougainvillea terrace, off-season, in none of its purple glory; and my small lawn reduced to five percent of its original size, the rest looking ploughed over.

I explain that the gardener who usually cuts the lawn was booked, so he sent his brother to do it. I indicated the area and disappeared inside my house, coming out twenty minutes later to a scene of pure horror. "Stop!" I said, running over to where my wonderful carpet of thick green grass had been just moments before. He'd taken it out with a hoe and loaded it into five buckets and a wheelbarrow. "Why?" I asked in disbelief.

"It's bush," he answered plaintively, telling me he'd rid the area of weeds, and it was now ready to be seeded with something useful.

Len laughs, which gets me laughing, and we take long sips of caipirinha as an electric cow-moo sounds from a horse-drawn ice cream cart up the street. Beyond is the sound of the fourth-ring traffic. It's been one of those overcast days, sewn into place at every edge, but a rusty glow now seeps through the gray and illuminates my mustard-colored walls and the brown veranda pillars. I look up the block, over the neighbors' clay roofs to where the pavement collapses into dirt—the gardener's house. It's a tiny, one-room shack guarded by skinny dogs and surrounded by a yard of dirt exactly like my new lawn.

"I want Salvador to be perfect," I say to Len.

The corners of Len's mouth rise into something approximating a smile, and he unpockets a pack of Cambas, removes one of the dark brown cigarettes, and lights it. "You heard how he came to fight for the Indian Territory?"

I think of the *patrón*'s whip, the ceibo tree, and the blood. "Yes," I say, but then realize I've gotten only snatches of the story. "No."

Len sits up in the hammock. He's wearing—as a kind of costume I presume—an olive-green park-ranger uniform, emblazoned with his name and PARQUE NACIONAL KEMPFF, and accompanied by black military-issue boots. He's not only FAN's public relations officer but its walking institutional history, having been with the foundation for a decade.

Len launches into the story. Through the seventies, eighties, and early nineties, large firms harvested a billion dollars of timber and palm hearts, but left nothing behind for the Chiquitanos. These companies were cronies of corrupt Bolivian officials in La Paz who gave them concessions in exchange for political support. By 1996, Salvador had seen enough and led the very first act of resistance in that part of the Amazon, putting enough pressure on the infamous Iténez Palm Heart factory to boot them out of Porvenir. Sultan-to-be Apollonius, a mere driver for the company, laid plans for a locally owned palm-heart factory. Salvador, flush with success, set his sights on much bigger game: the powerful Taruma and Paraguá logging companies.

First target: the smaller Taruma. The year was 2000, and FAN and the newly formed AMAZONA together filed a claim for a permanent Indian Territory. While the claim was under consideration, the government declared a moratorium on logging. But it wasn't long before a Chiquitano hunting in the forest heard chain saws. Taruma was busy felling mahogany.

Salvador rang the town bell—the same one the *patrón* used before a public whipping—and the whole village assembled. He mobilized eighty men, who marched to the logging site and seized the chain saws. The skidder operator tried to escape, steering his vehicle toward the main road. "Here Salvador did something remarkable," Len says. "He placed his body in front of the enormous orange skidder. That machine came within millimeters of crushing him but he stood firm." I think of that lone Tiananmen Square protester standing down a Beijing tank, as Len continues, "The driver stepped down from his machine. Salvador took him prisoner and marched to the company headquarters."

There, Salvador sat down with the Taruma boss, Carlos Blunder, who claimed his men had been logging without his knowledge, apologized profusely, and poured chicha. Salvador held the skidder operator for forty-eight hours in Porvenir and then released him. From then on, Taruma respected the moratorium.

But the larger company, Guillermo Roy's Paraguá, would prove much more difficult. They too broke the moratorium, but when Salvador complained, Roy was defiant, saying, "Take it up with the government in La Paz!" Instead, Salvador again rang the bell and Porvenir sprang to life. Ninety Chiquitanos descended upon the Paraguá loggers, confiscating two skidders and holding them in Porvenir along with four prisoners, all of them Paraguá loggers.

When word reached Roy in Santa Cruz, he was furious and took out an arrest warrant on Salvador. Meanwhile Salvador, fearing vigilantes, sent his wife and children to a secret location in the jungle and traveled under cover of night to Santa Cruz, where he telephoned Roy from a public plaza and insisted on meeting him there. The millionaire timber baron brought along his lawyer and the police.

"You whipped my men!" Roy bellowed, jabbing Salvador in the chest.

"Where are their lash marks?" Salvador demanded, explaining he'd freed the four Paraguá prisoners after the customary forty-eight hours, and they were treated perfectly. Sure enough, when the four were summoned and no lash marks were found, they finally admitted to spinning tales of being whipped by wild Indians.

The big-boned Roy turned to Salvador: *"Estoy malinformado, mi hijo."*—I've been misinformed, my son. "We're both *cambas,* you and I, and we understand each other, right?" Salvador agreed, laying on the charm, and telling Roy that he could pick up his unharmed skidders right away.

Chicha was poured, and Roy chuckled, "I was ready to arrest you, *mi hijo."*

"It would have been a vacation with four walls," Salvador replied, grinning.

"And I would have made you famous," the logger said somewhat prophetically.

By the time Len finishes, the sun has gone down and we've drained another pair of caipirinhas. Len leaves, and I listen to his Soviet Lada putter up my road and into the night, merging into the fourth-ring flow.

"Salvador para presidente!"

Len would shout this out sometimes during our long trips bouncing through the Indian Territory in the Illustrious Green Wagonette, and the rest of us would echo him in unison, *"Salvador para presidente!"*

"Gracias," Salvador would say, with a gold-toothed smile.

Then he'd clear his throat and say, "Distinguished ladies and gentlemen of the National Park Service, FAN, and the Indian Territory of the Paraguá Amazon . . . ," launching into a slow-worded and increasingly impassioned speech about the conservation of the park and the wisdom of his indigenous brothers and sisters. Applause marked different parts of his speech.

"Salvador para presidente!" someone would cry out at the end of his speech. We would then go on to designate cabinet posts: Gisela, head of the National Park Service; Len, his spokesperson; and *el amigo* Bill, in charge of foreign affairs.

At the time I viewed all of this as a joke, one of the many ways we passed the long hours of travel, but could it be part of a larger pattern? *Don't worry, Engineer. Now we're civilized barbarians.* I'd thought Salvador meant that he was trading traditional culture for civilization. But now I understand more of the history of his activism. In ousting the Iténez company and enforcing the logging ban, Salvador used a sophisticated blend of symbolism, force, and diplomacy. He took prisoners and private property, but returned both—at the exact point where his goals were achieved, deftly avoiding bloodshed. "He's adapted Gandhi to a savage Amazon," Len said at one point during his story.

Salvador para presidente! It all suddenly makes sense. Even as Santa Cruz snoozes away in hammocks, the Chiquitano has been refining his resistance tactics, traveling to La Paz, building a network of allies, and honing his stump speech. Salvador has national political ambitions.

CHAPTER 17

"EVERYBODY JUST CALLS me Goni," Bolivian president Gonzalo Sánchez de Lozada says in a documentary I'm watching with Salvador and others from AMAZONA at FAN. "They call me plain old Goni because they can't pronounce Gonzalo."

Here Salvador, who has been squinting along with his fellow Chiquitanos to read the subtitles as their president drawls on in English, explodes, "We can't pronounce Gonzalo? *Es mentira!*"

A lie indeed, and most curiously of all a completely unnecessary one. The documentary cuts to Goni with his wife, the Bolivian first lady, boarding an airplane. She's got gray hair, a heavily powdered face, and earrings set with rubies like small globules of blood. "This is Bolivia's Air Force One," the president tells the camera. "It's a little bit smaller than President Bush's Air Force One. But it sort of reflects the size of our economy. So it's only fair that I should have a smaller plane."

Goni flies from La Paz to Santa Cruz in "Bolivia's Air Force One," and as he crosses over the posh swimming-pool-strewn neighborhoods of Palms and Hammocks and Equipetrol, he quips to the journalist, "We lose in La Paz and Cochabamba, but we win all the elections in Santa Cruz."

"Never again!" one of the coca-munching Indians with me exclaims, to much murmuring of assent. One of the other Indians relates an oft-told piece of urban legend about Goni: The U.S. government, supposedly, identified new gold fields near Potosí during satellite surveillance and informed Goni about these potential riches so that he could develop them in the national interest. Instead, Goni quietly bought up the fields to add to his private empire.

Goni owns several gold mines and is rich beyond proportions imaginable here. He's a near cartoonish version of white rule in Bolivia. Short, stocky, and square-haired, he speaks immaculate English and embarrassingly poor Spanish with an accent resembling that of a tourist ordering *boor-ree-toes* on an Acapulco package tour. Goni was raised in the United States and schooled at the University of Chicago and is as comfortable with his foreign business associates as he is with the Bolivian gentry who own the other mines, concessions, and haciendas.

How did a guy like this win? He dug into his mining millions and hired pricey U.S. political consultants James Carville and Jeremy Rosner. An independent documentary, *Our Brand Is Crisis,* captures Goni's 2002 campaign. Carville, who orchestrated Bill Clinton's 1992 victory, gets off the plane in exotic La Paz with a posse of pollsters, adsters, lawyers, and strategists and quips that in this place his group "won't know whether to wind their asses or scratch their watches." They've come in the middle of Goni's campaign to boost his sagging numbers; with these kinds of numbers, Goni himself says, "maybe we should all be drinking Kool-Aid." Rosner too admits it's an uphill battle, explaining that for the majority of Bolivians "the only question is 'How high should the gallows be?'"

Despite the odds, the American consultants come up with a strategy: create another Goni. He had managed to become president of Bolivia from 1993 to 1997 and is best remembered for pushing through the controversial Enron-Shell gas pipeline to Brazil in his final days in office, and winning the global Dirty Digger Award for unsustainable mining in his own concessions. "We must own crisis. We must brand crisis," one of the consultants exclaims. Whenever asked about his first term, Goni is counseled to bow his head and say, "I know, I fell short." Rosner tells Goni to use these catch-phrases: "oppression of indigenous rights," "the have-nots of globalization," "the silver mines of Potosí," and "the treasure trove of natural gas."

It works. Goni wins 22 percent of the vote in a multican-didate field and takes the presidency, but the surprising second-place finisher, one percentage point behind Goni, is Quechua-speaking Evo Morales, who enters congress as head of the opposition. Copper-skinned Morales, whom everyone calls Evo, herded llamas as a child and played trumpet in a band. He is unusually tall for an indigenous Bolivian at nearly six feet and likes to sport jeans and polo shirts. Evo climbed from Cochabamba union leader to the national stage through organizing tight-knit groups of campesinos called syndicates that pressure against what they see as antipoor government policy through blocking highways with rocks, trees, and tire-busting nails called *miguelitos*. He's not coached by pricey consultants when he says, "Without empowering the Aymara, the Quechua, the Guarani, and the Ayoreo cultures, we'll never solve the problems of this country. We have to create a new state. I'm convinced that capitalism is the worst enemy of humanity and the environment, the enemy of the entire planet."

When Evo says this, a rowdy cheer rises from the Indians sitting around the television set with me in FAN's conference room. To them it's Goni versus Evo; corruption and greed ver-sus social justice and democracy. They see Evo as a poor man like themselves, speaking truth to power. Only one of the In-dians is not hooting it up for Evo but rather sits at the back of the group, slumped in his chair, a contemplative look on his face: Salvador.

Not that Salvador doesn't despise Goni. It's just that he's not much more comfortable with the other politician. Sal-vador's civilized barbarianism curbs his enthusiasm for Evo.

After all, Morales's radical tactics have gotten his own comrades killed at roadblocks; Salvador cringes at the thought of putting his followers in that kind of danger. And I suspect Salvador feels ambivalence about Evo's claim that "capitalism is the worst enemy of humanity and the environment," considering that his own fight for the Indian Territory and the adjoining park is financed by corporations. And what about Evo's growing reputation in the international media as "the rising star of the New Latin Left," his hobnobbing with Fidel Castro and Hugo Chávez, and his recent threat that growing antiglobalization movements will bring "another Vietnam" to the United States?

As he watches Goni and Evo on the screen, does Salvador imagine himself as another kind of leader? Goni says with a smirk, comfortable in his presidential chambers, "You know, it's a globalized planet. And I think Evo's got to join the world."

"Bolivia's got to join the world," Daniel says to me. "I'm having a supply problem." We're at a dinner in his garden in Santa Cruz's Palms neighborhood. Several servants shuttle among his guests with food and china. Daniel wears khaki shorts and an oxford shirt, and we're both sipping Chilean wine. "I've got the bloody markets," he says, leaning toward me. "Just don't have anything to send them."

Several months have passed since Daniel predicted that our sustainable logging business with the Indian Territory would be a "big bloody orgasm." But we haven't even made it to first base.

Wine flows. Laughter resounds from one of the several simultaneous conversations across Daniel's patio. He suddenly leaps up and takes my arm. "Follow me," he says, escorting me into his living room. "See this? This is what we call a 'component part.'" He's pointing to the wooden arm of one of his living room sofas. "Even fucking La Chonta can't fill a container. *La Chonta,* all right? And they're supposed to be the best.

"I needed three thousand of these, seven thousand of those, and thirteen thousand of these widgets," he says, walking around his living and dining rooms and indicating component parts of his furniture, "but they gave me too many of these, and too few of those! And they got it all into the container so damn late that the order was canceled. I'm wondering if I can even work in this country."

In the Indian Territory I've been having the same problem as Daniel. Though we've hustled to ship two containers of heart of palm to Chile, I shudder at having to reliably fill even a modest regular order of, say, two thousand cases per month. People seem to work only long enough to satisfy their present needs and then it's into the hammocks. *Tranquilo.* Exasperated, Apollonius told me he might need to resort to harsh *patrón* tactics of days gone by. Instead, he brought in migrant laborers who did in fact work—until they had enough money for the next month or so, and then they returned to their villages.

Even my own Santa Cruz home has become an eyesore because the carpenters I've hired to do a job show up for a maximum of two days—the amount of time necessary to accumulate enough money for the rest of the week. Foolishly, I've been continuing to pay the men their wage daily and listened to unfulfilled promises of *"Sí o sí"* showing up the next day. As I step over paint cans and trip on scraps of plywood, my frustration mounting, they lead the good life with chicha and a checkerboard.

In every society there is a tension between what the ancient Greeks called *otium* (leisure) and *negotium* (nonleisure, or what we today call work); Bolivians have resolved this tension in favor of the former. In an invasion by neighboring Chile during a war that lasted from 1879 to 1884, Bolivians allegedly refused to fight because it was Mardi Gras. Up until recently, almost no one in Santa Cruz would work if it rained, preferring fireplace to workplace. Many Bolivians embrace what the Italians call *dolce far niente*, a fine ambition toward doing nothing.

This very non-Anglo-Saxon perspective frustrates foreign businesspeople like Daniel who "have the bloody markets" in Australasia and elsewhere. They want to open up Bolivia's veins and let her resources flow overseas, but butt heads with the country's deep-seated penchant for *otium*.

I get frustrated too when I find *otium* slipping into our meetings with a national Indian network, known as Juntos. The insidious purpose of many meetings, of course, is *the meeting itself*. After all, such gatherings satisfy Maslow's entire hierarchy of human needs from food, rest, shelter, right up to a feeling of importance, so why go further and actually do something? But the classic meeting-for-meeting-sake rises to new levels of absurdity one day around FAN's conference table.

"It's the imperialist neoliberal model," a bigwig from Juntos says, as he snuffs out his cigarette in an ashtray. "It's Bush and Goni against the poor."

"This is class warfare!" another agrees.

"We need to nail down this Indian Territory now!" another angry Indian exclaims. "Salvador's territory is Juntos' top priority in all of Bolivia."

Here Salvador, who has been largely quiet, does muster up a weak "Not one millimeter," but his tone conveys ambivalence.

The skinny Juntos leader lays a hard look on Salvador, then says, "Goni's weakening. Now's the time to push harder for the ITs nationwide." Sure enough, President Goni's approval rating has slumped to record lows, while indigenous leader Evo's numbers have grown. In fact, I feel as if Evo were right here with us in recent meetings as the tenor changes: less about the wonderful national park, and more about the workingman's struggle; less Smokey Bear, more Karl Marx. The discussions move to the rhythm of "The people! United! Will never be defeated!" But nothing is accomplished. And now, after two hours of paraphrasing *Das Kapital*, I suggest coming up with a concrete plan.

Salvador nods in hearty agreement; less definitive nods from several others; a scowl from the Juntos leader. I get up and draw the most basic of planning charts on the whiteboard, with columns for Task, Who's Responsible? and By When?

Salvador urges the group to "complete amigo Bill's chart." But a colleague starts into a diatribe about the corrupt oligarchy. As a logical rejoinder, the boss recites with ire the woes of neoliberalism over two chain-smoked cigarettes, crescendoing with "I'm tired of the 'invisible hand of the market' giving me the middle finger!"

During these diatribes I try to grasp the room's shifting politics. The leader is the group's ideologue, filling the room not just with tobacco smoke, but also with resuscitated leftist rhetoric, which several others breathe in and mimic. Salvador rejects the ideology, but feels torn between loyalty to his native colleagues and his greenhouse-gas-sequestering allies. I myself feel the Indian Territory is slipping away. All of the fine oratory may be a smoke screen for a lack of leadership among the Indians, and perhaps an even more significant lack of political space in which to maneuver. Our twofold goal is stalled on both fronts: the territorial demand is mired in quicksand and Daniel's sawmills of salvation are stuck in Auckland.

Sensing brownie-point potential, Smithers tries to nudge things along: "Why don't we fill out the planning chart?"

Someone says that Goni's simply got to go. He's an imperial puppet. The leader abruptly stands up, looking at his wrist, which has no watch around it, declaring it's late, and, *Dios mío,* the cigarettes have run out. Before making his exit he declares he will personally accompany Salvador to a special encounter in the Indian Territory, "where the real decisions will be made."

CHAPTER 18

W E DUB THE upcoming meeting in Kempff as "the encounter." It's the first time national politics is front and
center in Kempff—the Juntos Indian network will attend. The
Amazon Project corporate partners are watching the encounter with interest since they are increasingly skittish about
their carbon credits as the Indian Territory land dispute settles
into firm gridlock.

A few nights before leaving for the meeting, I swing by
Daniel's to ask about the eco-sawmills. I bring it up after a romantic comedy he insists we watch. He says we *will* get the
mills and he *will* blacklist those logging firms grabbing for indigenous people's land, but it's just taking longer than he
thought. "I mean, just look at this mess!" CNN is now on
his tube, and images of Indian roadblocks in El Alto are
shown. The reporter explains that Goni has slapped a steep
twelve percent tax increase on Bolivians' already dismal incomes under an International Monetary Fund (IMF) demand
that Bolivia reduce its budget deficit in order to receive vital
loans. She talks about "increasing social unrest" and "what's
starting to be called the IMF war."

Daniel stares through his cigarette smoke at the television.
"When I was married to the Jamaican, I had this big sprawling
mansion in Dade County," he says. "It was *Architectural Di-
gest* house of the year. Ex-wife got it . . . Another beer? You
know where it is."

I walk downstairs, find my way into the kitchen, greet his
maid, Nancy, and pull open the refrigerator. Taking out a can

of Paceña, I stop, refrigerator door still open, and suddenly realize what Daniel is doing.

This is not about business and never was. Those portable sawmills might not be arriving. Daniel simply wants a friend.

It's a cliché: the megamillionaire who has everything but love. Daniel is on his third wife now, and they are having problems. She's back in Australia with their three-year-old son, Bobby, while Daniel shuttles back and forth from Buenos Aires to Santa Cruz every several days. During the romantic comedy we'd just watched, Daniel compared nearly every scene to his relationship with Gayle. "That's us!" he would cry out. "I'm sending this to her. This DVD will be in Australia in twenty-four hours."

I walk back up to the TV room, where Daniel is exhaling from a Marlboro and staring at a point somewhere above the television screen. He pours himself another Scotch and lets pieces of his life seep out as disconnected stories. There was his first wife, the Dade County Jamaican, who doesn't let him see their eleven-year-old son. Then came the second, from the Bolivian frontier region called Pando. "Never marry a *camba*," he says, using the term for people from eastern Bolivia, "unless you're willing to pay her a salary.

"When the *camba* and I first married and came to Santa Cruz, her entire family showed up at my house. Dozens of *primas*, aunts, uncles, her mother, her grandmother. All came down in the bus. Nothing stayed in the refrigerator for more than one day. After three weeks of this I kicked them all out. Every single one of them."

An undercurrent running beneath this evening with Daniel is that he has been loved for his money. The converse of this explains his conspicuous consumption: "I am only loved for my money; I want love; therefore I flaunt it."

Daniel thought he had found true love with his third wife, Gayle, who doesn't need his money. Her father is a Melbourne real estate tycoon, and she owns a few companies herself. But now even that relationship seems delicate.

A few days later, Daniel is off again, first to Buenos Aires as usual, but from there he just keeps on going. Rio, Cape Town, Majorca, Amsterdam, London, Hong Kong, Australia. I get e-mails from him. Stuck in the Cape Town airport first-class lounge, he writes, "I'm platinum on every airline and I couldn't get a seat. Completely overbooked." From Amsterdam: "I've got the Dutch market wrapped up!" New Zealand: "Will be with the portable sawmill people tomorrow. We're going to help your indigenous people. Went to the Great Barrier Reef with Gayle and Bobby. We're having problems."

Like everyone else in my Urby Lisboa barrio, I'm glued to my radio, listening to Goni insist, as firmly as he can during a press conference, "I'm not going to back down from these taxes."

E-mails crowd my in-box at work as Bolivia's middle class mobilizes against the "IMF tax." Goni's narrow legitimacy, which has rested on exactly this middle-class segment, is now almost completely eroded. Yet he drawls on in his grammatically poor Spanish, defending the IMF tax. I do sympathize with him. Like Bolivian presidents before him, he's found that tiny Bolivia has little bargaining power with the IMF. Yet the consensus of my colleagues at FAN is that Goni could show a bit more backbone. Even as Argentina's social democratic president Néstor Kirchner bucks the IMF and successfully reschedules that country's debt, the more conservative Goni seems all too eager to pander to the IMF by slapping taxes on Bolivia's working poor.

As the protests heat up, we head east into the heart of the Amazon for "the encounter." After another spine-busting twenty-hour ride we collapse into the refreshing waters of the Paraguá River in the Indian Territory hamlet of Florida. It's a ritual we repeat nearly every late afternoon while here; I've come to call them "lingering baths," which take place among colleagues and villagers in a river. Soap and shampoo are passed around, but the deeper purpose is to bond with other people in nature. The rushing water carries away banter, laughter, and spaces of silence, sweeping it downriver along with our tensions.

Now I'm in a water circle with Len, Smithers, two rangers, a ranger's wife, and several "Floridians," passing around the soap, exchanging jokes and stories. I feel my muscles relaxing, but there's one tension even the water cannot wash away. It's a missing presence: Salvador. Nearly every lingering bath I've taken has included him, but this time he has chosen instead to meet, and presumably bathe, with the radical Juntos contingent that has come along. And I overheard something I shouldn't have before our bath; another Juntos member said in an impassioned half-whisper to Salvador, *The only thing anyone cares about is the park, not you, not the Chiquitanos. You need to go after what they care about.*

Len lathers the peach fuzz on his chest and passes the soap to a Floridian as he says, "Every job has its difficulties. If you work in a bank, a hospital, driving a taxi, or plowing a field. But *here*," he says, the sweep of his arm taking in the whole of Kempff Park, "here the problems will never end. Protecting this park will never end."

As if on cue, one of the three-inch minnows that have been attacking our leg hairs and nipples leaps out of the water and nibbles Len's shoulder, perching there dragonfly-like for a stretched second before flopping back into the water. A few gasps of delight escape from the community members, and then I notice the rain coming. It begins as a saturation of mist in the air, accompanied by the wind, which swirls playfully through the assai, and ripples the river surface. I duck under the warm Paraguá waters, escaping the first drops.

The chilly rain sends the ranger's wife running in her dark blue bikini out of the water and up the embankment toward the ranger camp. I figure that we too will leave, but, quite the contrary, two more Floridians come down into the river to join us. We all listen to the plip-plopping, the metal shavings on glass, and a myriad of other sounds contained within water swept by wind striking more water. My arms spontaneously stretch out, palms up, to feel more of the rain.

Later that evening, a dozen of us, FAN and park staff and some community members, are relaxing in hammocks and on the edges of beds when a small boy shouts, *"Buenas noches!"* through the open tacuara bamboo wall and asks, "Are you coming to the thing you already know about?"

Salvador, who has left the Juntos group at their campsite, walks in behind the boy. I swallow hard when I see him. He scans the room, but avoids eye contact with me. Suddenly he sweeps the six-year-old up, folds him over, and grabs him by the ankles, the boy's tiny head dangling toward the floor. "Tell us," Salvador growls, "about this mysterious *thing that we already know about.*"

"The birthday party!"

"Is that code?" Salvador continues. "Tell me now what you mean by 'birthday party.'"

By now everyone is chuckling, and Salvador wrestles the boy to the ground and tickles him until they're both in hysterics. Smithers stands and says, imitating Salvador, "It's time for a Solomonic truce. We'll go to the party!"

Salvador and I walk side by side now across Florida's cow-pasture plaza, but neither of us says anything. We finally do make some stiff small talk as we pass the school and climb onto a candlelit porch, where plates of roast duck and pig are already laid out. We each take a plate and eat in silence. Meanwhile somebody puts a cassette tape in an antique boom box. Brazilian music kicks in, and everyone in our party of thirty or so oogles the full bottle of vodka on the ground between one community member's legs. Finally, Smithers's sister Lila, unable to stand it anymore, asks him about "that thing standing up between your legs" and if he's planning to "share it with me." He picks up the bottle, only to snuggle it against his chest.

Florida is a village of one-of-each-thing, and that is the only bottle of decent liquor in the village, a kind of prop that appears at various gatherings, the promise of something. We eventually gather up the bottle—which would not be opened that evening—and Florida's only radio, its batteries now dead, and stride through the drizzly night toward the schoolhouse for "the party." Several men struggle with a sputtering generator for a half hour in order to power lights and music—in vain.

Meanwhile I chat with a completely relaxed Salvador, who says, "What is a party without women?" Indeed there are five men for each woman present. "Is there anything more perfect than a woman? Look at her!" He gestures toward a lovely young woman from his own village. "The ride from Santa Cruz is long—a day in the mud. This is an eternity with only men. But if a woman is there in the jeep, it flies by."

The drizzling has stopped and the full moon breaks through wispy clouds over the river. Salvador follows my gaze toward the park and continues, "Yes, when a woman is present the whole world smiles. The trees, the leopards and borochi, the monkeys, all dance with joy and laugh when a woman is present."

"*Oy che!* Salvador's a poet," Smithers jokes.

The generator emits a final choking cough, and all hopes of a party end. We chat in the moonlight for quite a while and then one by one peel off, heading for tents and hammocks to rest for the next day's big event.

"Are you going to block the roads, Salvador?"

It's Len, the next morning, who rather bluntly asks the question on everyone's mind. The tension mounts as Salvador considers a reply. We're seated in a circle, but a fractured one.

The chiefs cluster together, community members on each side; Salvador sits with the Juntos folks; and Len, Smithers, the park director, and I have almost unconsciously grouped into a kind of eco-faction. Salvador's face first hardens at the question, then flushes with uncertainty, and he finally says, "Roadblocks would put my people at risk of being killed."

His Indian network colleague is much more decisive. Three Indian territories—this one, Monteverde, and Lomerito—are considering several options to pressure President Goni to title their lands. An irresolute look spreads across Salvador's face as the skinny Juntos leader speaks; a bit of Salvador's gold-rimmed tooth shows between parted lips, sweat beads on his forehead.

Meanwhile, Len regrets having asked Salvador such a direct question about the roadblocks. He launches into several minutes of platitudes, to massage his faux pas. The wonderful AMAZONA, he says, always makes wise decisions, especially when linked with the mighty Juntos. And Salvador himself is the paragon of leadership. Slowly circling the wagon, he finally wonders aloud if blocking roads is the best idea.

Salvador clears his throat. *"Bueno,"* he says, and goes on to compliment Len and the capable director of the spectacular Kempff National Park. He also rambles at length about how grateful AMAZONA is for all the help from FAN and the Amazon Project, but that, sadly, in the end "the fight for our homeland is our first priority."

Len praises the wise foresight of "Don Salvador" and "his Indian brothers and sisters," then gingerly prods the tender spot: Salvador is cementing an alliance with a group of migrants from the Bolivian uplands. These are the very people who are advancing every day deeper into the Amazon, slashing and burning their way toward Kempff and Salvador's own beloved Indian Territory.

After such lengthy diatribes, Salvador's response to this is surprisingly terse: "We need all the help we can get."

"We are all Indians!" the Juntos leader jumps in. "It doesn't matter if you speak Quechua, Aymara, or Ayoreo!"

A wicked silence, which I finally break: "Salvador . . . The most important thing to these colonists is getting more land, right?"

After a heavy pause, Salvador nods in agreement.

"If they help you secure the Indian Territory," I continue, "do you think they'll want something in return?"

"Of course," Salvador says.

"What do you think they will want?"

Silence. The obvious answer slowly sinks in. Salvador finally says, "We'll not give up a millimeter of our forests."

"What else," I ask, "do you have to give them?"

With this, the Juntos leader has had enough. "This is an internal matter for the Indian movement," he snaps.

Len is shaking his head. "Don Salvador!" he pleads. "We have been at your side for six years now. Six years. Who helped you set up AMAZONA? Who got the Indian Territory to where it is today?"

Salvador admits it was FAN and the national park that helped them.

Len continues, "After all this, you would turn your back on us?"

Here, Salvador manages to look slightly ashamed. He shifts in his seat and seems as if he is about to say something, but Len—comically costumed in his park-ranger outfit, like a little kid who wants to be one when he grows up—continues, "Where were all of these new friends at the beginning?" He shoots a sharp, slightly pouty glance at the Indian-network folks.

"Where were they *then*?" Len says, his voice rising. "Salvador, you are like a *quinceañera*. No one looked at you when you were thirteen and fourteen, but now, at your fifteenth birthday, everyone wants to dance with you, dance with AMAZONA."

145

Salvador jumps in now. He lavishes praise on FAN and the park, thanking and honoring Len and the quiet but wise park director. But despite his diplomatic words, everybody realizes Len's *quinceañera* metaphor nailed the underlying dynamic perfectly: AMAZONA has come of age and is finding new friends.

There is a delicate overlap between conservation of the world's last rainforests and the ambitions of indigenous peoples. Salvador was indeed our best friend as long as he exclusively needed the conservationists for funds, but as soon as he gained power, the thin land bridge that connected our worlds became submerged. AMAZONA has become its own island, connected in an archipelago of similar islands of indigenous peoples and campesinos hungry for land. And whatever is the romantic view of Indians, these people will not always steward this land for the seventh generation. They may leave much more than footprints.

We'd spent six years helping them secure the Indian Territory, that enormous swath buffering Kempff National Park, and now they are nearly sanctioned to do what they wish with it—for good or for ill. As if to underscore this very point, Juntos and Salvador declare a suspension of the meeting so that they can privately discuss strategy.

Naturally Len and I are not invited, nor is Smithers, who's evidently perceived as too compromised, so the three of us and a ranger decide to cross into the park to survey the oxygen ranch. More than to measure a few circumferences, my own goal is to escape from politics into nature. But as we inch the jeep onto a precarious contraption of oil drums and planks that is pulled across the Paraguá River with ropes and wind our way through the riverine forests, I know it is impossible to escape politics. Thoreau once said he could walk for thirty minutes and come to "some portion of the earth's surface where man does not stand from one year's end to another, and there, consequently, politics are not, for they are but the cigar smoke of man." Today you might walk for a year to reach such a place, such as the one we're in now, but even pristine Kempff is thick with cigar smoke. Does this contested terrain belong to BP or borochis? To a tiny Amazon tribe or the world?

We shoulder onto an embankment, threading some partially flooded forests, stopping in a high-tropical grove thick with monkeys, macaws, and tapirs. I wrap a tape measure around several tree trunks while Smithers takes GPS points—the handheld computer silently conversing with the sky—and then we motor the jeep along a narrow dirt road through thousands of acres of swaying grass, now capped with white flowers. This soft, white plain stretches for what seems like a hundred miles, only occasionally dipping, tracing the edge of a light blue sky. The hardiest, most fire-resistant trees and shrubs and occasional pockets of high forests texture the opposite, eastward view toward the Huanchaca mesa. The rest of the area is kept in white flowers by lightning-induced fires that continually beat back the advancing jungle.

There are many Amazons. Though I've traveled mostly in her rainforest bosom, this stretch of fire-gilded plain is her spine. We lurch across it in the jeep, unspeaking. Like a Montana high plateau, it seems to go on forever, and yet, for all its sheer breadth it is terribly fragile. Some of the world's last in situ borochi wolves live here. They feed on a type of deer called the *gama,* which munches tender grasses that spring up only after lightning fires blaze through the savanna.

As the first lighting flashes appear over the distant mesa, I think of the borochi, each requiring vast individual territories. Smithers and Len also seem lost in thought, so I wander off alone across the white carpet. More lightning bursts, and I search for traces of borochi and think about *connectivity,* certainly the most important concept driving twenty-first-century conservation. The idea is not just to conserve fragments of nature, or even large parks, but rather "eco-corridors" or "eco-regions"—vast and integral areas of wilderness. This is necessary because species migrate; borochi wolves require large individual territories, as do migratory birds like the cerulean warbler, scarlet tanager, and purple martin. All the major international conservation groups, as well as their junior partners in the third world like FAN, have abandoned species-based approaches for ones based on conserving robust ecosystems—and the species within them. The Nature Conservancy, for example, is disposing of many small parcels of forest willed or donated to it, in order to focus on connectivity. Preserving little islands of forest is akin to draining a natural lake and placing a few fish tanks in the dry bed; isn't it better to find a way to preserve the lake itself?

It's the lightning that's gotten me thinking about connectivity, because it's a planetary electrical wiring system that humans are creating. FAN, for example, focuses all of its work on three ecological corridors: the Chiquitano-Iténez (which includes Kempff and the Indian Territory), the Amboró-Tariquía, and the Amboró-Madidi. These three Bolivian corridors patch into neighboring grids in Argentina, Peru, and Brazil, branching in turn into a South American system of eco-corridors championed and funded by the UN, regional bodies like the Organization of American States, national governments, and conservation groups. Connectivity is psychologically appealing: a continental web of migrating species, carbon sequestration, biodiversity maintenance, freshwater, and sustainable livelihoods.

But there are blockages. The Juntos leader quipped, "I don't live in an eco-region; I live in a neocolonial prison." Even now, Juntos may be convincing Salvador and the chiefs to sever Kempff from the grid. Connectivity is being cut or maintained all the time by people's decisions. Will Salvador take an antipark posture or find other means? In his classic work about global warming, *The End of Nature,* Bill McKibben writes:

The end of nature is not an impersonal event, like an earthquake. It is something we humans have brought about through a series of conscious and unconscious choices: *we* ended the natural atmosphere, and hence the natural climate, and hence the natural boundaries of the forests, and so on. In so doing we exhibit a kind of power thought in the past to be divine.

He's not saying that nature no longer exists, but that it does not exist in the way we've come to understand it: as *a force independent from humans*. Through climate change we have literally altered the atmosphere in every square foot of air on the globe. Whether I measure carbon content here under Huanchaca or at the tip of the north pole, it will read 330 ppm instead of the 234 ppm it would have been in the absence of humans burning fossil fuels. Our airplanes, cars, and factories have destroyed the natural seasons, shifting the beginning of spring forward a week or two. Now it's "spring" in quotes, a human spring.

A tap on my shoulder, and I turn to see Len smiling. It's time to head to a part of Kempff I've never seen: the Irons. There's a camp there where we'll spend the night before heading back to "the encounter" at sunrise. The Irons Camp turns out to be more substantial than I expect: a few wooden cabins and a small water tower in a forest clearing. As we unload, macaws angle in from two directions, their vibrant blues, yellows, greens, and reds beautiful in the deepening dusk. After we eat and retire to stiff beds, I listen to thunder grumbling in the distance and crackling closer in. I stand up and walk onto the cabin's overhang, the rain flowing into a catchment barrel, springing up onto my bare feet. A burst of lightning illuminates the high forest that buffers the savanna just beyond. I feel much smaller in this wilderness but at the same time very large through a sense of connection with the whole. A close-in pop of thunder speeds my heart; oxygen spewed by the trees

149

around me feeds my lungs; I let rainwater fall into my cupped hand and swallow it in a big gulp, and I know that what we are doing is worth it.

The Amazon Project must succeed. This wilderness must remain, and the Chiquitanos must not lose their land and follow the Guarasug'wé into extinction. The alternative is too difficult to accept: humans spreading into these final wild spaces on earth, until we have consumed it all and are still no richer.

"Our objective has never wavered: legal rights, forever, to the Indian Territory. Sadly, we've been forced to revert to our final option."

Salvador's eyes are in his lap, his body slouched. It's the next day and we've gathered once again. There's a long, tense moment as the Juntos leader talks about "final options," waiting for Salvador to chime in enthusiastically. Instead, Salvador raises his head and says, "We didn't want it to happen this way."

I look at Len, the park director, and the other non-Indians gathered. We dread what's coming: *he's going to say they'll block the road.*

Salvador looks over to the chiefs, who nod in agreement, and then toward the park director and at me, and says, "Goni doesn't own us. We Chiquitanos are the legitimate owners of the house."

The Juntos representative, impatience growing on his narrow face, finally blurts out something that takes us completely by surprise. It's far worse than a roadblock. "Yes, the *final option* is to compensate ourselves for the two hundred thousand acres the logging companies are stealing from us."

I feel my stomach sinking as the Indian hammers it home: "If our demands are not met in thirty days, we will be forced to annex our stolen acres from someplace else. We'll invade the national park."

150

CHAPTER 19

W E'LL INVADE THE national park." Five words accomplish what five hundred years could not; Salvador finally has everybody's attention.

I board a flight to my old stomping ground, La Paz, and make the rounds. The Bolivian national director for climate change finds "this development deeply troubling." Colleagues in the Nature Conservancy are "alarmed." Not only is the park, a UNESCO World Heritage site, under threat, but the entire Amazon Project is at stake. The two hundred thousand acres the Chiquitanos propose to annex from the park form part of the expansion zone that delivers carbon credits to the corporations.

"The investing partners," Gisela says to me by phone from Santa Cruz, referring to BP, American Electric Power, and PacificCorps. "They can't hear a peep about this."

But news of the threatened invasion spreads like wildfire, making it all the way to President Goni. As he considers a response, I taxi across La Paz to the Hotel Europa, where I have a working lunch with a lawyer from the national land-titling agency, the Instituto Nacional para la Reforma Agricola (INRA); she's responsible for ITs nationwide, and I want to urge her to push Salvador's territory through once and for all. It could be just that simple. All the government would have to do is designate an alternative concession for the logging firms elsewhere.

My mind is so focused on the IT that I've hardly been noticing the scenery, but as we swing through Plaza Murillo, site of

the Bolivian White House—the aptly named Burnt Palace—I
notice the blackened walls from the recent battle over the IMF
tax. While we were off in the remote Amazon, protests forced
Goni to abandon the tax—but not before thirty people were
killed in clashes. One group to be slapped with the tax, po-
licemen earning just a hundred dollars a month, faced off
with a military contingent guarding the Burnt Palace, and
gunshots came within inches of Goni's chest. He's reportedly
left the bullet-riddled chair right there in his office, as a re-
minder to himself of just how close he came. Other ministries
we drive past, including Sustainable Development, look far
worse than the Burnt Palace; their façades charred by Molo-
tov cocktails, they remain evacuated for repairs. The streets,
however, are quiet. We pass *indigena* women in jaunty derbies selling trinkets; the llama-fetus stalls of Sagarnaga; the
sixteenth-century cathedral atop the bold Prado boulevard,
built a century back by Bolivian liberals trying to imitate the
grandeur of their beloved Paris.

Entering the Hotel Europa's sun-drenched dining room, I
feel awkward. I'd had lunch here before, in my lords-of-
poverty La Paz days, but now I feel a bit like a country cousin
as I navigate the tables of charming aid workers, businessmen,
and government officials on my way to a short woman in
slacks and a red blouse waving to me. It's the INRA lawyer.
We make small talk and pick up menus. My glance drifts off
the menu to one white-linen-covered table to the next, looking
for familiar faces, but finds none. It seems that my former aid
colleagues have sailed to other ports. I put down the menu and
say, "Here's an idea: Why not just sign the Indian Territory
over?"

"I hadn't thought of that," she says. She's a friend of Gisela's,
so we're informal from the start. "No, wait. There's just one
minuscule detail: the law."

"So Guillermo Roy's claim to the land is more lawful than
that of ancestral inhabitants?"

"He has a *legal,* forty-year concession—"

"—obtained through political favoritism. And under an archaic understanding of Indians organic to the landscape. Do
you still claim that the Chiquitanos have the same rights as
jaguars?"

A waiter places plates in front of us. "Look, it's not going to
happen that easily." Her voice drops and seems strained. "I've
been bending over backward for Indians, okay? I helped make
the Guarani IT happen, and you know how some of them
thank me? By illegally selling off their supposedly 'indivisible'
land once they got it."

"So they should all be saints?"

"And what is this about invading Kempff Park? That only
strengthens Guillermo Roy's hand. He's—" Her cell phone
sounds, and she answers. This is a funny protocol in Bolivia.
People answer their cell phones everywhere: meetings, social
events, even movie theaters—it's so annoying to me personally
that I stopped going to the cinema—but Bolivians never seem
to mind the interruptions.

"You're in luck," she says, snapping her phone shut.
"Goni's sending Minister Moira Paz to Santa Cruz to meet
face-to-face with Salvador."

Over a hundred people pack the room in the state-government
office-building complex on Santa Cruz's second ring, the vast
majority dark-skinned, dark-haired, dark-eyed. The rest include journalists, NGO officials, and logging-company representatives and their lawyers. A full hour passes—still no
minister—but everyone sits patiently. Finally, the doors burst
open and an elegant entourage sweeps through the door.

Minister Moira Paz leads the group, smartly groomed in a
black suit-dress and white silk shirt. Her skin is as light as her
boss Goni's. Behind her are several aides, the head of the land-
titling agency, INRA, and the state governor. They work the

first row, shaking hands, murmuring, *"Buenas tardes,"* then take their seats at a long table in front of us. Salvador is invited to join them at the table. He picks up his trademark roll of maps of the Indian Territory and joins the VIPs. The minister explains the purpose of the meeting—"not to come to a solution, but rather to listen to both sides and suggest ways forward"—and then calls on the Paraguá logging company to speak.

The tall, big-bellied president of Paraguá, Guillermo Roy, ambles up to a microphone in front. "I don't have legions of supporters, like the other side does," he says, indicating the lowland Indians from various Amazonian tribes who have come to accompany Salvador and AMAZONA. "I don't have a cheering section. I have only one thing on my side: a principle. Sure, it's my land and I have the legal papers to document that right. But way beyond my own self-interest, I am here to defend the fragile institution of private property!"

One of Roy's lawyers gets up next—imperially slim, hair slicked back. He assumes a more conflictual tone than his client: "To be frank, I don't even know why we're here. We have the legal right to that land. This is just another case of *los indígenas* trying to bully private landowners. I ask Don Salvador: Where is your documentation? We have a forty-year logging concession signed by the government!"

There is a saying in Spanish that sounds a bit like a Gypsy curse: *Entre abogados te veas* (May you be surrounded by lawyers). The logging company is; AMAZONA is not. The Indian group has only one legal representative, a fellow from Juntos, who wisely allows Salvador to speak for himself.

Salvador unrolls a map, which Lila and Smithers hold up behind him. He calmly explains that this swath of land, buffering Kempff National Park, is their historical land, their *casa*. He invokes the Bolivian Forestry Law, which says that in cases of two overlapping legitimate claims, the rights of those indigenous people already settled in an area trump other claims, such as concessions. He then presents the minister with documents showing that the Paraguá company is not even serious about the concession. They have not paid their taxes for several years, nor done any logging.

The loggers' lawyer jumps up: "Why should Mr. Roy pay taxes when *you* won't let us log the area?"

Salvador grants the lawyer only a vaguest of stares and lets the silence grow larger. *He's become quite a showman,* I reflect. "This theft of our land," Salvador continues more quietly, "would push Piso Firme and Porvenir up against the river. The cut practically eliminates Chief Gaspar's town of Cachuela. We are *indigenas* and need our entire territory to hunt, fish, collect medicines. How can we live if Mr. Roy comes in and cuts down our forest?"

The minister looks at her watch and says. "*Bueno*. I know everyone hoped I could come here today, wave my magic wand, and settle this, but I can't do that." A numbing silence overtakes the room. "I can't, and President Gonzalo Sánchez de Lozada can't. The reduced Indian Territory limits were established by legal procedures. The concession that the logging company now holds came about through legal procedures. To reverse this reality would mean changing the Bolivian constitution."

I notice the faces of the Indians in the room harden. The minister drones on, oblivious to the changed mood in the audience, "This process will not be decided today, nor in the next few weeks, nor in the next months." She then says that she has to fly back to La Paz, but asks if the two sides would be willing to sit down tomorrow to look for "a win-win compromise." The logging-company lawyer quickly agrees, as does Salvador, but much more grudgingly, and the minister is whisked out of the room.

Indians around me are rising, shuffling, murmuring. The Juntos leader says that this is Goni's typical "neoliberal love affair with millionaires" and that "Evo would give us the territory."

Gaspar, who sidles up to the conversation circle I'm in, puts it in a down-home kind of way: *"Ellos tienen los papeles, pero es nuestra casa!"*—They may have the papers, but it's our home. The pink elephant in the room for the past two hours has been the threatened invasion of the park; it's only reason such a high-level official came in the first place, and yet it was never mentioned.

The INRA lawyer from the La Paz lunch finds me and says, "Sorry it didn't work out better than this. But, I want to tell you something about Roy. He may go after more than just the two hundred thousand acres."

She guides me over to the side of the room. "The entire claim for the IT is based on ethnicity. Are your guys indigenous?"

"Of course they are," I say.

"Roy doesn't think so, and neither do some other important people. I hate to break this to you," she says with just the hint of a smile, "but it's an Indian Territory without Indians."

I don't want to believe her, yet certain things nag me. On my last Indian Territory sojourn I sat down with Apollonius in his mahogany mini-mansion for a cup of Nescafé. I'd brought Riester's *Guarasug'wé* along, since the anthropologist mentions something interesting about Apollonius's Porvenir: it seems that a single Guarasug'wé named Frey broke off from the rest of the tribe after their last cacique and shaman were killed and settled in Porvenir. There may have been others as well. So I asked Apollonius, "Do you recognize any of these names?" I pointed to the section where Riester lists Guarasug'wé birth names next to the Christian names they used to use with whites.

Apollonius reads aloud in his squeaky voice: "Francisco Frey . . . Savu'i . . . Maria Frey . . . Hapik'wa . . . *Hapik'wa!*" He started giggling nervously and shaking his head.

"Do you know anyone named Frey?"

"These were the barbarians," he said. "The savages."

Not a bit of irony in his voice. A blunt fact. He takes a sip of his coffee, places the white china cup back on its saucer, and says, "We've civilized most of these people."

"But you're indigenous," I said. "Chiquitano."

Here he just shrugged and offered me more coffee.

Apollonius and Smithers, of course, are the sultanic exceptions. The vast majority of the folks living in towns like Porvenir, Piso Firme, Florida, and Cachuela live at subsistence level, fishing, hunting, and clearing small agricultural plots as their ancestors did. However, almost none of them still speak Chiquitano; just as Kusasu is the final Guarasug'wé speaker, only a few dozen Chiquitano elders can still have in-depth conversations in their own tongue. Could Guillermo Roy use that against them to revoke their entire legal claim to the Indian Territory? I page through the legal code, and the definition of *indigenous* underlying ITs is dangerously ambiguous.

"It's an Indian Territory without Indians," the INRA lawyer said to me. But what exactly is an Indian? Compounding my confusion, I bump into a thirtysomething American from Colorado who has settled in Bolivia. He's got long, blond dreds and says he's "living in the spirit of Crazy Horse." His name is Christopher Columbus.

"Is that your real name?" I ask. He's selling what he calls fiber art on the Santa Cruz plaza. He's got a welcoming smile, as does his thin Bolivian wife, Kelly. Their two young children play under the table displaying his wares. Above, the sun filters through the plaza's assai, cambará, paquío, tajibo, and almendrillo, freckling the face of the cathedral with dime-sized points.

"You don't choose your name." His wife attends to a couple admiring a necklace, as Columbus says to me, "I know the original double-C was a conqueror, but Kelly and I come in peace. We live like the Indians here did before they were corrupted." He says he and Kelly purchased thirty acres of rainforest for five thousand U.S. dollars and "live off the seeds." All of his jewelry comes from nuts, barks, stones, and twine that he gathers in his back thirty. "Our rainforest *provides*. We're also harvesting gold."

"Gold?"

"I just figured out how to harvest twenty-two-karat gold from butterfly cocoons. I get one twelfth of a gram out of each cocoon."

I choose not to pursue that thought with him any further, letting my eyes wander to the other booths. Lots of earth-tone clothing, cascading hair, incense swirling in the tropical air. Dozens of itinerants, who refer to themselves as locos, are selling woven and beaded jewelry, performing magic, or juggling fire for loose change. This is a small part of a tribe of Argentineans and Colombians, Belgians and Israelis, who wander South America slowly, perhaps a year or two per country, living off their homemade items, and gathering together in the evenings around fires to dance and play bongos, guitars, and *zampoña* flutes. Some, like Christopher Columbus, end up settling down along the road, buying up land and growing and gathering a livelihood.

Intrigued, I would later visit Columbus's jungle homestead, an hour outside Santa Cruz in a hamlet called Bermejo, and indeed he and his family live in the rainforest without electricity beside a rushing stream. Across the way an Israeli couple, graduates from a kibbutz in their own country, have a similar setup. They, and hundreds of other international transplants wanting to live "in the spirit of Crazy Horse," are accomplishing it in Bolivia, at least in the sense of living as lightly on the planet as aboriginal people. "A lot of so-called Indians here are 'apples,'" Christopher Columbus says to me at one point. "They're red on the outside, white on the inside."

I try to say that it's more complicated than that, but his wife jumps in, "They've sold out!"

"But they don't always have options."

"They can revert," Columbus says. "We did."

Revert. The Guarasug'wé tried, but the rubber tappers came into their jungle and murdered them. Same with the Ayoreo, now known as asphalt nomads, who are commonly seen on Santa Cruz footbridges begging with bow-and-arrow props.

I've not seen much of Salvador lately since he's been either off to La Paz or with Juntos, but I'm able to catch him one day after work outside FAN's office, a bit after dark, and ask him how it's going.

"I'm tired, amigo Bill," he says, and I notice he's got large bags under a bleary pair of eyes. "Tired." We walk together across FAN's parking lot toward the "old road to Cochabamba," where he's to catch a micro into the Santa Cruz center. I ask him about the planned invasion of the park.

"We don't choose our tactics," he says. "Our opponents do." *Where have I heard this?* Only later do I realize it's apartheid-era Nelson Mandela. "Amigo Bill, I trust you, so I think I can tell you something in confidence."

I nod as we both stop at the main road, the taxis whizzing by. Here we'll both get our separate micros. "You know us, the Chiquitanos, and you know Kempff. Do you really think we're going to invade?"

Salvador's looking at me, his lips slightly parted, a gold front incisor picking up the gleam of headlights. "I've convinced my Juntos colleagues that the most we'll do is slash and burn a tiny area, for the TV cameras."

He looks up the road for his micro and says, "But we'll take any action to defend our home. The Kempff expansion zone was our hunting ground. We signed it over on the promise that our core acres, all 740,000 of them, would be legally ours. That promise, until now, amigo Bill, has unfortunately not been kept."

Salvador sticks out his hand to hail his bus. He climbs aboard and I watch him place a coin into the bus driver's palm, then grab a handrail since all the seats are taken. He looks just like any of the hundred others squeezed into the bus. I lose sight of him as his bus's taillights blend with all the rest, and I turn the other way and search the oncoming traffic for my own micro, number 83. As I'm waiting, it strikes me that I arrived in Santa Cruz for this job one year ago this month, which gets me feeling nostalgic. I find myself tapping my toe to some rhythm, something I heard in the Indian Territory—I don't remember which village or which trip—but that is soon absorbed into the sounds of the moment: the zoom of motors, swaying of palms overhead, and my bus's brakes grinding to a halt in front of me. I step on board, pay the fare, and squeeze into a seat. The bus is thick with the smell of sweat and coca, and there's some good-natured laughter from a few seats behind me, and I'm suddenly feeling a bit bitter toward fiber artist Christopher Columbus, who would certainly have lumped Salvador into his apple category. Columbus has reverted into a splendid rainforest niche by choice, his American passport always at the ready. Salvador's choice is between extinction and an imperfect survival—while he gently cradles Kusasu's bony fingers in one hand, he's gripping a spiked club with the other.

PART III
Rebellion

CHAPTER 20

H AVE YOU SEEN today's paper?"
"No," I say to Daniel. "And why are you ringing me
at"—I squint over at my alarm clock—"six thirty in the
morning?"

"It's evening in Hong Kong and my workday is just ending.
Next question: Is anyone passing your house on mule or oxen
selling newspapers?"

"I don't think so."

"Do you own an espresso maker?"

"Yes, but what does—"

"I'm coming over with the paper. Make coffee!"

When Daniel arrives, he waltzes straight into the kitchen
and throws *El Deber* newspaper at me, saying, "You won the
Harvard prize!" Sure enough, out of several hundred appli-
cants worldwide, the Amazon Project has received the prestigious Harvard University Roy Family Award for innovative
global initiatives. As I trip over the words for the details,
Daniel is saying, ". . . and my wife is going to love this, she's
going to love *me* for this. We're throwing this indigenous-
people thing into overdrive, mate!"

At FAN that morning the mood is elated. Lots of hugs
accompanied by *"Felicidades!"* but soon the phones start
ringing, the meetings commence, and there are e-mails from
donors to answer. For the whole morning it's as if the prize
never happened; such is the dramatic change in productivity
since I arrived a year back, thanks in large part to FAN's director, Gisela. In a fairly *machista* society she was not only

tapped to be FAN's first female director—and definitely the first with a nose ring—but she took on FAN's all-male board of directors, imposing a code of ethics to reduce possibilities for nepotism. Meanwhile, she controversially fired nearly half of FAN's deadwood staff and systematically built a solid team around her. She cut out red-tape bureaucracy and turned the organization's eight departments into "independent businesses." Her leadership aside, a local NGO like FAN is inherently nimbler than international organizations; low budgets and high workloads force local groups to become scrappy and resourceful. We're on the front lines—shipping the palm hearts to Chile, equipping park rangers with motorbikes, holding the seminars with illiterate community members—there is rarely enough time to do it all.

Gisela announces a celebratory lunch and we pile into Len's Lada and other equally defunct vehicles and head a mile up the road to an outdoor duck feast. Fifty of us sit around a long table with pitchers of chicha, piles of yucca, and steaming roast duck. All hurry has evaporated. *Tranquilo!* Two-hour lunches in Bolivia are still sacred, usually with the whole family, and often with a twenty-minute siesta snooze. Unlike quick sandwich-shop grabs, lunch in Bolivia is a separate space. The office busybodiness metamorphoses into laughter and good-hearted jabs.

When we are all completely stuffed, the speeches begin. After Gisela and several board members, Salvador stands up. He's surrounded by a few AMAZONA colleagues at the far end of the table. He "gives thanks for the Amazon Project," which has protected the park on their border and "is helping them finally to have a home." Everyone around the table now knows his park-invasion threat was a strategic bluff. At the same time we also suspect he may be planning other acts of civil disobedience along with the national Indian movement.

But the national conflict seems far away; we're celebrating success. All things considered, there has been extraordinary progress. A vast piece of the Amazon, three *million* acres, has been protected. Some of the world's biggest energy companies are bankrolling this giant oxygen ranch and are conserving rainforest in their own financial interest, not through fleeting charity, as the rules of the global economy are gradually greened. And even as another arm of globalization—Big Timber—threatens, it's incredible to have other multinationals and the Indians together opposing it. Local incentives too have changed; heart-of-palm harvesting is in full swing, an ecologically benign living for the Chiquitanos. Women have begun to speak more forcefully and even take leadership roles in the Indian Territory. And Salvador organized several community work groups in an effort to establish and mark the IT's boundaries—a job that is now complete. Legal recognition can't be far away.

FAN representatives fly off to Cambridge, and the Amazon Project comes into the spotlight, in full view of global policy makers. But soon the celebration ends, and I find myself again driving the Illustrious Green Wagonette due east, Amazon-bound, through the harsh reality of an internally colonized republic. Smithers is sitting shotgun. We're well past Concepción, just two hours from the Indian Territory boundary, when we witness a startling change.

Fresh waves of settlers have chopped down swaths of virgin rainforest on both sides of the road, with help from the Catholic Church. Bishop Ramón has been doling out church land—a slice Amazon annexed long ago by the Church under rights-of-conquest law—to rural families from the western altiplano and valleys. "Go east!" he's been telling them, trading land for souls. Granted, he's one of the more traditional of the country's eleven bishops, each of whom has tremendous autonomy over his own vicariate. About half of Bolivia's bishops have a social-justice perspective on poverty, while the others believe in old-fashioned charity. Ramón falls squarely in the latter camp; he's said to visibly swell with pride as he buses

· illiterate Quechua peasants to their new home in the Amazon, naming the places New Hope and Heaven on Earth.

But it's hard to slash-and-burn your way to salvation. Bishop Ramón falls prey to the myth that if land grows trees, it must also grow crops. Quite to the contrary, the World Bank says that less than ten percent of existing rainforests grow in soils good for agriculture. Huge areas of tropical soils are composed of nitrogen-poor silica—the fossil sands of ancient oceans. In other rainforests silica dissolves out of underlying rocks, and alumina, iron oxide, and magnesia accumulate, yielding the typical tropical "lateritic" soils infused with the bright reds and yellows, and, while containing adequate nitrogen, they don't have much calcium, phosphorus, or potassium. Rainforest plants draw their nutrients not from these pitiful soils, but rather from themselves—by penetrating directly into rotting logs. When the forest is cleared by peasants, torrential rains quickly leach away what nutrients there are, often creating gullied badlands. The bishop might as well christen the new towns Hell on Earth.

What's more, the settlers often fall prey to malaria and other tropical diseases for which their high-altitude constitutions are ill-equipped. But with nowhere to return to and their poverty often worse, they are forced to fell deeper into the Amazon as their soil erodes, thereby inadvertently acting as shock troops clearing the jungles for cattle ranchers. More ironic still, some of the peasants the bishop so yearns to help are only pretending to be landless. They are *traficantes de tierra,* or land traffickers, who already have small holdings. In front of Bishop Ramón they bow their heads and mouth the Lord's Prayer and then deforest the jungle. Once felled, it's theirs, and they hawk the land off to cattle ranchers and others.

As we drive through these clear-cuts, Smithers whispers of another large change in the works: "The Mennonites are coming." Having exhausted their soils closer in to Santa Cruz, the blue-eyed Dutchmen in overalls are said to be scouting out fresh expanses of Amazon. The same kilometer-long soy-farming strips that jut out from Santa Cruz might someday replace the jungles clear to the Indian Territory. I've struggled to understand the Mennonite mentality and have spoken to several of them, but they either don't see, or most likely don't want to see, the disconnect between their professed Quakeresque stewardship and this wanton destruction of God's creation. They say they're living "outside of the mainstream" where they can avoid the moral hazards of consumerism—and yet are the ones creating the choking dust storms descending over Santa Cruz, topsoil blown off their desertified farms.

But neither conservative Catholic nor myopic Mennonite fells trees in a vacuum. The Bolivian state is supposed to be the bulwark against such private excesses. Where is the state?

Smithers and I arrive at the only checkpoint along this vast Amazon frontier, the gateway to the Indian Territory and Kempff. It's the government timber-control station, which used to have a certain grizzly-looking fellow on duty, checking all timber. The checkpoint had nearly eliminated pirated wood, but it's now been abandoned. It's just a shack, a wooden door swinging on its hinges. Did timber barons like Roy pressure to have the gates opened so that his timber might flow out unimpeded?

Smithers and I both find this too disheartening to comment upon. We simply slip through the collapsing checkpoint in silence. But after a while Smithers is talking rapidly, anxiously: "Ten years ago there weren't any cars back here. No buses even, because the roads were so terrible. We had to take the occasional cargo truck. We'd sometimes get stuck in the mud for a week. So we love the road but . . ." *But.* We dip into the coca leaves, and as we chew, Smithers vents his anger about the very road we're on. It's what's bringing the clear-cutting outsiders; it is destroying the Amazon as he's known it. I've never seen Smithers so passionate.

By the time we arrive in Piso Firme it's late, but we find Salvador still up, *very* up, dancing and playing drums with a group of two dozen villagers. An oblique moon, a few days off full, hangs over the river. Salvador cries out when Smithers and I walk up to them, and there are backslapping hugs all around, and someone pours a Huari beer into two cups, handing them to us.

"*Como fue el viaje?*" Salvador asks.

"Fine," I say. "Except for the bishop's settlers and the Mennonites." My brow knit, I continue this tale of woe until Salvador interrupts.

"Can't you just celebrate?"

I don't know what to say. Salvador goes on, "We're celebrating the award. And . . ." He pauses and looks out over the moonlight-bathed dancers, among them the diminutive headman Gaspar in a ten-gallon cowboy hat. Salvador's got a grin on, only slightly tipsy. "And we're just celebrating."

"*Salud,*" I offer, and we tap beer glasses together. Before long I've joined in the dancing. They've put down the drum and flute and a cassette of Brazilian country music is playing. I notice Salvador making a round of farewells, and when he comes to me, he says, "Can I show you something tomorrow morning?"

"Okay. After the meeting?"

"Before." He's grinning. "I'll get you before sunrise."

I'm following Salvador and a Piso Firme farmer through a pitch-black patch of forest; the moon has sunk, and the first glow of dawn is not yet penetrating the jungle canopy. Branches scratch my arms; leaves and flowers swab my cheeks. At last, Salvador leads the farmer and me out of the forest to the edge of a cornfield, the huge ears looking overripe in the gathering light. The first streak of sunrise, an artificial-looking pink, joins with a rather warm breeze coming out of the jungle beyond the wide river. As the farmer and I freeze alongside Salvador for several long moments, it occurs to me: *We're hunting something.* But what? The cornfield's floor is choked with pumpkins and squash to control weeds, and black beans pole themselves on the cornstalks, spiraling up around the ears. *It could be tapir,* I think, *or something smaller like pheasant or painted hochi.*

Salvador has not moved for an eternity, and I scan for an animal silhouette in the gathering light. Nothing. My ears are the first to tune in—parrots! First one, then two, right before me on the ground munching on an ear of corn. Salvador signals to the farmer, and just before they move, I see it. Not just a few, but *hundreds* of parrots. Their electric green wings merging into chartreuse with splotches of vibrant red. Everywhere, parrots—in the trees, on the earth, amid the corn.

I follow as Salvador and the farmer burst forward into the corn, their throats emitting a primordial *"Raaahhhh!"* that clashes with the alarmed cacophony of the terrified birds. Above, behind, all around us, their cries crescendo with a confusion of brush strokes—green and red on a deep blue canvas—the texture of cornstalks on our skins as we race up the rows until we're still running but the fireworks have ended, and it's just us, laughing and panting.

"Scaring parrots!" Salvador says, explaining that these beautiful pests eat the corn, and it's a morning ritual this time of the year to flush them out. "But this isn't what I wanted to show you. Come on."

We move out of the cornfield, the farmer peeling off, perhaps to scare another fieldful of birds, and eventually Salvador and I arrive at the riverbank, where we sit. He points toward a brown body swimming against the current and suggests I watch.

We both sit in silence, and Salvador eventually slips away, but I remain there as the sun inches up, another couple of swimmers passing. Nothing else. Sure, there's the usual beauty of the river separating Piso Firme from Kempff Park, and the mundane sight of villagers swimming by. And this is supposed to be the main act after the parrot extravaganza?

I attend the morning's meeting. Salvador doesn't mention anything. But my curiosity grows during the day, and that evening I sit in the same spot and watch. Nothing. The next morning, again sitting there, something finally strikes me.

I stand and follow one swimmer upriver until he disappears up a feeder stream. Then I follow another, and another, carefully watching their motions. These swimmers, mostly men and teenage boys, but also some women, never take the same route twice. They are always improvising, adapting to a river that is never the same. In these Amazon tributaries, current, speed, and volume change with little warning. The swimmers adjust, feeling their way into benign currents, following sandbar and shore, sometimes side-stroking to the river's center and taking it from there.

The swimmers always have a purpose. Something practical is to be done: baiting fishhooks hanging from twine tied to riverside branches; crossing the river to check a papaya grove; visiting an upstream relative to ask a favor. But despite the job on hand, the Amazon swimmers are never in a hurry, never take a straight shot toward their goal.

"You won't be seeing me around here too much anymore," I say to Salvador in his cottage the next day. "I'll be traveling a lot. All over."

He's hugging two of his kids, one under each arm. "I know," he says, smiling. "Enjoy it!" Salvador's been hanging around FAN enough to sense the change. Even before the Harvard award, world interest had been coalescing around the Amazon Project, and in a larger sense around the potential of Bolivia as a green nation, economically grounded in "ecological services." The Chicago Climate Exchange (CCX), a kind of oxygen stock market, has been born, and credits from our project are now being bought and sold voluntarily—even before rainforest carbon is officially included in the Kyoto accord. The World Bank just offered to buy up such credits at five dollars a ton. And other oil companies have started jumping on board, sniffing profits. I've been tapped to advise the Brazilian petroleum giant Petrobras on how to replicate the Amazon Project in their natural-gas concessions in Bolivia's southern dryland forests.

At the same time, Evo Morales, Salvador, and the rest of the Indian movement—boxed into a neocolonial regime for so long—are forging ever stronger alliances with European and North American groups, gathering both expertise and cash. This is finally forcing the Bolivian government on the bandwagon; they are sponsoring the first national ecological tourism summit on the banks of Lake Titicaca, and I'll be going.

"Ever heard the saying 'Think globally, act locally'?" I say to Salvador. He shakes his head. "It was a slogan in the U.S. back in the sixties. I've been thinking that now it's completely reversed: 'Think locally, act globally.' "

One of Salvador's daughters places plates of *masaco* in front of us, along with mugs of coffee from their own farm. I thank her, but Salvador is silent as he ponders the wordplay. Watching Salvador lead marches and speak to crowds, I sometimes forget he barely finished high school. He's a novice to abstractions but struggles with this as he does with everything. He finally gives up on the puzzle, saying, "What do you mean?"

I use other words. Only through acting in places far away, as we're doing with multinational corporations and conservation groups, can we ever hope to break through local racism and exclusion.

Salvador is nodding now, his eyes brightening. "I like that," he finally says, nodding. "And, amigo Bill, I really like you."

Salvador's never said anything like that to me, and I find myself lapping up his compliment like a thirsty man. It would take me some time to unravel why I so deeply crave Salvador's approval.

CHAPTER 21

S ORATA SHRINKS BEHIND us, the colonial town's red
teja roofs and white houses blending into earth and snowy
Andes. Our van crests the ridge and dips below it, and the
only thing we can see of Sorata is the icy pinnacle of Mount Il-
lampu, which soon disappears into a wake of cirrus clouds,
their silky filaments ending in hooks.

We're squeezed into a twelve-seater minibus, me and three
other conservation officials along with a dozen community
ecological-tourism leaders, including two from AMAZONA,
on our way to the Titicaca Tourism Summit. We're following
a dirt road along the Royal Range that has dropped out of
alpine tundra into the stunted trees of an elfinwood and finally into a wide cavity of Andean piedmont where Lake
Titicaca stretches out like a sea. It's the world's largest high-
altitude lake; I squint to see the far Peruvian shores, but cannot. Up close, we pass Aymaras clad in colorful ponchos who
farm yellow-green corn in the tidal flats, and fish with nets
among reeds that rise by the thousands like long flutes, attached to their reflections in the still, cold water.

Lila from AMAZONA is moaning in pain behind me. She
and Gaspar have never made it farther from their Amazon
home than Santa Cruz. Suddenly we're twelve thousand feet
above sea level, and climbing, up a now-paved road to a
peninsular butte within the lake. Lila says she's got a pound-
ing migraine, and a colleague from Conservation International tries to peddle some *sorochi pil* on her, and I see a
disaster coming. "That's like bringing your speeding car to a

halt by slamming it into a brick wall," I say, knowing from having personally ingested the stuff during my first days in La Paz; the medicine is a confused brew of uppers and downers.

A Quechua among us suggests a local remedy. He passes forward a bag of coca leaves. Lila and Gaspar stuff the light green leaves into their cheeks and within ten minutes say they feel fine, just in time to savor the sight around a curve so sharp that we take it on two wheels: our destination, Copacabana, a bustling colonial village nudging into Titicaca, with the Islands of the Sun and the Moon shimmering in the distance like two chestnut-colored contact lenses floating on saline.

In town, a line of spiritual pilgrims winds out the door of the Church of Copacabana, clutching *alacitas,* or miniature trinkets, for the priest to bless before they are placed beneath the Dark Virgin, patron saint of Bolivia. The little *alacitas* represent big dreams: a two-inch health-insurance policy for someone feeling insecure; a tiny suitcase and thumb-sized passport for hopeful travelers; statuettes of crowing cocks in the palms of young women in search of husbands—the bird's beak is brown or white, depending on ethnic preference. The priest douses all of these *alacitas* in holy water. Inca and Christian sources of spirituality blend; beyond the cathedral walls vehicles covered with garlands of flowers line up before a traditional Aymara priest, who performs a *chall'a* with Titicaca holy water to protect travelers.

The hotel lobby and conference room are jammed with hundreds of Bolivians from all corners of the country, all here to ensure Bolivia's still nascent tourism industry grows democratically. The key buzzword is the awkward sounding *eco-ethno-tourism.* Instead of Club Med–style hotels controlled by outsiders, Bolivia's majority Indians seek to create and control a multimillion-dollar low-impact sector shaped around megadiversity.

It's definitely a case of the reversed slogan "Think locally, act globally." The Indians are not alone here. Peppered into the mix are international diplomats from the United States, European Union, Japan, and the UN, who are funding the event, along with their NGO partners like FAN who work directly with the Indians. The odd ones out, those feeling squeezed, are the Bolivian government officials. These elites would love business as usual: hand tourism over to their wealthy cronies in exchange for votes and kickbacks. After all, that's the way it's been done with mining, timber, and petroleum.

Scholars are calling this shift in geopolitics the "human rights revolution," where rich-country governments are pressured to act humanely by their own voters' heightened humanitarian and environmental concerns. Whereas the Bank, the Fund, and first-world governments used to encourage countries like Bolivia to "modernize" and "civilize" the Indians, now to internally colonize a country is frowned upon. Apartheid is just a little too difficult to watch on CNN. So the wealthy countries, the ones with the clout, are allied with the Indians and helping them democratize tourism from the get-go.

This explains why I, a six-foot, strawberry-blond gringo, stride into the Titicaca hotel conference room flanked with a pair of confident-looking Indians on either side. The UN gave FAN funds to create two eco-ethno-tourism sites near Kempff and Amboró parks. The world community is paying for me and the community members to my left (Gaspar and Lila) and right (Ernestina and Fidel, two new participants from the Amboró-bordering village of La Yunga) to be here. It's a tiny piece of millions of new dollars flowing into Bolivia around responsible tourism, particularly "CO_2 rism," where the rainforest is a two-layered cake, both layers providing value: the first, through sucking carbon dioxide out of a warming atmosphere; the second, through the jaguars, tapirs, quetzals, and Lost World waterfalls that Amazon safari-goers are eager to behold. It's an ecological double billing, where pristine rainforest should generate so much income that everyone will laugh hysterically when someone proposes to cut it down and "develop" it.

Tourism has the power to treasure or trash Bolivia. The multibillion-dollar global tourism industry hosts 664 million vacationers around the world, set to double in twenty years to 1.6 billion, and is the top foreign-exchange earner for nations like Costa Rica and Guatemala. "Bolivia is where Costa Rica was twenty years ago," an ecotourism expert tells me. "It's brimming with promise." Bolivia already takes in $175 million in tourism each year, even with just 350,000 visitors. The Ministry of Tourism wants to raise that to a half million by 2008, creating one hundred thousand new jobs, a substantial chunk of Bolivia's labor force. The people gathered here are intent on shaping those new jobs around a thousand community-based enterprises, run primarily by Indians.

Speakers talk about shaping the tourism around trips certified and sold by e-retailers like Responsible Tourism.com, Escape Artists, and Trees for the Future. Travelers do not need to go through tour companies anymore, but can now easily weave together a community-based itinerary on one of these Web sites, eliminating go-betweens and keeping more profits with local people.

Between sessions one day, my four community friends and I head out on a motorboat for the Island of the Sun. The wind feels amazing on my face as we race forward into a clear sky, splitting water that looks like blue lacquer. As the island grows before us, its appearance increases in intensity from lucid to glowing, and then positively flaring red clay. I put on sunglasses to cut the glare, revealing the island's ribbing, ancient Inca terracing that also appears in Machu Picchu, across the lake in Peru. Our plan is to disembark and explore the island's ruins and feast on fresh trout prepared by Aymaran islanders. But abruptly the captain cuts the throttle.

"We have to turn back," he says, explaining that the mainland Aymara are on the march. If we don't get back soon, we could get walled into Copacabana by road blockades. The Aymara campesinos are protesting an "illegitimate" Goni government and have already cut off access to Peru.

"This is why we'll never get more tourists!" Lila says, back on land. "We keep scaring them off." She lashes out against Salvador, how he's now too cozy with the *bloqueadores*. I look to Gaspar for his opinion, but the little old man simply shrugs and says with a smile that he's just the "tail of the Indian Territory and does what the dog wants."

But the two Amboró Park community members disagree. One, Fidel, says to Lila, "Sure we want travelers, but we've been exploited by the oligarchy for five hundred years."

"I've had the same five hundred years as you!" Lila says. "I'm Chiquitano, but you don't see me blocking roads—it hurts *us*. I want to work."

"So do I," Fidel says, "but roadblocks are the only language Goni understands."

"And English," his colleague says, with the hint of a grin. "Roadblocks and English."

Back at the hotel, the reception desk is slammed with guests wanting to beat the roadblocks back to La Paz. On line myself, luggage in hand, I feel a bit of Lila's pain. Bolivia loses millions for every day of roadblocks. Even Daniel was affected. He'd organized three tour groups of "very wealthy Australasians" who would have left hundreds of thousands of dollars in Bolivia, taking away with them only photos of unicorn birds. All three groups canceled when the protest images hit CNN. Daniel was furious: "We were going to fly from park to park in Cessnas! They're not blocking the *air*." But demand for tourism is highly elastic—just a whiff of something amiss reroutes itineraries to Zimbabwe or Brazil.

* * *

I beat the altiplano blockades, catching a bus along rough dirt roads, eighteen hours to the world's largest salt flats located in Bolivia's southwest, where the country joins with Argentina and Chile. I can't seem to catch five consecutive minutes of sleep the entire night; meanwhile dozens of Bolivians snore away blissfully, not just in the seats but also covering every inch of the floor. My seatmate's large head rests peacefully on my shoulder as I stare out into the moonlit landscape that has dropped out of the Andes into scrub and then desert. By dawn it's as if we're driving through cream—smooth yellow sand under the tires—into a pristine morning. The bus driver pulls over to relieve himself, and I'm out the door behind him, feeling for toe space between the dozen bodies on the floor. The brisk autumnlike air is a welcome change from the stale odors of the bus.

Finally, Uyuni. It's a desert town where salt speckles the sand like coconut grated onto butterscotch icing, and boxy, white buildings clamor for space, vaguely evoking Morocco. A colleague and I board a Toyota 4×4 and head off with our driver and a Canadian tourist couple into the salt flats, the world suddenly bone white on metallic blue. Our guide, a Quechua named Mamani, explains through a mouthful of coca leaf that we're caravanning with another 4×4 because of "the unfortunate recent deaths." It doesn't seem as if he'll elaborate.

"Deaths?" I query.

"Swedes," he says, explaining their vehicle broke down mid-salt-flat. "They tried to cross the salt on foot but died in the freezing tidal pools."

I can see how that would have happened. After two hours driving, plowing through the frequent washes of salty water, I feel as if we're at sea, until some hazy islands appear on the horizon. We stop at one of them and hike past twelve-meter cacti on our way to a rock perch, overlooking what could be an ice sheet. We also stop at another break in the *salar,* the appropriately named Salt Hotel. Its dozens of rooms, lobby, and restaurant—and even the beds and other furniture—are constructed entirely of salt. Unfortunately, we can't stay there. Local Indians have shut it down until the wealthy La Paz–based owner includes them in the operation.

During the rest of our four days we encounter only simple B&Bs and pensions run by the local people. My colleague and I are, theoretically at least, here on work, so we crunch the numbers. Yes, it's natural capitalism. The entire area, about five percent of Bolivia, runs on ecology. This thanks in large part to Eduardo Avoroa National Park, the only one of Bolivia's seventeen parks that is totally sustained by the forty thousand visitors coming through each year. It gets that many because it's linked to neighboring Chile's far more developed tourism industry—Europeans and Americans cross the border for a few days during their Chilean adventure.

We both see the enormous potential. Even with this relative trickle of tourism, thousands benefit. It would be no great thing to double the numbers while still having minimal impact. "And it's a virtuous cycle between economics and politics," my colleague says, explaining that the local rangers, tour guides, and B&B operators will vote their pocketbooks—electing officials who will protect the area in order to keep it prosperous.

We pass lakes of otherworldly hues: red, green, yellow, and streaky blues. We're out of the *salar* and into rugged moraine landscapes like none I've seen. The Canadians rave that it's "ten times better than Patagonia" whence they've come and wonder aloud why no one knows about this. The answer is that it's not been promoted, beyond best-kept-secret mentions in backpacker bibles like the *Lonely Planet* and the *Rough Guide*. Bolivia is just beginning to imagine itself as a tourist destination.

Early one morning we hike amid geyser fields. I'm fully relaxed after soaking in natural hot springs and find myself alone, wandering amid scree and talus as an Old Faithful–style geyser jets fifty feet into the sky. But I'm more drawn to the bubbling witches' cauldrons on the perimeter, what geologists call fumaroles, and the streams of boiling water winding into deep vats like sleek-bodied animals. I pull off my T-shirt and sink down beside one of these vats, letting the sulfurous vapor warm my face and chest, as the sun heats my back. I'm hypnotized by fifty points of fizz, burst, and bubble, hot water doing all sorts of things, and there's one lonely vulture riding the rising warmth.

"Bolivia is both the poorest and richest country in the Americas," Anaí wrote to me recently from Brussels, where she's working on the global-warming treaty. "It's the soul of South America." Anaí's idea of richness is the megadiversity around me: wild ecology and radicalized culture. Galleno wrote, "Of all the Latin American countries, Bolivia is the one with a furious sense of dignity." It's a myth that material poverty must lead to apathy; Bolivia is turning into a geyser field.

My parents have had a trip to Bolivia planned for some time, but are thinking of canceling because of the social unrest. The plan was for me to meet them in La Paz, and from there go to Madidi National Park in the far west. But when I phone my father in Chapel Hill, he sounds skittish. "Can we reschedule? I'm watching Bolivia blow up on TV."

"Just come. We'll fly over the roadblocks to Madidi." They agree to make the trip anyway.

At first it seems the only berths I can reserve from La Paz to Madidi are on the infamous "meat plane," which caters mostly to not-so-finicky peasants and philosophy-major backpackers. You can't argue about the fare—as long as you're skinny. The meat plane is an Aeroflot relic that transports slaughtered beef between La Paz and the rural area beyond Madidi Park. Pricing is simple: you step on a scale and pay by the pound.

My mother says it sounds splendid, but Dad is firm: "I'm not getting on a scale."

I eventually locate a small Bolivian carrier that makes runs to Rurrenabaque, and we board unweighed. Soon we've landed and climb into a motorized canoe, racing upriver for five hours into the middle of Madidi, stopping once to watch capybaras sunning themselves. The Chalalán Lodge is luxurious. My parents share the "honeymoon" cabin, constructed in Uchupiamonas Indian style—a steep-pitched roof with exposed tacuara-bamboo supports bound by strips of dried vine. The beds are covered with eggshell-white sheets and have a single fresh flower on each pillow. We share Uchupiamonas meals—typically fish or pheasant with yucca and forest herbs—at a mahogany table in a longhouse fitted with flush doors and windows screened to keep the anopheles mosquitoes at bay. Between the buildings a grassy meadow slopes into Lake Chalalán.

Amazingly, Chalalán is one hundred percent Indian owned and operated. The four hundred Uchupiamonas and Quechua Indians living in the park's boundaries serve not just as cooks and maids, but also as accountants, certified tour guides, and even general manager. This miracle didn't happen overnight. The Interamerican Development Bank and Conservation International invested several years and over a million dollars to help the Indians put this in place. They even sent a dozen Indians off to La Paz for degrees in business, nature interpretation, and culinary arts. The Uchupiamonas have catapulted from pauper to trust-fund kid, with the international community as the benevolent uncle. For two years Chalalán has been turning a profit, and the pride—and newfound economic clout—of the Indians here is obvious. It has become a Latin American model for what can be done by local indigenous people in tourism.

But at least one visitor is not wholly satisfied; my father begins to complain after the first few of our five days at the lodge. "We're urban people," he laments, adding that he's tired of awaking at five A.M. to pursue jaguars and tapirs. He misses his libraries, theaters, and daily *New York Times*. He sleeps in the fourth day, and my mother, who couldn't be happier to be out of civilization, creeps behind me as I point to the sight of a hundred capuchin and squirrel monkeys crashing down from the canopy where they'd slept. Branches snap and leaves flutter down to us along with the monkeys' musky odor. That evening I'm canoeing with my father on the wide Lake Chalalán. We scan the lake perimeter with flashlights, catching the red eyes of caiman crocodiles. As we approach the lodge, still scanning the water, we catch another set of eyes in the light. Not reptile, but mammal: "Mother!"

"The water is wonderful!" she shouts, not ten meters from the piercing eyes of a crocodile. I inform her that she's bathing with caimans, and she calls back that she has some strong American students to protect her. Sure enough, she's treading water with two coeds, part of an ecological study tour of the Amazon. Meanwhile my dad is muttering that a couple of sophomores won't be able to save his wife and adds wistfully, "Just think. In three and a half days we'll be home."

On our last day, our guide, a young Uchupiamonas woman who knows the park's flora and fauna inside out, has led us to an escarpment overlooking Chalalán Lake and the humid forests beyond, which stretch unbroken to the horizon.

"There's a plan to dam this for hydroelectric power," she tells us. "The dam would put half the park underwater."

Along with us is a Bolivian economics professor who now lives and teaches at a prestigious university on the U.S. west coast. She's got a few of her students in toe, including the ones swimming with my mom and the crocodiles last night. The professor is in her midthirties, a blond-haired, blue-eyed Bolivian who grew up in a walled-in house in La Paz's exclusive South Zone. Her father is a politician in Goni's Movimiento

Nacionalista Revolucionario (National Revolutionary Movement) party, and close friends with the president. She's frowning in mock-dismay at the Indian guide and then turns to her students and says, "Bolivia might have *too much* land under protection. We may need to dam this for our development. There are trade-offs."

"Dam the national park?" one of the students says.

"I'm not saying to dam the whole . . . *darn* thing," the professor says. "It's just that we must be reasonable people."

I point out that the park contains forty-four percent of New World mammal species and forms a vital link in the globally significant Vilcabamba-Amboró ecological corridor, adding, "By keeping it intact, hundreds of poor Bolivians are earning a living from tourism."

With each word I utter the professor's scowl deepens, and she finally snaps, "We're *not* just a view for gringos. We have a right to develop. *You* did."

My father says, "You know she's right, Son. Bolivians do need money more than they need trees."

Our Indian guide has learned enough English to understand this and slowly says, "The tree are . . . our money." She gestures back toward the lake, eco-lodge, and rainforest beyond.

Our heated little debate goes on. To the eagles flying above we probably appear as the small herd of chattering mammals that we are. Or maybe they hardly notice us, our voices absorbed by a million acres of wilderness. And yet so much depends upon this discussion, and others like it, because it is one species that gets to shape the planet's future for the rest. Nothing is clear. The professor is right that Western wealth was built on conquering nature; and if ecotourism employs hundreds here, the dam might generate power for thousands. Yet it goes deeper than trees versus dollars or environment versus development. We're really talking about "Development for whom?" and, more fundamental still, "*What*, pray tell, is development?"

The two Bolivian women with us form a stark fault line: the La Paz heiress and a shorter, darker Uchupiamonas. The professor is a *hidalgo*, literally a contraction of *hijo-de-algo* or "the child of something." She's benefiting from the rights of conquest of the New World, and this Indian is out of line. One woman's parents quite literally owned the other's several decades back. The Uchupiamonas woman is an *hijo-de-nada*, "the child of nothing."

"It's all a lie," the professor would say to me later that evening. Her face reveals her worry; her family and class privileges are under attack along with Goni. "She's not even Indian, that . . ." *bitch*. She's itching to say it but holds back, staring over the dark lake. She says that the guide is "just a *campesina*, a *mestiza* farmer masquerading as an Indian to take advantage of the project."

Or is the world changing in a way that allows her to be Indian once again? My parents and other Americans and Europeans, through paying taxes and donating to nonprofits, paid for the Indian woman's ecology and English classes—something upper-class Bolivians have been unwilling to do. And by staying here, instead of at a Hilton, they support her growing economic clout. I'm pondering this on the canoe ride out of Madidi. Gripping a gunwale, I zone out a bit on the jungle as it rushes by, then turn around and catch my father hugging my mom against him. They're content. My dad, to be sure, is thrilled to be going home. But it's more than that; he would later admit that Bolivia got under his skin. During this and another visit, the country's wild nature and feisty rural people touched them both.

Here's the mental photograph of this moment I still carry with me: My parents crush into each other, forming a soft pyramid, their eyes cast slightly downward, toward each other's center. Their faces glow in the day's breaking light. Behind them, a white wake on the river rushes into a riot of green forest. My love for them blends into the landscape around them, around us. An invisible presence heightens the photo's mood. It's the Uchupiamonas woman from the ridge who got in the last word with the professor—her people will not let anyone dam their forest; she will fight to defend Pacha Mama.

CHAPTER 22

I'VE NEVER SEEN so much commotion in the sleepy hamlet of La Yunga, tucked away in another national park, Amboró, far from Madidi and Chalalán Lodge. It's one A.M. and we're still working. We scrape whitewash off fat guadua-bamboo beams; sweep out the new bungalows and install mattresses; and buff the new restaurant's large glass windows, which overlook a moonlit pueblo.

I'm with a dozen community members, and each of us has something in hand, be it broom, brush, or hammer. Below, the women prepare tomorrow's feast. They bake bread in clay ovens and smoke pork in shoveled-out pits. Above, in the giant-fern forest, another community crew finishes off the trail work. It's a big day tomorrow. We expect several hundred people to drive up the mountain, among them television and print journalists, for the official opening of La Yunga's community ecotourism project.

My boss, FAN's director, Gisela, looked at me skeptically several weeks ago when I told her I was going to raise the bamboo superstructure in La Yunga. "You're an *obrero intelectual*," she said. "You don't need to actually build these things."

" 'Intellectual worker?' " I said. "That sounds kinda Marxist."

"Look. You've got a bunch of new projects. Shouldn't you hire staff and control budgets? Stuff like that?"

Of course I'll do that, I told her. This is after-hours volunteer work. I enjoy the overtime. Barriers between people come crashing down when you've all got your sleeves rolled up and labor together. Even the project architect, a friend from La Paz, has donated her designs and time and is right alongside us in the moonlight. This project helps people living on less than one dollar a day—the measure of "extreme poverty"—earn money for their education and health. I feel buoyant, the endorphins flowing along with our banter, and I think of Paul Farmer's observation that all philanthropy "comes from a desire to relieve some psychic discomfort."

I manage to catch a few hours of sleep. The next morning five hundred people come up the mountain, most of whom heard about the event through word of mouth. After speeches by local politicians, FAN, and community members (including both Fidel and Ernestina, who had traveled with me to the Titicaca tourism event), we cut ribbons on the two bungalows and restaurant, feast together, and then head into the giant ferns.

La Yunga's cloud forests are packed with thousands of fern trees. Walking among them, even though for me it's the twentieth time, I feel I'm treading on another planet. I bounce along on the spongy mosses under a multistory canopy dotted with purple and phosphorescent pink orchids and bromeliads. The gnarled fern trees are six and seven hundred years old— some as much as a thousand—and grow in such an otherworldly, misty atmosphere I half expect a pterodactyl to swoop overhead. Our group's community guide, the twenty-three-year-old Fidel, explains that the unique, stunted plants, and relative lushness, result from the year-round clouds blanketing the area, keeping everything constantly damp and dimly lit.

Watching Fidel, Ernestina, and the rest of the community guides in action fills me with pride. FAN has been working for two years to train them in nature interpretation, business management, and guest services. Even before this, the official inauguration, visits jumped three hundred percent, from five hundred last year to two thousand this year. People's incomes have doubled, raising dozens of families out of poverty.

Len manages to burst my bubble. Sporting his trademark Kempff Park ranger uniform and black army boots, he strolls up spinning an orchid flower between thumb and forefinger. "This is wonderful," he says, a mischievous smile on his face.

I nod, my face tightening for the blow.

"Wonderful," he repeats. "If I had hot dogs and mustard, I'd never leave this place."

Fidel points to jaguar tracks—fresh in the mud—and indicates the "long walk" trailhead that leads down along the San Rafael River to Devil's Tooth Mountain, chock-full of immense condors and the Andean spectacled bears.

"*Eco*tourism," Len says quietly, as Fidel continues. "There must be a catch. Did you come up with the idea?"

"Of course I didn't come up with it," I say.

"So it's what you *know how to do,* not what works."

This is interesting. I stop and watch Len spin his orchid. He says, "I'm just thinking about the other incentives out there, the destructive ones. This is good; but is it good enough?"

Enchiladas. Three of them lined up next to Mexican beans and rice, dollops of guacamole and sour cream. I'm with twenty FAN and national park friends at a Mexican restaurant in Santa Cruz's fashionable Cristo district, back after long days leading up to La Yunga's inauguration, and am ready to unwind. And Santa Cruz certainly has that in the offering. It's called *la joda*: a sacred hedonism. Similar to what the Irish call the crack, *la joda* is a reverence for the art of the spontaneous good time. And, just as they say you've not been to Ireland if you've not been to the pubs, Santa Cruz is only fully experienced after dark.

Everyone raises a Corona or salty margarita to toast, knowing that this ten P.M. dinner is only the warm-up. We're dining early; Santa Cruz's sidewalks are just starting to fill with metal tables and chairs, and celebratory sounds begin to fill the city: corks pop, beer bottles fizz to life, laughter percolates. Santa Cruz has more than a million people, and on Saturday night nearly every single one of them is *out*. The same starry tropical night vaults over rich and poor, from the fancy Palms and Hammocks to the poorest seventh-ring barrio, and everywhere the dancing begins. It's the latest house and techno in the Equipetrol clubs; in the low-income fourth-ring joints it's ranchero and Brazilian country, with hundreds of couples holding each other over a cement patio, or nursing a single twenty-cent mug of beer. Those who do not drink are out too; legions of evangelicals stick to maracujá juice and Inka Cola, as do pregnant women and Bahais—but they're dutifully in *la joda,* around tables playing the yatzee-esque *cacho,* strolling, gossiping, and dancing.

Our Mexican meal, however, feels awkward from the start. Salvador and the chief of Cachuela, Gaspar, have come along, joining others from the FAN office. All of the rest of us are *licenciados,* ye licensed ones, while Salvador barely squeaked out a diploma and Gaspar finished grade two with a gold star. They're both dressed in rough country clothes: roadblocking garb. Gaspar doesn't utter a single word during the meal; he looks with quiet wonder at the margaritas, nibbles the free and ubiquitous tortilla chips. When the waiter asks what they want, Salvador says that he and Gaspar "want a couple of *majaditos,*" an Eastern Bolivian dish. The waiter says curtly that they only have *Mexican* food and points to the menu.

Salvador looks at it for another moment, and the illiterate Gaspar stares at Salvador looking at the menu. Words like *chimichanga, enchilada,* and *flauta* sound like Swahili to them. I interject that the burritos here are great, and Salvador readily agrees that's exactly what they'd like.

Daniel phones me during dinner, and he's as excited as a kid with a pile of new toys as he talks about the night he has planned for us. I agree to meet him in Equipetrol. Salvador declines, heading to a simpler locale, but I extract a promise from him to meet us later at my favorite Santa Cruz nightspot, a Cuban-owned salsa joint called Manizero. The unpretentious Manizero packs after two A.M. with Bolivians, Columbians, Venezuelans, Guyanese, and Trinidadians, and a few European and North American adventurers. I figure Salvador will love it.

I meet Daniel in Equipetrol. He's just touched down from a "round-the-worlder" à la Jakarta–Cape Town–Brussels–Rio. He buys us drinks at the Latin-rock bar Varaderos, where a band cranks out decent Maná covers. Then we shoot over to Manizero in Daniel's private cab, but the salsa joint is so packed you have to squeeze in sideways. Pepe, the six-foot-three-inch black man from Havana who owns the club, comes over to give me a cheerful handshake. At the bar, Daniel and I tuck down tequila shots, then sip into some *mojitos*. Several dozen couples spin on the dance floor to Celia Cruz, Oscar D'Leon, Willie Colon, and Tito Rojas. Everyone is *down*. The music is at once intricate and essentially rhythmic, a unique quality resulting from European and West African styles fusing in the Caribbean. Daniel and I toast and sip our *mojitos*, and my friend Ligia approaches us, her black hair tied up in a tumbledown bun. She grabs my hand and pulls me onto the dance floor.

At some point Daniel says farewell, that he's too much of an old guy for all of this, but I do notice he's grinning as he says this; he ducks out with a woman for whom he'd been buying drinks. I just keep dancing. After Ligia, it's Silvana, Noella, Tania, and a string of other women friends with similarly soft-sounding names ending in *a*. It's after three when Salvador and Gaspar finally arrive. Salvador bows to the first young lady he sees and asks her to dance and is soon doing off-rhythm salsa spins with gusto.

We leave the floor together and join Gaspar at our table,

both of us soaked in sweat. Gaspar is quiet and looks somewhat sad. But Salvador raves about the music. He tells us
about his recent trip to Germany, his first time on an airplane.
The UN flew him there as an "Indian authority" on global
warming, but he tells us about an uncomfortable moment at a
disco: "Two German women from the meetings asked me and
a *compañero* from Peru to dance. *'Bueno!'* we thought. Then
they started giggling and left us alone dancing together." He
stops here to sip his beer; Gaspar, now solidly plastered, is
speaking Chiqitano into his mug: *la joda*'s grand finale is crying in one's cups.

Salvador slams his mug down, stands, looks left and right,
and then chivalrously extends his hand to another woman,
who accepts. As the two fumble through the Caribbean dance,
I think about how *la joda* is an essential part of the civilized
barbarian. Salvador tries to sniff out joy wherever he can. He
drinks a little, but not too much, and though he loves women
("they make the borochi and the parrots sing for joy") has
never, as far as I can tell, cheated on his wife. But these
thoughts are interrupted by a startlingly high-pitched call
from beside me. I turn to see Gaspar wailing my name: "Biii-
illllllll!"

His chin falls against his chest, and he goes on mumbling in
the ancient language; I feel as if he's shrunk in size. Maybe it's
because Manizero is filled with large people: Afro-Caribs, Europeans, mestizos. Gaspar's doll-sized face has the highest of
cheekbones, typical of Amazonian tribes, and his shoulders
are like bent elbows. I touch one of them and he does it again:
"Biiillllll!" I look around desperately for Salvador. The sound
hits me at the core. It's as primal as a woman feeling the life
and breath stolen from her newborn, not wanting to touch the
still body.

Salvador, dancing, glances over at us just as Gaspar's tiny
head falls forward and thuds against the table. I shake him a
little, but he's out cold. Salvador chivalrously bows to the

beautiful girl and is immediately with us, taking charge. In one motion he has Gaspar hoisted over his shoulder and simultaneously fishes his free hand into a pocket for some coins, which he drops on the table. He takes the scenic route through the very middle of the dance floor, as couples disengage and stand aside. At the entrance he looks left and right, then shouts "*Compadre!*" to a dozing taxi driver stationed a bit up the road. The taxi's engine sputters to life, and Salvador has Gaspar in the back.

"Can I help?" I ask Salvador.

He shakes his head and is off.

Another cab pulls up. "Where to?" asks the cabbie, a bulge of coca in his cheek.

I get in and say, "Fourth ring. Urby Lisboa."

He nods, and that's the end of our conversation. I'm thoroughly confused. Sure, Gaspar was a drunken mess and needed to go home. But Salvador's reaction was just too over-the-top, *as if he wanted everyone to notice him.* He rescued Gaspar as if he were a wounded man on a battlefield. But a sound in my head pierces these thoughts—*Biiiilllll*—like a drill bit entering my temple, and I'm thinking about Pygmies.

Pygmies? It's five A.M., just before dawn, and we're rolling along the now vacant second ring, going through red lights and green lights alike. It takes a minute to make the connection; it's a moment from Philip Gourevitch's *We Wish to Inform You That Tomorrow We Will Be Killed with Our Families.* Though I read the book a year ago, one image from postgenocide Rwanda has stayed with me, and Gaspar has brought it to the surface. A Pygmy—about the size of Gaspar—offered Gourevitch a theory in a Gikongoro bar, admitting it's far-fetched: "My theory is '*Homo sapiens.*' Do you understand me?"

Gourevitch hazards a guess: that all humanity is of the same species.

That's the theory.

CHAPTER 23

A MBORÓ NATIONAL PARK strikes a dramatic contrast
with Kempff. Kempff is on Bolivia's isolated Amazon
edge; Amboró at its Andean core. Kempff's beauty is hori-
zontal: smooth and expansive, with waterfalls bridging long
lines of rainforest and mesa. Amboró's beauty is vertical: its
volcano-shaped mountains fortressing a dense, prickly interior. If Bolivia were a jaguar, Kempff would be a sleek curve
of musculature; Amboró a bared set of claws.

Amboró is a splendid place. This single park contains even
more biodiversity than the entire country of Costa Rica. While
the much celebrated Costa Rica has nine life zones, Amboró
alone has thirteen and contains the largest recorded number of
birds in the world: 780 species, including such rarities as the
quetzal, horned curassow, cock of the rock, chestnut-fronted
macaw, and cuvier toucan. Covering 630,000 hectares, Amboró lies within three distinct ecosystems: the foothills of the
Andes, the northern Chaco, and the Amazon Basin. The park
brims with mammals, including capybaras, peccaries, tapirs,
several species of monkey such as howlers and capuchins, jungle cats such as the jaguar, ocelot, and margay, and the increasingly rare spectacled bear, the only bear species found in South
America. New species are regularly discovered since only fifty
percent of the park has been thoroughly explored.

But Amboró has enchanted more than adventure travelers
and the global conservation groups that have placed it alongside Kempff as a key world conservation priority; it is also
eyed by thousands of marginalized Bolivians who dream of

reclaiming their own lands or gaining new ones. Founded in 1984 as the German Busch Wildlife Reserve and expanded in 1990 under the efforts of Bolivian biologist Noel Kempff and British zoologist Robin Clark, Amboró began to come under attack by farmers, loggers, and hunters and has since been prioritized by the Nature Conservancy as one of the world's twenty-five "parks in peril." Clark, with whom I spoke in his private bird reserve near the park's northeast boundary, spent eight years doing battle with those intent on exploiting the area. He helped establish what is known as Amboró's "red line," a reduced boundary that encompasses the still intact part of the park, and then began arresting anyone trespassing beyond it, confiscating chain saws and guns. Clark was for a time forced to leave Bolivia for his native Britain because of alleged threats to his personal safety.

The story of Amboró and the people around it is central to Bolivia's current struggle to invent itself. If Kempff is past and possible future, Amboró is Bolivia's turbulent present, as I find out the hard way when I am accosted by an angry Quechua peasant near Amboró's red line, his machete raised as if to behead me.

I'm just over the hills from La Yunga's fern forest visiting a different Amboró gem: a cloud forest owned by FAN. I'm with my field officer, Jesús, and a private landowner. We have been blocked on the road for an hour by several dozen Indians brandishing sharp machetes and threatening us in Quechua. The leader turns his machete away from me and points it toward Jesús's chest. I can tell Jesús is scared. We're nowhere near any authority that could protect us. The men's leathery faces, Asiatic eyes, angular jaws and limbs, stained *ropa usada americana* clothes—their whole appearance contrasts with the pleasing tonality of Quechua, which, even when shouted, has some of the melodious appeal of French.

We've accompanied the Santa Cruz landowner in order to

advise him on how to turn his several hundred acres into a nature reserve that would border FAN's own private reserve. But these Quechua campesinos want neither the landowner nor FAN anywhere near what they consider to be their land. No matter that FAN has the legal title to these twenty-five hundred acres of fragile cloud forest, nor that the landowner is in the same position. As in other parts of Bolivia, these poor farmers have begun to ever more strongly insist that the land belongs to those who work it.

These folks belong to a national campesino organization called Movimiento sin Tierra, or the Landless Movement. It's not a political party, but more like a union of disenfranchised Indians and mestizos, who have chosen a radical path. Having tired of lobbying the La Paz government to hurry up with the long-stalled land-titling required by the Agrarian Reform, they've taken things in their own hands. Their tactic: occupy and begin to farm private lands that they claim are "underutilized." Like ours. Jesús tries in vain to explain that they are conservation lands, being secured for all Bolivians. That FAN's twenty-five hundred acres harbor wildlife, attract ecological tourism, and provide a watershed for the whole municipality.

I don't need to understand Quechua to catch the gist of the campesinos' response to this: This is *our* land now! Land to those that work it! Land for our cousins and second cousins and nephews and their nephews' children. The ones who are here. The ones who will come from the valleys outside Cochabamba, Sucre, Potosí, from the dry, stingy lands that breed tooth-rot and pinched ribs to God's country: Amboró Park, where the Andes tumble into the eastern jungles.

Ambiguities hover just below the surface. Neither farmer nor environmentalist is pure. Some of these "landless" folks are actually smallholders elsewhere who want more land, and politicians are also sometimes behind these territory grabs, wanting to swell the rolls for their own party in certain districts. Nor is FAN emphasizing at this particular moment that the property was purchased with foreign funds as a Nature Conservancy "colonization break," intended to stop the penetration of slash-and-burn settlers like these so they cannot raze the giant ferns and enter the heart of Amboró.

I use conflictual language: advancing colonists, penetration, invasion. At the front lines of tropical conservation it begins to feel like so many battles. But my colleague Jesús calmly navigates the tension in his smooth Quechua, and the campesinos retreat fifty meters back up the dirt road to conference. One intones vigorously to the others. Jesús, the landowner, and I lean against the pickup in silence, waiting for the mob to issue its verdict.

A full nerve-racking hour passes. They've stopped deliberating about us and seem to be in a general meeting when I spot among the faces someone I know personally: Placido.

FAN, ironically, has given a full decade of assistance to the small community of migrants that have settled here in our cloud forest reserve, including Placido. We gave them part of the territory and helped increased their income by introducing better agriculture. We thought we had exemplary relations with them—how did it come to shouting and raised machetes?

I first came to this cloud forest a year ago for a country fair. The community displayed a dozen FAN-sponsored activities, including their organic-honey production. One farmer displayed six hundred thriving peach trees. In the ten-meter gaps between his rows grew nitrogen-fixing trees that would be harvested for wood in six years, thereby reducing deforestation while suppressing weeds. Other farmers displayed compost making, row irrigation, and intensive vegetable production.

These minor miracles had been wrought by a committed FAN field-extension officer: the very Jesús held hostage with me now. Over the years he'd won the community's trust. At the demonstration day, I remember Jesús laughing and joking with some of the same farmers now blocking us. But a fresh wave of "landless" farmers have since arrived and convinced our friends that Amboró Park is getting in the way of dreams they didn't even know they had: conquering yet more land.

Finally the machete-wielders return and tell us they have decided to "liberate" us on the condition that the landowner never again appears on "their" lands.

A few days later I'm just up the hill in La Yunga's fern forest to evaluate progress since the big inauguration. It's going well. The spunky sexagenarian Ernestina and twenty-three year-old leader Fidel beam with enthusiasm over the income they're earning from tourism. But Fidel is concerned about something and leads me to the edge of the fern forest and says, "Look over there." He's indicating an area near the next ridge to the west, toward FAN's cloud forest. I do not see anything out of the ordinary. It's the same shimmering blanket of green dropping down toward—

"*Mierda,*" I mutter. Other Landless Movement colonists have clear-cut a rectangular swath of rainforest on a distant hill, its rounded end giving it the appearance of a brown tongue.

Fidel calls a meeting that afternoon in La Yunga's schoolhouse and says, "We have to stop the *colonos.*" When another community member from their ecotourism association scoffs it off as "just a few acres," the others pounce, saying that if they do nothing the *colonos* will spread right down into the valley, ruining the landscape the tourists come to see. And then the next target could be their precious fern forest itself.

These Inca-descended people *do* have an idea of the future—and immediately make plans. They will hurry to finish their "individual land-use plans," which give bolstered legal protection against invaders. They will bring this up with the network of other "community tourism providers" around Amboró to give themselves strength in numbers. And they will speed up talks with a Swiss investor interested in putting a rustic, but somewhat higher end eco-lodge in the valley. Excited by their spontaneous defense of their environment, I unthinkingly slip into the parlance of the dismal science, exclaiming that this will "further increase the land's existence value over agricultural-use values!"

Blank stares, as I peter out with ". . . thereby internalizing ecological services."

After an awkward silence Fidel says, "Let's go find the mayor!"

Down in the municipal capital, Mairana, the mayor is unfortunately out, but we do get a meeting with the most powerful of the town councilmen, a moon-faced man with oddly small shoulders and a round belly. The community presents its case: these *colonos,* they say, are illegally invading lands in the Amboró Park buffer zone.

"Honorable councilman," the ever-earnest Fidel says, "the tourists won't like it."

The councilman nods gravely throughout the meeting and says he will certainly look into it and take all necessary actions. Before I know it, he's shaking our hands and showing us the door. But when he gets to me, he says cloyingly in my ear, "*Compañero americano,* can I have a word with you alone?" His face is as round as a pie, and slicked with sweat and facial oil.

Feeling a mix of curiosity and unease, I agree. The councilman leaves me alone, walking out with the others. I hear laughter and backslapping. Soon he's talking to his secretary and then on the phone, repeatedly murmuring, "Uh-huh." The town hall has a kind of Old West quality, with dust covering the wooden floors. Out the window, the plaza is barbwired to keep the cattle out of the shrubs. My wooden seat begins to feel harder. Does he want to cut me in on some kind of deal? I imagine him trying to absorb me into a petty corruption racket, maybe some kind of bogus tax on giant-fern peepers.

At last the large man comes back, excusing himself and settling in behind his desk. "What I want to ask is your opinion on something very important." He uses one hand to flatten out his hair. "Can you give me your candid advice, as an American?"

"I'll try," I offer. I stare out into the plaza, wishing I were somewhere else.

"Good," he says. "I wish to know how I can be more like Bill Clinton."

The calendar behind his desk is a faded artifact from 1999. Maybe he doesn't know Clinton has been out of office for several years. "You wish to be more like Bill Clinton," I repeat.

"Exactly. He's macho. A *toro*!" The councilman gets a dreamy look in his eyes. "He rules the world, and he has beautiful young women. Like Monica Lewinsky."

"You wish to know how to be more like Bill Clinton."

"Monica." He repeats tenderly, adding, "Isn't she *una belleza*?"

He calls for some chicha, and we drink and get down to the serious business of "being more like Bill Clinton." I seize the chance to point out some of Clinton's environmental achievements: the roadless initiative in national forests, protecting the Arctic National Wildlife Refuge, expanding national monuments, and signing the Kyoto climate treaty. We talk about how he's so lucky to live right next to Amboró, a globally important eco-corridor stretching to Peru. After several cups of chicha, he's pondering what Bill Clinton would do about the folks illegally entering Amboró Park.

A month later Fidel tells me that the councilman—mini-Clinton—has started confiscating produce from trucks coming out of illegally colonized Amboró lands. And he's overheard pompously insisting at a meeting that these measures are harsh but "of global ecological importance."

But this kind of environmental diplomacy can only do so much. Up the road from La Yunga in FAN's cloud forest things worsen. "They've invaded," Jesús is telling me through a statickey phone connection to my office in Santa Cruz. After our showdown a few weeks back, the Quechua *campesinos* who'd held us decided to machete trails through our property. Every hundred meters they've sunk tagged stakes, each labeled with a family's name. I recognize this practice as the age-old precursor to slash and burn. Each *colono* family receives one hundred meters of width and can clear a length as far as they are able.

Since FAN's private land doesn't fall directly under my authority, I visit my Bolivian colleague Rodrigo, who is responsible for it. Yes, he's heard about the invasion and plans to visit—next week.

"Next week! But they've marked off their plots."

Rodrigo, leaning back in his chair: *"Tranquilo."* I go above Rodrigo's head to Gisela. As alarmed as I, she calls a quick meeting, which leads to another with the Amboró Park director. We ask him if he'll put two full-time guards in the cloud forest.

"It's just too dangerous there now," the director says, shaking his head. He adds that he has only two dozen rangers for the 630,000-hectare park, and ours is just one of many flash points. Compared to the mere two thousand people living in villages around Kempff, twenty thousand people live in one hundred communities *inside* the Amboró buffer zone. And every day more settlers arrive and push more forcefully against the park's fragile defenses, a next-to-impossible challenge for a handful of unarmed rangers.

The next day, Gisela and I rise at six A.M. and make the three-hour drive to the cloud forest. There, several dozen farmers have gathered in the community schoolhouse, their faces solemn. I exchange handshakes with Placido and the others I know, as well as with municipal and syndicate leaders I do not recognize.

The community leaders launch their assault: FAN is an imperialist organization, funded by *los yanquis,* with a mandate to tie up productive land so that poor farmers can't work it. Moreover, FAN promised a honey production center and other goodies that were not delivered. The farmers we've been working with for a decade know this is false but say nothing.

The ride back to Santa Cruz is muted. The sharp ridges of the Amboró buffer zone rise to our left and the deforested hillsides to our right. Dusk is deepening as Gisela says, "We'll have to pull back from the cloud forest." I remain silent. Even the optimistic Gisela is basically writing off this key buffer protecting Amboró. *The people have come.* The discourse in Bolivia is radicalizing, and she fears risking FAN's national reputation over this particular spot. It's triage. We've been outflanked and will concede the territory.

CHAPTER 24

ONSIDERING HOW ADVANCED we are in the early
twenty-first century, it's remarkable how little we know
about conserving rainforests. So all of FAN's projects double as
laboratories. Cap-and-trade for rainforest oxygen; national eco-
ethno-tourism; a model third-world national park system—we
share these experiences in journals and at conferences around
the world.

One day Salvador surprises me when he says, "In Senegal
the tribes won their traditional lands, their *casa*, by focusing
on . . ." I have to do a double take; Salvador is throwing
around cross-continental references? Sure. After traveling to
Europe as an Indian expert on climate, he received a delegation of African community leaders in Santa Cruz to compare
notes. Meanwhile, as excitement builds around the Amazon
Project, I too am asked to present papers, including two in the
same week. Unable to do both, I ask Smithers if he would go
to Argentina's Patagonia to present one of them there.

He stalls, hems, haws; I finally figure out that he's afraid.
He's never been on a plane, nor does he possess a passport. I try
to reassure him, but his face tells me he's not convinced, and I
eventually pry out the real reason for his hesitance.

"They'll think I'm stupid," he admits. "Just a dumb *indio*."

No words of mine can erase this feeling, so we finally arrive
at a truce. Old-timer Len will go with him to hold his hand.
The trip goes beautifully. Smithers returns networked into the
Mapuche Indian movement in Chile, and he's sending e-mails
around to friends from other South American tribes.

While Smithers is in Patagonia, I give a talk on Amboró at a trinational desertification powwow in Santa Cruz that compares the success of a fern forest with the failure of a cloud forest. Why did La Yunga ecotourism flourish while FAN's private reserve, just miles away, floundered? In the former we used indigenous thinking; the latter, industrial thinking. Ecotourism in the ferns employed natural capitalism, while agriculture in the clouds used traditional capitalism. The results could hardly be more polar: in one, the community defends nature while in the other they destroy it.

Then I pause, cringing before delivering a controversial, politically incorrect idea: "Reducing poverty will not save the rainforest."

There's a bit of background here. For nearly two decades the world community has channeled billions of dollars through ICDPs, or *integrated conservation and development projects.* It's neither fair nor feasible to protect rainforests in the face of human misery in the tropics, so let's do both at once! Well-meaning Americans and Europeans grab their checkbooks and donate to the World Wide Fund for Nature (WWF) or CARE. And we pay our taxes, which also go into ICDPs by the millions. We feel warm and fuzzy over the results: fabulous photos of (choose your own combination) Africans or Asians or Latin Americans; harvesting papaya or palm hearts or assai; in harmony with a rainforest or dry forest or wild savanna. With so much colorful clothing, sparkling eyes, and earth-toned wilderness, you're bound to reach once again for pen and checkbook. But your money could be better spent.

Mountains of evaluations detail the abysmal failure of ICDPs to sustainably protect the environment. Like FAN's work in the cloud forest, thousands of ICDPs around the world fail to enter the dark, scary, and completely necessary caves of economics. Don't be shy; it's really not as bad as it seems. We just need to get the incentives right.

The fern forest changed incentives; the cloud forest did not.

ICDPs must raise the existence value of the forest above its destruction value. Let's say rows of corn or board feet of timber in a given acre add up to $500 a year for a family. The destruction value is $500. A project must raise the existence value above the destruction value—that is to at least $501—if that rainforest is to stay. This means hard work for conservationists, who need to make the rainforest work in economic terms through "ecosystem services" such as stabilizing climate, providing watershed for towns and families, harboring genetic material for medicines, producing nontimber products such as fruits, nuts, meats, and fish, and yielding aesthetic value for tourism. Unless some combination of those existence values add up to $501, all the cute pictures of organic-honey production won't help.

After the Santa Cruz meeting, the World Bank invites a biochemist colleague and me to Paraguay, where tropical conservationists and eco-businesspeople from around the hemisphere discuss blending economics with ecology. A Brazilian talks about how entrepreneurs made millions from the asai fruit, its exotic and healthy juice sought-after from New York to Tokyo. The fruit grows in healthy forests; its value is higher than slash-and-burn. Green venture capitalists show how they channel socially conscious investor funds into earth-friendly projects like asai.

My colleague and I leave Paraguay enthusiastic about a new idea: communities can be taught to extract a valuable endemic moss from the Amboró cloud forests. The extract from that moss is needed for medicines in Germany—and they're paying $50 an ounce. The moss depends upon intact forests, and the communities will depend upon the moss. A proposal is put together, and the moss project is quickly under way.

But as these new ideas begin to take root, Bolivia is sinking deeper into the morass. Racism and inequality are still the order of the day. President Goni huddles in the Burnt Palace brainstorming strategies for salvaging his presidency. Meanwhile Evo Morales plans new roadblocks to thwart Goni's plan to ship Bolivian natural gas to California through archrival Chile. Salvador finds himself pondering whether to block the eastern highway toward Brazil as part of the national protests. Annual foreign investment in Bolivia has crashed from $1 billion to $134 million over the past four years, corresponding to the period of protests, which have made skittish investors leave and deepened the economic crisis. Unemployment is up; education and health care down.

So yet another cleavage develops in Bolivia: those who get on planes and those who do not. We in FAN and AMAZONA, linked with wealthy organizations of global solidarity, board pressure-controlled cabins and float in and out of the turmoil.

Salvador and I find ourselves on the same flight. We're seated side by side, and I'm looking down into the virgin valleys inside Amboró Park, before we cross over a Cochabamba clogged with protests. We're both heading to La Paz. I'm en route to a conference in California, and Salvador, well, he's been a bit vague about his trip. I know two things: one, that he's accompanied by several other eastern Indian leaders; and two, that I'm paying for his trip out of FAN's budget. The form he handed me to sign listed under *purpose of trip* "legally securing traditional lands," but I know that he knows that I know (wink, wink) that he's involved in the revolution abrewing. I sighed—and signed—figuring that bringing the Indian majority to power is at least remotely connected to securing their ITs.

Good-natured teasing is traded among the Indian leaders on the plane and continues in our taxi. We've all got cheekfuls of coca leaves to adjust to the altitude, and one tribal leader boasts with macho bravado that he's got an enormous wad of coca in his mouth, so big that it's "blocking the sun and casting a shadow across La Paz." As the others snicker, Salvador takes things in a serious direction, passing me a photo of a man, dark of skin and hair, a sturdy-looking Quechua—whose leg has been severed at the thigh.

"This is Frutoso," Salvador says, explaining that Mr. Frutoso is a poor coca-leaf farmer from the Chaparé region near Cochabamba. I pass the picture to another of the Indians in the taxi, who asks Salvador, "How'd he lose the leg?"

As we thread our way into the center of La Paz, Salvador tells us Frutoso's story. U.S.-funded and -trained Bolivian soldiers eradicated the man's coca-leaf crop as part of the War on Drugs, driving him from poverty to the brink of starvation. Like tens of thousands of other Quechuas in the tropical Chaparé region, he lives in a mud hut full of children, surviving off his few acres of coca leaves, the only crop with a strong enough external market to maintain his family.

The United States and Europe offer Frutoso and other Bolivian coca farmers "alternative development" to help them switch to crops like papaya or heart of palm. But such trades are often disingenuous. There is often no market for these crops; this was the case for Frutoso. He planted "alternative development" bananas, tended and harvested them—but there was no one to buy them. He and other frustrated Indian peasants blocked a highway with rotting fruit. U.S.-paid Bolivian soldiers gave the Quechuas two minutes to clear the road before spraying the group with bullets. The protest leader was killed, and Frutoso's leg was filled with shrapnel and had to be amputated.

As Salvador finishes the story, we're coming to the Plaza Murillo. Salvador and the Indians will get out in front of the Burnt Palace, and I'll continue on to the U.S. embassy to pick up a replacement passport, my current one waterlogged beyond recognition during my adventures in the Uyuni salt flats.

"What happened to Frutoso?" I ask, before the bunch gets out.

"It's hard to keep up a farm with one leg, but he does," Salvador says, adding that Frutoso is not bitter, but there is one small thing he asks of President Bush: "He'd like a good orthopedic leg."

Frutoso is one actor in an intricate drama being played out in the War on Drugs in Bolivia. For a moment, forget about blue-eyed action heroes battling wealthy Cali and Medellín drug barons. In Bolivia it's a war on the poor.

I am by no means defending cocaine, a drug that has ruined countless lives through addiction and crime. Among thousands of others, one of my own second cousins, of whom I have fond childhood memories, was a cocaine user and tragically shot to death by drug dealers in Washington, D.C., in 1999.

Like me, the U.S. DEA thinks it would be great to reduce cocaine use. To that end they have poured $1.3 billion U.S. taxpayer dollars into Bolivia over the past decade for counternarcotics and development assistance, the lion's share for helicopters, weaponry, and other military assistance to the Bolivian army to eradicate the coca plant, the base ingredient for cocaine, in fields. This investment led to what the U.S. State Department boasts as its "Andean success story": from 1995 to 2001, a whopping seventy percent of the country's coca fields were eliminated.

But the policy did nothing to reduce U.S. drug use, nor its attendant social problems. Six million Americans continued to use the drug regularly (34 million have tried it at least once) because cocaine use is demand-driven. Think of it as a balloon. If you squeeze the balloon in one place—say Bolivia—you always end up transferring the coca fields someplace else as long as the same six million people want it. The Andean success story was successful only in transferring coca-leaf production to Peru and Colombia.

If the policy had scant impact in the United States, it was a disaster for Bolivia. Tens of thousands of poor Quechua farmers went from a subsistence existence growing the leaf to severe food insecurity and even starvation. Studies have shown that "alternative development" assistance was far insufficient. Frutoso lost his leg trying to demonstrate that no one was willing to buy his bananas; dozens of other farmers have died in similar protests against the policy.

Moreover, the coca leaf is sacred to Andean Indians and predates cocaine by centuries. It is used in spiritual and social rituals, and as a mild stimulant to reduce hunger and altitude sickness. Anyone who has been to the Andes knows that it is sold everywhere and chewed by the majority of the country's campesinos. Coca is as dear to the Bolivian heart as tea is to the British. Hence, even those in favor of the policy acknowledge that the image of Uncle Sam going after Quechuas and Aymaras who have been growing the plant since Inca times rankles deeply with many Bolivians.

Evo Morales: "I don't admire the U.S. president. Bush represents the culture of death and intervention, of massacre." Evo vocalizes something that resounds with millions of other Bolivians. The more sober voices, such as middle-of-the-road political scientist and former Mexican foreign minister Jorge Castaneda, talking about the impact of the drug war and other U.S. policies, puts it like this: "Very clearly electorates across Latin America have moved . . . toward a more strident anti-American stance."

The failure of supply-side measures to reduce cocaine use should cause us to rethink the policy and explore demand-side efforts. For starters, why is use so widespread in U.S. culture? What is lacking in our lives that we try to fill with a coke high? (In Bolivia, interestingly, the street price of the powder is one hundred times less than in the United States, but use is virtually nonexistent.) We might redirect some of the $1.3 billion squandered on eradication in Bolivia to increase "healthy lifestyles" education for teens to prevent future use. And to the extent that we do continue to attack coca-leaf supply in Bolivia, we must provide true alternatives to coca farmers to avoid the hunger and disease resulting from deepening poverty caused by the current approach.

Sadly, instead of revamping the policy, Bush's head of Latin America in the State Department, Otto Reich (yes, Otto Reich of contra-scandal renown), pushes on with more of the same. In the end, these policies are carried out with tax money, and most Americans are completely unaware of it. I had to search hard to find a single newspaper, the *Baltimore Sun,* that recently covered the story of the War on Drugs in Bolivia. The *Sun* piece profiled Victor and Gomercinda and their eight children, reporting that Bolivian soldiers, all of whose salaries are paid by the United States, cut down the family's small coca crop for the fourth time. Each time the couple would doggedly replant—underscoring the futility of such efforts—but were left with several months without money or food.

"How can they cut down all our plants?" cried Gomercinda. "I have eight children. What are we going to live on? Our coca is gone."

I've got a new passport in hand, and my California-bound flight departs tonight. I'm sitting across a glass coffee table from a U.S. embassy acquaintance, Dwayne, whom I knew during my La Paz days. His office is spacious and silent.

"The drug war here creates anti-Americanism," I say, "and does nothing to stop supply to the U.S."

"Hmm," Dwayne says. He's in his midforties and wears a white shirt and dress slacks. Dwayne's got a bad knee—a jogging injury, he told me. He's been taking it easy since the operation.

I talk about the missed opportunity. The $1.3 billion spent represents something significant that will *not* happen. We could use that same money to revitalize women's groups recuperating traditional Andean weavings or to replicate the Amazon Project in the Andean valleys to further help control global warming.

"I know, and I agree," he says, "in my more utopian of moments."

"The European Union is utopian?"

He shrugs and gets up, limping over to his window, which looks out over manicured lawns and bushes—and a thick, white wall blocking the city from view. He knows that Holland, Belgium, and others from across the pond are supporting Bolivian Indians' fight to organize themselves and gain land rights, thereby winning goodwill. It's part of a larger picture: Northern European nations give more that .7 percent of GDP to poor countries; the United States gives only .1 percent, beat out in generosity by twenty-three countries including Turkey.

I touch my new passport—not a single stamp yet. I feel a stab of homesickness and can't wait to get back. I'll see my family, my old friends. Yet that emotion is twisted up with that familiar sensation that many of us feel abroad: there's a growing disconnect between my love for Bolivians and care for their future, and the direction my government is pursuing here.

Dwayne doesn't say anything for a while. It's so quiet. Hard to believe that several hundred people work here in this embassy, designed for maximum security in bunker-style architecture. I look at Dwayne's wall clock; my plane leaves in three hours.

"What are we so afraid of?" I say.

"Why do they hate us?" he replies.

"Why is this embassy stuffed with DEA agents and starved of nutritionists?"

"Oh, I see . . . a round of questions." Dwayne limps to the other side of his window, reminding me of Frutoso's request for a new leg. He turns and says, "Wouldn't it be pretty to think so?"

Out Dwayne's window, beyond the bunker walls, the nightly protests would later begin—bitter slogans chanted against Bush, Goni, and globalization—that would lead to the terrible Indian massacre that would come to be remembered as Black October.

CHAPTER 25

J OHN REID MEETS me at the San Francisco airport. He's a Harvard-trained environmental economist and noted director of the Conservation Strategy Fund (CSF), but from the very start he surprises me. With his tussled dirty-blond hair, faded jeans, and wrinkled T-shirt, he seems far humbler than I'd imagined. Straightening to his full five feet eleven inches he gives me a strong handshake and grabs the larger of my bags.

Walking with him to the car, the culture shock hits. Advertisements wallpaper the terminal, one for a combined mouthwash and toothpaste ("2in1") from Colgate, presumably intended for those too busy to do both. Other ads display the Cheerio-coated cereal bar with a real milk filling—eliminating the need for bowl and spoon—and Pasta Anytime, a packaged product that includes already-cooked pasta. Just pour the sauce on top and microwave for two minutes. I'm definitely no longer in Bolivia.

John drives us the one and a half hours to the redwood-forest retreat center along the coast where our environmental-economics conference is to take place. The next morning, again in a casual T-shirt and sandals, he kicks off the event he's put together, his speech unadorned. Gathered around John are twenty-five conservation professionals from a dozen "highly biodiverse" countries from Peru to Nepal, Congo to Canada. We're here to figure out how to better hardwire economics into our projects. The debates are lively and we all leave twelve days later with a wider network. But most fascinating of all is John himself, precisely because, on the surface, he is so thoroughly unexceptional.

The man is quintessentially American, in the most sublime sense: an unpretentious, pragmatic idealist. Though a tad dry—when not out surfing, that is—he lives the principle that we should treat each other and nature with deep respect. John took a risk and quit an excellent job in Washington, D.C., to start up the nonprofit CSF; he's since gathered millions of dollars from other American visionaries, mostly in private foundations, wanting to do better human development and conservation through applying economics.

The conference farewell ceremony doubles as the five-year anniversary of CSF. We toast to the organization's success. Even in this moment of glory, there's no alpha-male posturing from John; does he have an ego? He's embodied the mission and lives for it, and for his family, who've come along for the celebration: his artist wife and two kids. They live in the country in a modest book-filled, TV-free home.

The contrast between my days with John, and the next few with Taylor, couldn't be starker, as I move from a sheltered subculture in the redwoods to a very different America.

Taylor and I were inseparable windsurfing buddies in high school on Long Island, and he invites me to stay with him in San Francisco, where he now lives. I've got two free days before heading back to Bolivia, so I accept. He pulls up to our agreed meeting place downtown in a brand-new Forester. I get in and he drives me to his other car: a kelly green Bronco. He left it there after a drunken party the night before: Could I help him out and follow him back to his place?

It isn't easy, manipulating the stick shift of the monstrous SUV in San Francisco's traffic and hills, but we eventually make it to Taylor's pad. His garage is his gear closet, stuffed with rock-climbing ropes, mountain bikes, Rollerblades, and a vintage Harley. I touch the smooth curve of a windsurfing boom, the mast, several jibs, and we talk boards and breezes.

Then I ask Taylor, a philosophy major who managed to hit the jackpot in the Internet boom, how he justifies his gas-guzzling Bronco.

"I bought it to keep it *off* the road. If someone else owned it, they'd be driving it all the time," he explains. "I usually drive the Forester and my gas-sipping Harley, so I'm saving the world in my own small way."

We take the Forester to the Haight, and I begin to enjoy Taylor's world. We drink Bloody Marys blooming with a salad of veggies while walking through an art festival. Among the funky masses, Taylor points out one hippie hoisting a sign with a single word: DEMOCRACY. Each of the letters in the word has been extracted from a corporate logo: Disney's *D,* Enron's *E,* the yellow *M* from McDonald's, and so forth. With a smirk Taylor says, "The *Y* is from Yahoo!" His company.

"Seen the pimp movie?" Taylor asks at one point.

I haven't, so we rent it, returning to his three-thousand-dollar-a-month loft. The pimp documentary rolling, he passes me some Ben & Jerry's Phish Food. The movie is hip. Real pimps talking with pride about their work; real hos talking about their pimps. The ice cream is good. Taylor's an interesting guy: makes Plyboo (bamboo plywood) tables, cooks Laotian food, and attends Burning Man each year. I savor a spoonful of Phish Food. A pimp is saying something funny. I'm just now comfortably settling in when Taylor retires to his home office for a previously announced stint of work before that night's "trash party." I take off into San Francisco.

Union Square. I feel claustrophobic. Unlike a lazy Latin America plaza, this one is wall-to-wall marketing, storefronts and billboards cajoling me to invent a shtick, carve out a distinctive "me." I wander into a six-story Gap store, a solid piece of glass dotted with ultramarine and mauve clothing on mannequins. I'm up to the fourth floor on the fast-moving escalators, passing people all dressed slightly differently, yet wearing more or less the same clothes as the mannequins. I begin to feel self-conscious. When was the last time I thought of clothing? We adapt to the environment we're in, and my world has taken on a totally other focus; I think of Salvador's generic jeans and button-up shirts.

"Where's the men's department?" I ask a clerk.

She points through the glass front to another temple of clothing across the street: "This is the women's Gap."

Outside again, in the press of fog, there's a homeless man on every corner, each with a different spiel, including one who's mastered understatement: "Could you give me a penny?" I've got my radar set on the men's Gap, feeling a new desire to update myself in some way.

My parents' asceticism, including a strict TV protocol, inoculated me from consumerism more than many of my peers, but I am far from immune. There's the Gap, its doors revolving, consumer in, consumer out, and I hesitate. Harvard sociologist Daniel Bell warned us in 1976, our bicentennial year, about "the cultural contradictions of capitalism," arguing that while capitalism hinges on such virtues as asceticism, thrift, and self-denial, it produces social surpluses that lead to luxury, deepen materialism, nurture acquisitiveness, and turn self-indulgence into a birthright. Tocqueville too predicted that self-centeredness and egotism would be "democracy's temptation."

Have we succumbed? George Bush just dropped a bomb: he's pulling America out of the Kyoto Protocol on Climate Change. He states on television that he will not do anything that could affect our economy, as European and other world leaders look on in horror. The Gap doors before me, spinning faster. This is how an economy grows. I am not surprised Bush has snubbed Kyoto; his environmental philosophy has evolved little beyond Reagan's famous claim that "trees cause pollution," or that of James Watt, who told Congress, "After

the last tree is felled, Christ will come back." But I am saddened because Bush's move puts the Amazon Project in jeop-
ardy. The carbon credits lose their value; the corporate
investors throw up their hands; and Salvador and the Chiquitanos, their green economy spoiled, have no choice but to let
in the loggers. Are the doors spinning off their hinges?

Taylor hands me the invitation to the evening's "trash party."
We're to dress as either white trash, Eurotrash, or plain old re-
fuse. Taylor goes as the first, wearing a T-shirt that reads I
FORGET . . . WHICH ONE OF US WAS ON TOP LAST NIGHT? I
pull on one of Taylor's black turtlenecks.

"*Very* Euro," an obviously gay man says to me at the party,
extending his hand. "I'm Divan. *Encantada!*"

We chat. Though he's now draped in Hefty bags, it turns
out that the thirtysomething Divan owns an exclusive clothing
store downtown and studied political science at UC Berkeley.
We talk about the Iraq war, Divan saying, "I didn't want us
going into Iraq, but now that we're there . . ." He goes on to
say that his best clients support the war. " 'The hidden hand
of the market will never work without a hidden fist. McDonald's can't flourish without McDonnell Douglas.' "

I excuse myself from Divan and Thomas Friedman and start
looking for Taylor. House and techno blast from eight-foot
speakers in the living room; the DJ wears dark glasses and a
hooded sweatshirt. I track down Taylor in the kitchen with the
party's host. Not surprisingly, knowing Taylor, he's telling the
same goofy camel joke he loved in high school fifteen years ago.
It cheers me up immensely, especially watching the long-faced
Taylor pucker his lips like a camel wanting a good smoke. He's
hamming it up, and the circle around Taylor tightens to catch
every word. But my eyes are drawn above the group to Divan. I
spot him on the porch now—snorting a line of coke.

I lose the thead of Taylor's camel joke and find myself back in Bolivia, just a few weeks back, in Santa Cruz's dreaded Sunny Palms Prison.

NORTH AMERICANS—ERADICATE YOUR NOSES read some graffiti scrawled on a wall outside the prison. I'd come along to Sunny Palms with a lawyer friend who works with inmates. On the local TV news, disparate prisoners had temporarily taken over the prison and begun crucifying themselves on wooden crosses. As I entered with my friend, an obese guard asked me if I had any concealed weapons and, before I could answer, began laughing hysterically as he waved me through.

Inside, Sunny Palms is a Darwinistic world of corruption, poverty, and vicious inequality. With a budget of just pennies per prisoner, the facility is kept afloat only through an inflow of criminal money. In this open-air village-prison, the richest of the three thousand inmates build themselves two-story mini-mansions, while the poorest, mostly Indians, clean those homes to earn scraps of bread.

Ninety percent of the prisoners are held for cocaine-related charges under U.S. DEA–imposed Law 1008, many without trial. While Palmasola's narco heavy-hitters purchase weekend furloughs and reduced sentences, Bolivia's poorest are trapped inside by the draconian law. I talk to a woman, Eliana, who couldn't yet be thirty, but has three children under seven. They've grown up in the prison. She admits to having transported a small amount of cocaine—as a mule within Bolivia, à la *Maria Full of Grace*—"but do I deserve to be in here for so many years?" She can't afford the harsh "liberation fee" of one dollar a day for time served, and each day beyond her sentence the fee increases. In her tiny, plywood cell she strokes her youngest daughter's hair. The place stinks of urine. "Because of your drug habit," Eliana says to me, "we're stuck here in jail."

* * *

"Divan can snort coke if he wants," Taylor says when I bring it up the next afternoon. "He's only hurting himself." We're back in his loft on a Sunday with the shades shut against the gray, foggy day.

I tell him about Eliana in Sunny Palms, and the connection with U.S. policy. "Why do users like Divan only get slaps on the wrist for possession, when Bolivian women and children spend their lives in prison? If coke is to be illegal, the rules should apply equally to everyone."

Taylor says he "didn't vote the radical nationalists into the Oval Office" as he puts in the next DVD. We've been watching episodes of 24 on his wide-screen TV. There's a terrorist plot and I feel I'm at the very center of all that gripping violence and sexual tension. When we're numb from the special effects two episodes later, I ask Taylor if he's happy, and he says that he's in a rut at work and he's been better, but he'll soon be wrapping cars. "You know how they wrap buses with ads? The sides of people's cars are the next frontier. Imagine, all that open space just waiting to be personalized." As he talks about the idea, he seems increasingly unconvinced about it. When he calls wrapping cars "a revolution," he becomes slightly choked up, as if suddenly feeling the hollowness of the scheme, and looks away toward the shaded window, his eye glowing electric blue-green from the television.

Looking at Taylor's profile, I remember a moment from when we were seventeen and in love with no other thing more than wind. We took a much awaited windsurfing trip to Cape Cod's Wellfleet Bay and never left the water. When the breeze went flat, we'd stand on our boards and make up prayers and songs to the wind gods. One time it worked; the winds rose to a howling thirty knots and blew our sails straight across the bay. It was impossible to tack back, so I hitched a ride to our vehicle while Taylor watched the boards. I returned with the car to see that same profile, the one now framed by TV haze, snoring away in the whipping grasses.

CHAPTER 26

W HEN I GET back, Santa Cruz is hotter, drier, dustier, and smokier than anyone can remember. A record number of forest fires blaze, and that smoke combines with the dust from eroded Mennonite and World Bank–sponsored soy farms to blanket the city in a haze.

"Seen Salvador?" I say to Lila, sticking my head into the AMAZONA office on the far side of the FAN compound. She shakes her head to save the energy required to speak. Half our air conditioners are on the fritz, and those that do work are on full blast, sending our computer screens into headache-producing pulsations.

I locate Len in the HF radio room. He's perspiring as he listens to incoming traffic. I ask him if he's seen Salvador, but he shushes me. "Welcome back, but give me a sec. I'm talking with Gaspar!"

I smile, picturing the tiny Chiquitano chief yelling into the radio. Len and I strain to hear the communication. "Forty head! Forty head!" Gaspar is saying.

"You want forty head shipped to Piso Firme. Copy," Len replies.

"Yes, forty head!"

Len pauses and considers this. "Of cattle?"

"No! Chicken."

"Forty head . . . of *chicken*?"

"*De pollo, de pollo!* Forty head of chicken!"

Len stops chuckling and presses the transmitter. "Copy that, Gaspar."

FAN biologist Rene Frank walks by the radio room and sees

me. "Hats off to your president on Kyoto. And by the way, *this*"—he lifts his arms to show the wet patches—"is climate change. Ten of the twelve hottest years in a century in this past decade, and we need more studies?"

FAN's senior staff meets on the Amazon Project in the afternoon. If the United States doesn't participate, it could have grave consequences, causing BP and AEP to pull back. After all, the United States contributes thirty percent of the world's greenhouse gases (though it makes up just four percent of the world's population), so its nonparticipation could mortally wound the treaty.

The meeting ends early. It's just too hot and humid to think. I check messages on my cell. One from Daniel: "Why don't you talk to your blokes about whether they've got information about medicinal things from their particular part of the forest. It's interesting. And come by for seafood."

Daniel's Santa Cruz home is trying to be a jungle.

Not only are his patios covered with clay pots containing an immense diversity of Amazon plants, but his gardens burst with colorful flowers, and his living room and dining room are filled with the aroma of dozens of vases of cut flowers.

"I love flowers," he's telling me over the empty shells of crabs and lobster. Just back from another round-the-worlder, he swings his arm in a wide arc over his garden. "I buy them not for wives, not for mothers, not for grandmothers . . . I buy them for myself."

He pauses for a moment, then says, "Highgate Hill Cemetery, in London, where Karl Marx is buried. We used to live right near it, and there'd be conferences about Marx, people leaving hundreds of red flowers around his grave. I'd nick the fucking flowers, steal from Marx's grave. You should have seen those roses and carnations all over my house."

Daniel's appearance has changed over the past several

months. He's gotten even thinner than his usual wiry self; his beard is a bit longer and much more disheveled; his skin, paler. Our relationship has taken several turns—from pure business, to drinking buddies, to a period when I felt deep suspicions about him. Now I feel a genuine affection for Daniel, a real friendship. His innate goodness rises around me, like the scent of so many flowers: his profligate generosity, his insistence that domestic staff eat at his table even when important guests have come to dinner, and his often comical, but ultimately genuine, attempt to help indigenous people. I think of a saying I once heard in Africa: "To look at a king you'd never think he sucked his mother's breast." But standing here before me, this potentate of the global economy is a child.

"Let me show you something," he says, jumping up and leading me into his gardens.

Back in the jungle sometimes, I think of Daniel.

We're stuck behind yet another fallen tree on the road out of the Indian Territory. I'm a sweaty, tired mess, having just handed off the ax to Smithers. A ranger is on machete duty. Every twenty minutes or so there's another tree blocking us. This particular one is so enormous that we've been at its hardwood trunk and branches for nearly an hour. A few miles back, we were stuck in a deep pit; I wrapped the hauling chain around a tree and we pulled our way out, flailing left and right. But the trees are worse. They crisscross the road, hunched like monsters in the headlights. With each one we stop. Cut the engine. Get out with the now familiar disheartening prospect of facing another little battle with ax and machete.

On this trip back to the communities, the roads have worsened. Perhaps the far-off municipality has completely run out of money to keep trees at bay. Or had the logging companies who had been clearing some of these roads now stopped, retaliating against the communities fighting to reclaim their lands? Whatever the reason, it has become almost impossible to get to the communities we serve, at least by road. Next time I'll have to take one of FAN's Cessnas, which I try to avoid since it creates yet another gap between us and them—*licenciado* environmentalists who swoop from the sky and local Indians who fight back trees.

The inconvenience I feel (three A.M., hurling an ax into another fallen tree) may be a kind of resistance. The trees block the road, as if to tell us we do not belong here. "This," say the trees, "this last corner of the Amazon is *ours*." The blocked roads are blood clots, a healing of wounds as nature reclaims its wholeness, sealing two thousand Chiquitano people back into their Indian Territory. As the forest reverts to its natural state, so too, I imagine, might the Chiquitanos—into their traditional world of myth and survival, a world where seven skies rise over the Amazon; where all of the animals used to be people; where a tree holds up the world.

Sometimes in this lost world, at moments like this, my mind wanders to the globalizing ninety percent. Its flow, ease, swiftness, and power become personified: a pair of clear blue eyes, a concealing beard, limber movements. Movement, constant movement. *Daniel.* I picture him swooping into Hong Kong, Singapore, London, Nairobi, Buenos Aires. Chilled take-off chardonnays and hot showers in red-carpet lounges.

My shirt is torn in several places; blood beads on scrapes on my forearms and neck; salty sweat burns my eyes—we've cleared another tree. Smithers drives the truck past and we get in. We can move another few kilometers, maybe. Stuffing coca leaves into my cheek as we move forward in silence, the vocabulary I was using for Daniel (flow, ease, swiftness, power) changes quite subconsciously to something else: erratic, individualistic, greedy, unhappy, isolated.

Expelled.

* * *

"You touch these plants and they go to sleep," Daniel says. He's led me into his lush gardens, where we are standing in front of a raised flower bed. It's a leafy plant with small thorns, a variety of which I've seen many times in Central and South American jungles. He touches one, and its hundreds of fernlike leaflets fold in against its woody stem.

"The thing is that they sleep for different amounts of time. I've watched them. It's like they have individual personalities, different levels of fear. Some wake up in a few minutes, others take hours. This one," he says, pointing out a shriveled plant toward the back, "never woke up after I touched it."

The philosopher Hölderlin wrote about the anguish of the first man who realized the following paradox: we are part of nature, born of her, and yet are distinctly separate from her. Freud too spoke of our subconscious fear of two opposite, equally terrifying realities: being captured and being expelled. Captured, in the sense of reconsumed in nature, once again a part of her; and expelled, cast forever out of her, rejected, banished.

Daniel fears the latter. He has dedicated a good part of his life to the global capitalist endeavor, thriving off the mining and export of natural resources, existing in airtight airplane bubbles. As with our race to destroy the world's last rainforests at an acre a minute and our simultaneous creation of rainforest theme parks, so too does Daniel make of his home a mini-jungle. It's a kind of atonement.

Putting a few more plants to sleep with his hand, Daniel muses, "I always buy my flowers from the indigenous women in the market. Yesterday, one of them chased me down, laughing and bonking me on the head with a bundle of flowers because I didn't buy from her.

"I love indigenous people, and they like me." He gets this sad look in his eyes. I wonder if it's the stress of separation from his wife, or something else. Then, almost imperceptibly, a fragile smile spreads over his face as he puts a few more plants to sleep with his fingers.

CHAPTER 27

T HE INDIANS BLOCK Santa Cruz off from the rest of the country.

It happens suddenly, and the change on the streets is palpable. I am familiar with the feeling—what I call *the buzz*. It's as if everyone's had four cups of espresso. There's an edge to each conversation. I had a similar feeling in Croatia during the Balkan wars and in post-Wall Berlin. I sensed it too while working both in Chiapas during the Zapatista uprising and in West African conflict zones.

Expatriate friends murmur about evacuation. The protests are building in numbers in front of the U.S. embassy in La Paz. The first few Indian bodies have fallen in pools of blood in El Alto. Shop owners close without notice at the slightest hint of mobilizations. At one point I'm in the Shopping Norte center on the Santa Cruz Plaza when a student protest goes by. The shopping center is sealed shut with iron bars, locking me in for an hour. Meanwhile, President Goni switches to offense. He is the steward of law and order, the constitution, and democracy itself against a growing anarchy instigated by uneducated Indians. For the first time I see Goni sweat.

I switch off the TV and head up to my balcony. The moon is nearly full and casts two shadows from my mismatched palm trees onto the saltillo tiles. I switch on some *zampoña* music; the Andean flutes get me thinking of the tens of thousands of mostly Quechuas and Aymaras now shutting down the nation with roadblocks. I try to recall an example of my countrymen blocking our interstates for a cause, but can think of none. Yet these, some of the poorest folks in the hemisphere, have the whole country hostage. The *zampoña* pipes crescendo with the high winds, and I remember a moment at a roadblock two years back while still working out of La Paz.

"Look, I don't care about myself. But there are *wawas* here," my Bolivian colleague said to the obstinate Tarabuco. He used the Aymara word *wawas* instead of the Spanish *bebé,* a lovely onomatopoeia that mimics the *waa-waa* cry of an infant.

The Indian man just stared at us, expressionless, sucking a tremendous wad of coca leaves.

"Look, the *wawas* are going to cry!" My colleague's attempt at sympathy was not working. Neither this Indian, nor his several dozen companions, were going to move a single of the boulders blocking our way. In fact my colleague's minor tantrum was having the opposite effect, as two or three other Tarabuco men gathered in front of us, arms folded across their chests beneath brilliantly colored ponchos. None of the Tarabucos topped five feet six inches, but there were a whole lot of them.

My colleague opened his mouth to argue some more about the poor little tiny babies but then thought the better of it. It was the solemn way the Indian men were starring him down. The silence stretched on, and, indeed, a *wawa* did start to cry from inside one of the cars and micros stacking up behind us.

National roadblocks were scheduled for midnight. Fine. We had plenty of time to do our work on a project back in Yotala and still make it back to our hotel in Sucre. But at eight o'clock, navigating the mountain passes, we were shocked to see the protesters gathered on the road—a full four hours early. It was already midnight, give or take a few hours, Indian time.

More vehicles piled up in the queue behind us; more restlessness, tension. Everyone wanted to get out of here before dark, before things could get nasty. In previous *bloqueos* dozens of people had been killed in bloody triangles of pro-testers, military police, and blocked civilians. The first fire was lit, and a rainbow-checkered *huipala* flag hoisted above the jagged granite.

I nudged my colleague and we gathered back at the Toyota pickup along with our two female colleagues. We decided to secure and abandon the vehicle and slid through the road-block into the silent gap beyond. Walking into the darkening silence, the only noise was the hollow sound of our boots on the dirt road. In the distance, flames: the second blockade. We yanked down on wool hats to fend off the growing Andean chill. On the other side, we managed to board a cargo truck, and I watched the fires shrink behind us, the road boomerang-ing around the mountain like the arch of a question mark.

"We're locking down the compound," Len says to me.

The chanting crescendos beyond FAN's now clamped-shut iron gate and high walls. I can't see anyone, but I feel the rush and press of bodies. The protest responds to a specific issue: Goni's plan to export natural gas to the United States through Chile, a historical enemy that grabbed Bolivia's coastline in an 1879 war. Most Bolivians feel that Goni and giant firms such as Brazil's Petrobras, Repsol of Spain, and British Gas will benefit from the deal, not the Quechua, Aymara, and Guarani majority. In a larger sense, the protest is an explosion of rage over a historical string of similar swindles.

I am the only foreigner in the FAN compound and begin to feel vulnerable. Could the protests wash over the walls? Only half-aware of the irony, I peer over the walls through the *New York Times* Web site on my office computer. Their front-page article on Bolivia begins:

The many Indian protestors who choked the streets and highways of this Andean nation . . . have a powerful message. It is this: no to the export of gas and other natural resources; no to free trade with the Unites States; no to globalization in any form other than solidarity among the downtrodden peoples of the developing world.

One protester, an unemployed miner, is quoted: "Globalization is just another name for submission and domination. We've had to live with that here for centuries, and now we want to be our own masters." More news comes in. Goni decided to suspend the Sixth Commandment and flew government helicopters over the city of El Alto above La Paz, firing into street crowds and killing protesters. Hunkered down in the FAN conference room, we watch the images on Bolivian television. Mothers of slain Aymaran teens crying for revenge against Goni and his defense minister, Sánchez Berzaín, also from the white elite class. Goni appears on television and tries to quell the unrest by offering huge concessions to the protesters—to no avail. "The blood that has been spilled is something sacred," Aymaran leader Felipe Quispe says in a televised speech. "So we can't negotiate and we're not even going to talk."

I'm on my cell phone nonstop. The lines to La Paz temporarily down, I finally get through to friends there. One is holed up in his apartment as military personnel and protesters face off in the streets right outside his building. Daniel calls from South Africa: "Get your bloody ass out of that place," adding that "Brits, Kiwis, and Aussies are being evacuated." Meanwhile, no one is sure about Salvador's whereabouts. We suspect he's with the protesters narrowing in on Santa Cruz's plaza. Smithers tries to track him down through colleagues in the Indian movement.

Still trapped in the FAN compound, I get through to two other friends in La Paz. The first, a Dutch medic, doesn't spare the sarcasm: "What are we fighting for? *We don't know!* What will we get out of it? *Nothing!*" He adds that all the stores are empty, and he's been subsisting on crackers. He knows some of the Europeans who were trapped behind Aymaran roadblocks in Warisatwa for several anxious days. "This is Zimbabwe all over again," he says. "It achieves nothing."

Another friend, Rob, a thirty-two-year-old aid worker from Washington, D.C., has a different take. Though saddened by the deaths, he is elated by the display of people power. He himself has been out in the streets every evening for the past week right beside the campesino protesters. "Goni's going down," he says, heading off to a rally in front of the U.S. embassy.

In a larger sense, Bolivia's nationwide revolt is a verdict on the Washington Consensus—shorthand for the privatization and free-market policies imposed throughout Latin America by the IMF, World Bank, and United States. These policies rest on crucifixion economics: you have to kill yourself economically and socially in order to be born again, clean and healthy. Bolivia was one of the first Latin American countries to adopt this approach, back in 1985. State-owned companies were sold off. Government spending and regulation was scaled back. Foreign capital was courted. All on the promise of a new epoch of prosperity.

Twenty years later the average Bolivian is worse off than before. The liberalization policies made millions for oilmen and industrial soy farmers (neither sector creates much employment) but has not reduced inequality. Exports have declined. Bolivian incomes are stagnant, and half of the population lives on less than two dollars a day.

Bolivia is part of a Latin American region similarly questioning the Washington Consensus. Remarkably, a full three quarters of the region's 678 million people now live under leftist-populist governments. Labor unions and women's, civic, and student groups have voted in a new generation of leaders—Luiz Lula da Silva in Brazil, Néstor Kirchner in

Argentina, and Hugo Chávez in Venezuela—who express similarly grave doubts about a laissez-faire version of globalization. The situation in Bolivia is especially worrying to elites throughout the region that have similar racial and class tensions between whites and Indians, such as Paraguay, Peru, Ecuador, Mexico, and some Central American nations. In Lima and Quito people are said to be whispering about "pulling a Bolivia" in their own countries.

Salvador is missing.

Smithers and Lila look troubled after contacting a list of Salvador's friends and colleagues. As fresh images of carnage keep coming in, I increasingly share their concern. I avoid the blocked main strip that night, taking the back roads home. I wind my way through several barrios, crossing the seventh, sixth, and fifth rings to my house. The streets are empty, most people huddled in their houses, though many are downtown tangled in the knot of protests. I follow the same back roads back to FAN the next morning, but when I arrive, the office is unusually silent. I pour some coffee and then make the rounds; ninty percent of the staff has stayed home.

The nation is clenched in a tight fist, and no one knows how it might slam down. A military coup? More violent repression and marshal law under Goni? Unable to concentrate on work, I step outside. FAN's front gates have reopened, and I cannot see or hear protesters. I circle around the main building and step into FAN's "live collection," Bolivia's largest assemblage of orchids and bromeliads outside the jungle—thousands of them under translucent burlap. I take a deep breath of oxygen-rich air. This year alone, FAN biologists have discovered a dozen new orchid species in Bolivia's jungles; one of them is right before me.

Looking at the orchid, I marvel at the diversity of life still revealing itself in the twenty-first century. This green orchid has sent forth the tiniest of orange flowers, petals dotted with black. Its tag has no name, just a number, but the orchid will probably be christened with a North American name (perhaps *Orchis mcnamara*) under FAN's Biodiversity Godparents auctions where the highest bidder receives a piece of immortality by having a newly discovered species named after them. The funds protect the Bolivian rainforest habitats where those orchids thrive.

Leaving the live collection, I dial up Smithers on my cell phone. *"Como andas?"* I ask him.

"Bien, no más, en casa."

"Qué tal Salvador?"

He still hasn't heard anything, but says he'll call me as soon as he does. I find myself out in the sunlight, walking around through some mini-ecosystems FAN calls its natural classroom. In moments I cross the dry Chaco, Andean altiplano, and humid Amazon. It is designed to teach kids about their country's ecological diversity. But the small armada of botanists and gardeners needed to collect the flora samples nationwide and create this mini-Bolivia was not cheap. Luckily BP, number two on the Fortune Global 500 list, was there to pick up the tab through the Amazon Project.

There's a single tree, a hundred-year-old flowering tajibo, in the very center of BP's Bolivia in Miniature. I stop in front of it, watching the tree move slightly in the warm breeze, some of its flower petals fluttering down to my feet. As I touch its rough bark, I know that it is no longer the Guarasug'wé tree that holds up the world. It doesn't emerge out of their animate earth or send its flowers into seven skies. It grows out of and flourishes into globalization. In a sense, the ground below our feet and the air we breathe have *become* global capitalism. We live within Jamison's "postmodern hyperspace," where the great expansion of capitalism in our era internalizes the exterior world, just as the Epcot Center seeks to internalize its exterior, aspiring to be a total space, a complete world. Globalization absorbs traditional culture and wild nature and spews forth a heteronomy of fragments such as carbon ranches, green companies, and capitalist Indians.

But within this all-encompassing hyperspace there are struggles. And looking at the tajibo tree in front of me, I get an idea. Perhaps Salvador is a strangler fig, and the modernizing sultan Apollonius a liana. Both of these plants compete for the tajibo tree before me. But whereas strangler figs, like all hemiepiphytes, begin within the tree canopy and work their way down to the soil, the thick, woody liana is a vine that starts in the soil and climbs up. Both plants use the tree for structure, and both kill it, but in very different ways. A group of lianas can eventually bring the tree crashing down under their weight; strangler figs take the suffocating tree into themselves, and, remarkably, the new organism retains the shape and verticality of the tree.

Bolivia's protesting masses are not noble savages battling an evil corporate globalization. Everything is tainted. Salvador and hundreds of thousands of others come together as a strangler fig from within the branches of the ancient tree of indigenous culture and wild nature, shoot their roots down into the ground of globalization, and use it to entomb the tree. The new is shaped around the old, but is an entirely different species. The strangler races against time with the lianas: the forces of monoculture and extinction that simultaneously inch up the tree and threaten its collapse.

CHAPTER 28

T HE SOCIAL PROTESTS force Goni to step down.
    After a defiant resignation speech, he boards American
Airlines Flight 346, first-class to Miami, accompanied by his
wife and three of his top ministers. A cheer breaks out among
my colleagues at FAN and across the nation.

But there is still no word from Salvador, and for the first time
an ugly thought clouds my consciousness: maybe his body *is*
among the as-yet-unnamed dozens of Indians gunned down by
military helicopters and killed in the on-the-ground clashes.
Len says that if Salvador was martyred—God forbid—he
would be exalted as the unsullied Chiquitano who bucked giant timber companies threatening his people's land; who died
while peacefully advocating for new Indian leadership. In
death, Salvador would be scrubbed clean of inconsistency and
paradox, celebrated as an Amazonian Stephen Biko.

Meanwhile, oblivious to Salvador's whereabouts, the country explodes with euphoria over what millions of ordinary
people have wrought—bringing the country to a halt, stopping
an enormous gas-export project, and overthrowing a president. "They may still say that we are only Indians," one car-
penter in El Alto says, "but now we can see what the Aymara
nation can do when it is united."

I get a call from Daniel, from the London Airport Red Carpet lounge. "Just had a hot shower and am popping raspber-
ries into my mouth," he says in his Australian accent. "I am
bloody happy Goni's gone. I know him, and I've known
his type for decades. Those were the same guys throwing

Guatemalan Indian corpses into the volcanoes. They see indigenous people as shit!"

I tell him how worried we all are about Salvador, but he says they're boarding first class, and he has to go. "Majorca, next. Tying up some certified-timber shit. It's all going to help indigenous people in the end. But listen, mate . . . I'll be back in Bolivia in a few weeks and have something important to tell you."

"Good news or bad news?"

He pauses for a beat and says, "Gotta go. We'll do dinner at my house, and I'll tell you."

It's several nerve-racking hours later when FAN's reception door bursts open and Salvador strides in, unharmed.

"*Salvador!*" Smithers exclaims. Hugs and backslapping all around, as Salvador recounts details of the protest. He can't hide a sense of pride when he remarks that *"nosotros los indios"*—we the Indians—have changed Bolivian history.

Meanwhile, Vice President Carlos Mesa is hastily sworn in as Bolivia's new president. Mesa, a journalist and historian (whose best-selling book, *Presidents of Bolivia: Between the Ballot Box and the Rifle,* would now have to include its author), is generally seen as more trustworthy than Goni. He selects a fourteen-member cabinet that, while overwhelmingly white, is composed of independents. He warns his cabinet than any errors they make could "consign the country to the abyss."

When Daniel comes to the door at his Palms home, the first thing he says is "I'm moving to Argentina!" As we cross his house to the back gardens, he explains that he's closed on a house in Puerto Ángel. His garden is in fuller bloom than during my last visit here several months ago, I notice, as Daniel takes a sip of Scotch and then reaches down into a flower bed to put some of his sleeping-plants to rest. "It's perfect there. Plankton-filtered air; beach. And I'm an hour and a half from a *real* international airport, with direct flights to Europe, to the U.S.—if I ever want to go there—and to Australasia."

He's smoking more heavily now than ever. "Argentina, my friend. You're welcome anytime. They've got real motorways; you remember them, right? And there are toilets that flush, even in the small towns. You know, paper right there next to the toilets."

I ask him if he'll miss Bolivia.

"I'm not going to miss *anything*. I've got friends there—intellectual people—doctors, professors . . ." he says.

But later he admits, "Yeah, I'll miss it here. But, I have no choice. I can't do business in Bolivia. When I first got here, I wanted to crack this place open like a nut. But you can't; shell's too hard. But Argentina . . . Argentina *wants* progress.

"I'll miss the ladies in the market. You know, the ones with all those flowers."

Back in the living room later, some jazz playing on the stereo, Daniel is smoking a joint. The room is cool, the whole house has central air-conditioning, something nearly unheard of in Bolivian homes. "I can talk to dogs and children, even to my plants," he says, staring at a white wall. "Just have problems with adults."

I look at him, the smoke rising up, lightly obscuring his bearded face. I jiggle the ice in my Scotch glass and am about to say something, when Daniel tells me he has cancer and is dying.

He says, "Bill, I can shortcut you to what *is* important. Not what should be important but what is. We all have a role. We're creating this world and can make it better. I'm dying, so I can't do the work, but I can connect you." He snuffs out his marijuana cigarette, gets up to smell one of the flower bouquets in the room. Before I leave that night, he tells me that he can be the lightning, but that others will have to rain.

Not long after the euphoria of the uprising and the shock of Daniel's news, it is time for me to move on as well.

My father is about to turn seventy. That's when it really hits me that I've been away from my country for five years, two in Africa and three here, and am losing a sense of home. My contract comes up for renewal, and I have to decide whether to stay another full year. I know I need to go back—and for more than just my usual two weeks of vacation. Gisela tells me there will be a job for me at FAN whenever I return. I keep my farewell party low-key. Salvador is gone on a long break in the Indian Territory, so I do not get to see him before leaving.

I depart for the airport at dawn on a Saturday. Santa Cruz is still very much asleep, and the taxi zips along a second ring blooming with tajibo and assai, turning left up the new Cochabamba highway. Amboró's mountains are hued with gold, and her beauty seems to spill right into the city around me through the hundreds of tree species that line the city's rings, planted decades back by biologist Noel Kempff. I feel as raw as this new day, still finding its light and color; so much is unfinished. The revolution has brought us closer to securing the Indian Territory—Mesa has signaled it could happen soon—yet nothing is signed. Average Bolivians are beginning to grumble that Mesa, who made millions turning his PAT television news into a national network, hails from the same elite background as Goni and will not reach out to help them. "We are willing to give them this last chance," says an Aymaran from El Alto, and Felipe Quispe puts the president on strict notice: he has ninety days to break with Goni's policies or he will meet the same fate as his predecessor.

Bolivia remains radically contested. Eighty protesters were killed during what people are now calling Black October, including the eleven-year-old Mamani and seventeen-year-old Rosita, whose families cry out for revenge. The airport coming into sight, I sense the vengeance that runs thick across the land. One of the protesters called it "our ideology of fury," a feeling that too many Indians have died for too long, and someone must pay. I wonder if any kind of atonement is possible; if a positive nationhood might still arise out of exclusion and strife.

PART IV
A Delicate Space

CHAPTER 29

One year later

IT HAS HARDLY stopped raining since I returned to Bolivia a week ago. Water from the hills swells the pond behind my house. A haze blankets the picturesque colonial town of Samaipata below, softening the edges off the old church, *teja* roofs, and cobblestones. The jaguar-shaped Inca temple of El Fuerte crouches unseen in the fog above town; and beyond the jaguar are the drenched fern and cloud forests of Amboró.

I've been gone from Bolivia longer than planned. Personal and professional commitments took me through the States, Europe, and Africa, but all the while I had one ear cocked toward the deepening crisis in Bolivia. I was looking to head back anyway when a Bolivian-Dutch arts foundation generously offered me a fellowship, including a house and writing studio in Samaipata, a splendid niche where the Andes, Amazon, and Gran Chaco ecosystems merge. "You'll be in the center of Bolivia," the foundation director told me, "in the middle of the revolution."

But so far it doesn't seem like a revolution, just a lot of rain. Each day I duck in from drizzles and downpours for lunch at Marcelo's little restaurant on the plaza. His old house is little different from the others: high-pitched roof made of skinny tacuara bamboo; whitewashed adobe walls; family portraits and a statuette of the Virgin. It's a good place. The food is fresh, and I'm usually the only customer.

But I know this sense of peace is illusory; the rain is holding back a bigger flood of pent-up rage. Former president Goni has formally been charged with genocide for the slaying of eighty indigenous Bolivians during the Black October protests. The Bolivian congress insisted on the charge of genocide, a term ususally reserved for the systematic and planned extermination of an entire national, racial, or ethnic group. Fifteen of his former ministers are also accused of "complicity." If convicted, Goni could face up to thirty years in prison.

The proceedings against the former president seem permanently stalled. The gray-bearded President Mesa used to be, of course, Goni's *vicepresidente* and sees little reason to push forward to prosecute his old pal despite the condemnation of Amnesty International and the mounting frustration of ordinary Bolivians. Aymaras visit their dead daily. The TV news that I watch in Don Marcelo's restaurant shows the photos, including those of children gunned down by helicopters.

Mesa has not only stalled on Goni proceedings but also on the citizen demands known as the October Agenda. Of the demands, only one, a referendum on what Bolivia should do with its natural gas, was satisfied, but the questions were vague and the results difficult to decipher. The referendum was manipulated by Mesa and others for political interest, further compounding average Bolivians' frustration.

The national political stage is shaping up around petroleum; more specifically, Bolivia's vast natural-gas reserves, South America's second-largest. BP has now quintupled its estimate of Bolivia's proven reserves to 820 billion cubic meters, worth a staggering $250 billion, giving the Indian civil rights movement a specific target. They've seen what neocolonial elites have done with the country's enormous tin, silver, and gold reserves—sell them off at sweetheart prices to the global economy, leaving Bolivia the continent's materially poorest nation—and do not want to see the same thing happen with gas and oil.

Under what he called capitalization, Goni sold off state-run firms in the 1990s, including the Entel phone company, Lloyd Bolivian Airlines, and, most significantly, Yacimientos

Petrolíferos Fiscales Bolivianos (YPFB), the national petroleum company, equivalent to Mexico's Pemex or Brazil's Petrobras. Goni's logic seemed sensible enough: the firms were corrupt and inefficient, so selling off a controlling interest of each to multinationals would both capitalize them with new technology and give more transparent accounting. Though Bolivia would lose direct control of these industries, Goni's argument went, a rising economic tide would lift all boats.

It didn't work that way. Bolivia's petroleum coffers were forty million dollars per year lighter after capitalization as compared with before. This was partly due to the questionable deal Goni made on behalf of his countrymen: eighty-two percent of profits went to the foreign companies and only eighteen percent to Bolivia. Ordinary Bolivians have come to see capitalization as a rip-off, and everyone suspects Goni had personal stakes in the eighty-two percent giveaway, but he now lives with impunity abroad. The social movements demand renegotiated contracts with the multinational oil firms that benefited from capitalization. They want to reinstate the neither new nor radical fifty-fifty split on oil profits that existed before Goni—an arrangement common in other countries such as Venezuela and Mexico. However, less accommodating Aymara and Quechua leaders begin to call for something else beyond a fifty-fifty split. They want *nationalization* of petroleum without compensation to the foreign companies who have already sunk $3.2 billion in unrecoverable investments in road building, pipelines, and wells.

Mesa, the light-skinned president and media millionaire, can't imagine renegotiating contracts and will hear nothing of nationalization. Cheered on by the IMF, Mesa takes copious margin notes in his copy of Machiavelli's *The Prince* and tries to divide the Indian movement through stalling, bluffing, cajoling, and most of all diverting attention. Rather than focusing on the October Agenda, Mesa directs his rhetoric toward an external enemy: Chile. That country captured Bolivia's sea access in the 1879–1884 war, leaving the nation bitterly land-locked. Bolivia still maintains a navy that patrols Lake Titicaca, waiting for the someday-soon when Chile benevolently returns the coast, and the green-yellow-and-red flag once again flies proudly over the Pacific.

At the Organization of American States meeting in Mexico, Mesa squanders political capital by insisting to twenty-two heads of state that the Bolivian coast be returned. He raises the issue with Kofi Annan on his visit to La Paz. And before long everybody is laughing. Chile's foreign secretary says, barely suppressing a grin: Sure we'll return the coast—right after the United States returns Texas and California to Mexico. Several European countries and the United States announce their nonsupport of the return of Bolivia's coast, adding that Bolivia must respect the 1904 treaty that established current boundaries. But Mesa quixotically presses forward, his angular face and beard looking almost like Lenin's: "We Bolivians will regain our coast from Chile!"

It becomes, as Orwell put it, a case where words and meaning have parted company. By the time I return to the country, Bolivians have realized their president is deflecting their attention. And if it weren't for the rains—warm, slate-gray sheets washing the Amazon, freezing drizzle sending Andeans into their huts, and the steady, chilly chorus here in the heart of the country, slicking the Spanish tiles of my new home in Samaipata, filling my pond to bursting—if it weren't for all this water, the streets would be awash with people. Even with the rains, which lets up in pockets, the social movements have begun taking to the streets, their sights set on the oil multinationals.

The eastern Indian networks join farmers, women's groups, the Landless Movement—a thousand people all told—and descend upon Transredes, one of Goni's capitalized firms now owned and managed by Americans. There, they dance, play flutes, sing, and symbolically burn tires around the company's gates. Salvador is there in the thick of it, as one of the protest organizers and head of security. It looks extremely tense for a while as police and military swarm in, but thanks in large part to Salvador's knack for maintaining discipline, no one is seriously injured and the demonstration eventually breaks up.

After the protest I try to track down Salvador, but he's busier than ever. Off with national protest leaders, he is rarely found these days at FAN or AMAZONA. "Salvador's lost touch with his own people," Smithers says to me, at FAN, after a warm round of hugs and catching up with him, Gisela, Len, and the rest of my former colleagues. "Burning Transredes' gates! He does *not* have our support."

Smithers catches me up on a fissure forming in the Indian Territory. The chiefs just convened in secret without their president, Salvador, and unanimously called for a new election for the AMAZONA presidency. They feel Salvador is too worried about petroleum, too little concerned with their own land struggle. While he's busy burning gates, the two logging firms have not budged from their concessions in the Indian Territory.

I also talk with Smithers's sister, Lila, a former friend and ally of Salvador's who has changed her tune: "I'm running against Salvador for the presidency. I'll be the Indian Territory's first woman leader!" she says, lamenting that Salvador has become a La Paz jet-setter and roadblocker, forgetting his own people and becoming "half-*collya*."

Coming from an Amazon Indian like Lila, *collya* (pronounced COY-ya) is a racist slur, and her use of it explains a lot about the growing antagonism toward Salvador. A sharp regional divide has severed east from west, Santa Cruz's sweltering jungles from La Paz's snowcapped Andes. Those from the east (the lowland states of Santa Cruz, Pando, and Beni) call themselves *cambas,* while westerners (from the six valley and upland states including La Paz and Cochabamba) are *collyas.* Stereotypes abound. *Cambas* are lazy Amazonian hammock-dwellers; *collyas* are tightfisted businesspeople, and too politically radical.

Salvador sees the divide as white-Indian, while Smithers, Lila, and several chiefs view it as *camba-collya.* At the same moment Salvador was burning the gates of multinational oil, others from the Indian Territory were marching along the second ring chanting, "Autonomy now!" Bolivia's eastern states, including Santa Cruz, have called for referenda toward autonomy from La Paz, and it all comes down to who controls oil. Not coincidentally, most of the vast gas and oil reserves are in the east. The Indian movements, their numbers and power centered in the west, see this as another racist policy that would impoverish them. Should eastern regions simply say, "Tough, we've got the oil and will sell and tax it here," the Indian west would become even more destitute.

Even amid all this turbulence, the Amazon Project has leapt forward in two areas over the past year. First, the Indians' sustainable timber business is booming. Smithers talks about the progress for two solid hours: "This year will be our test of fire," he says. He's all facts: they've cut the first 1,507 trees this year and milled 681. He shows me photos of their newly installed sawmill in Porvenir, with dozens of people hard at work. AMAZONA owns the factory and has hired a technical team to manage the business. "We're the boss of forestry engineers and accountants," he says, not disguising his pride. "We made $34,000 in profits this year. Next year we're running on a $350,000 operating budget and hope to double profits. I'm optimistic because we're opening our own lumberyard in Santa Cruz and won't have to go through middlemen." Smithers says that by next year AMAZONA will be precertified as ecological by SmartWood; in two years, completely certified and selling at a much higher world price. This is particularly heartwarming to me since I helped AMAZONA develop the proposal that purchased the sawmills.

The second development is just as incredible: AMAZONA will be comanaging the entire Kempff Park along with the Bolivian Park Service and FAN. Here's where all of our capacity-building pays off; others now trust the Indians enough to bring them on board. Salvador argued at the meetings leading up to the decision to include the communities that they are not only "the original inhabitants of the land" but now have modern skills to help manage those lands.

Yet it's not all rosy. As I talk with Gisela and others, a more ambiguous picture of the emerging Indian Territory comes into focus—and at its center is the entry of the powerful Catholic Church.

Even as Bishop Ramón's *colonos* slash-and-burn their way to Heaven on Earth in the jungles approaching the Indian Territory, a large Catholic foundation from Spain called Hombres Nuevos—New Men—has penetrated right into Porvenir, Piso Firme, Florida, and Cachuela. It began last year with a visit from the bishop himself along with New Men functionaries from Madrid. Salvador accompanied them on a missionary plane into the Indian Territory. The bishop got off the plane in Piso Firme and immediately doled out coins to gathered children before announcing his creed as "nothing for the poor, everything with the poor." Then he said that New Men has a million dollars available to build a paradise for them.

I met this Spanish bishop over a year ago in the dean's office at the Catholic University in Santa Cruz when the idea was first taking shape. Smithers sat beside me on one sofa, the bishop and dean facing us across a coffee table. The bishop was draped in billowy black, and the dean's pointy beard screamed conquistador-chic. The bishop began by crooning his mantra: "Nothing *for* the poor, everything *with* the poor," the dean gravely nodding. "There's a lot of support in Madrid to build the biggest high school possible in Porvenir. How many students are in the area?"

The question was aimed at me. My chest tightening, I told them the numbers. Their idea included not just the Catholic school, but free Brazil-style wooden houses for everyone and satellite dishes to connect the Indian Territory with Bolivian television "to integrate them into the rest of the nation." It sounded like another wave of dependency.

And across the border in Brazil was not New Men, but New Tribes, a group based in Stanford, Florida, "composed of born-again believers dedicated to the evangelization of unreached tribal peoples," they write of themselves on their official Web site, adding, "Our focus is on finishing. And we are not truly finished until the day there are believers from every tribe. Of the earth's 7,000 ethnic groups, 3,000 are still unreached." Their newsletter has been until recently called *Brown Gold*, an insulting reference to outwardly "unclean" brown-skinned people who nevertheless have divine gold inside. Our Amazon Project has brought the obscure Chiquitanos into the open where Jesus has spotted them. The focus would be on finishing—polishing Salvador's brown body until the holy shine gleams forth.

CHAPTER 30

S ALVADOR STANDS SILENTLY under a flowering tajibo, gazing across the fourth ring toward some trees blowing in the distance. He's outside the Juntos Indian network office and doesn't see me when I pull up in my taxi. I get out and gesture to him. "Amigo Bill!" he exclaims as we embrace.

We get into the taxi and spend the first moments exchanging compliments and catching up. It's been a year since we've spoken. His wife and five children are all in good health. "Where to?" the taxi driver interjects. Salvador looks at me. I feel tense, knowing that if I suggest a chop shop he might feel slighted, yet I recall his discomfort in the hip Mexican place, and that eliminates others of its type, such as the Middle Eastern and Japanese restaurants in Hammocks and Cristo. I name a four-star hotel—not five-star, but certainly no dump—and study his face for a reaction, but his thick features reveal nothing. When we arrive, the maître d' smiles pleasantly to me, but his face tightens when he sees the dark-skinned Salvador behind me. I immediately regret the decision. A few others are staring too. We open menus, and I wonder if Salvador knows he's being noticed.

After ordering—Salvador asks for a big steak—he says, "They want to get rid of me." He's shaking his head. "*La hermana* Lila, who I've helped so much. And the chiefs, they've gone behind my back to call this election."

He looks out the glass wall over a turquoise swimming pool but doesn't seem to notice it. Then he shrugs. "I'm studying our Chiquitano language, Besiro, and all they can do is sing

Brazilian songs and dance lambada! They don't think they're Indians anymore."

I congratulate him on AMAZONA's progress with the sustainable timber business, adding, "And you'll soon be co-managing Kempff."

"I had to get out my spears to make that happen," Salvador says. He explains that FAN and the municipality had dropped AMAZONA from the arrangement, some feeling that AMAZONA needed more time to mature. But Salvador would hear nothing of it: "I stuffed my leather bag with laws, and at the meeting I pulled them all out: the forestry law, the environment law, and I read the appropriate articles."

I chuckle, imagining the dismayed looks as Salvador literally laid down the law. His voice crescendos as he recalls the meeting: "I told them, 'Our rights are not under discussion. We are the legitimate owners of the house!'" Salvador's voice now booms through the exquisite dining room, and a hush overcomes the restaurant. A businessman at the next table flattens his tie, trying not to look our way. The waiters glance at each other nervously. Silver clicks against china, and Salvador retreats to a whisper; I have to lean in to hear. "Leadership," he says confidently. "You're either born with it, or you learn it. But neither Lila nor the caciques have it yet."

"You mean they're not leaders," I say, noticing the conversations starting to resume.

"Exactly, *amigo Bill*. They're trying to push me from power because they're jealous. And because they don't understand the national Indian struggle. *La lucha! Ay,* they're still like our parents, *los pobres inocentes,* who cheered when the heart-of-palm companies came to take all of our richness."

I want to take issue with him here; we both know quite well he's been the one delaying elections. Even AMAZONA's constitution calls for a maximum four-year term, and Salvador's been president for six. He's hemmed and hawed and found technicalities that have allowed him to stay. And even if he is the most capable leader in the Indian Territory, Salvador needs to let democracy reign. Necessity, said Pitt the Younger, is the excuse of every tyrant.

Anticipating my reaction, Salvador assures me that he "fully supports the elections."

Now that they've forced them out of you, I think, but only say, "How do the others feel about your burning the gates?"

"It was a symbolic act," he says in clipped words, seemingly annoyed. "And anyway we didn't commandeer the installations."

We switch to more pleasant topics, and after two hours it's like old times. When we're on dessert, he's more relaxed and segues back into the multinational-oil protest. "I was in charge of security, that's the third in command. My role was to make sure everything went peacefully, without any of our *hermanos* getting killed."

Salvador then surprises me. He says that for several years he served as a Christian minister in his village. The same Iowa missionaries who converted Apollonius had a temporary success with Salvador. He talks at length about how Christianity helped him get *"la figura clara"* about peacefully resolving conflicts, and those few years on the pulpit built his public-speaking confidence. He says he left the church because he "couldn't give up dancing," but still has positive feelings about what he learned from the missionaries. Listening to him chastens my own reaction to New Men and New Tribes; human relationships—under whatever banner—can have either positive or negative consequences, depending on the hearts of the individuals involved, as well as a certain amount of serendipity. In this case what I would reflexively have called intrusive proselytization ended up helping Salvador obtain the tools to reclaim his own culture.

We've drained our coffees, and a hard, gray rainy-season light angles in over the swimming pool, catching the gold glint of Salvador's front tooth. He says, "Do you think I want any of us killed? I'm the last one who wants violence. But we're going to keep blocking roads. Making people *feel* us."

His face clouds over. "Blocking roads," he says, gesturing around us, for the first time acknowledging where we are, "is the only language some people understand."

I'm walking past a *salteña* café in the Cristo district after my conversation with Salvador, and there's Evo on the television news, as he is every day now. Talk of fresh roadblocks is everywhere. People have dubbed the inevitable coming showdown "the final battle." As Len puts it, "If the country is blocked again, it's either going to be the first Indian government in the hemisphere or a complete and definitive massacre."

White faces line the outdoor cafés and restaurants of the Cristo strip. This is the collective living room of upper-class *camba* society, and as I pass by, I try to nonchalantly catch conversation murmured over cappuccino and red wine. Bolivia's rich huddle ever closer; there's not only the usual common enemy now but for the first time a formidable one. The city is now cleaved into "*camba* Santa Cruz" more or less within the third ring, and "*collya* Santa Cruz," or the Indian-migrant hinterlands beyond the third ring. No longer is hospitality *la ley cruzeño,* at least not for the swelling hordes of migrants from the interior who now have a numeric majority even here in the eastern capital.

I take a detour off the strip and stick my head into my favorite salsa club, Manizero, and ask for my friend Pepe, the tall Cuban owner.

"Pepe?"

"Yes, Pepe."

"Pepe." This is a typical exchange; things take a long time to sink in.

"Is he around?"

"Who, Pepe?"

"Yes, where is Pepe?"

"In Cuba."

No one can say when he'll be back. I make my way back to the main strip, little surprised that Pepe's fled considering the political and economic uncertainty. I pass the Pro–Santa Cruz Committee building right behind hip Alexander's Coffee and bump into a gathering of a few hundred Santa Cruz separatists. As I navigate this crowd, I feel a bit as if I were strolling through a certain Munich *Bierhaus* in 1923. They're exclusively male, and many of them wear jeans, leather belts with enormous buckles, and full, macho mustaches and sideburns reminiscent of seventies cop shows. Their meeting has just broken up, and some carry green-and-white Santa Cruz flags. None of them look particularly chipper.

One of the men I pass spits out the word *indio* the way I imagine a Klansman might say *nigger*. I earn a few gruff nods as I pass, since I've got the right complexion. Some of those gathered are teens along with their fathers. A few days later the red-haired teenage leader of this group's youth wing, Santa Cruz Youth, would start appearing on television to announce roadblock-busting tactics and call for autonomy from an increasingly *collya*-run Bolivia.

CHAPTER 31

I BECOME ANXIOUS during the first weeks of my writing fellowship in the colonial village of Samaipata. I feel I should be doing something, *serving* someone. During three years in Bolivia I've led training courses, raised funds, and managed exciting projects. But now *nothing* is happening. How can such quiet exist in the very center of a country chock-full of roadblocking radicals? The locals talk about the weather—a way of gossiping about the planet—smile a lot, and rarely amble beyond a three-block radius from their homes. The entire town goes comatose during the three-hour midday meal and siesta. The evenings are a bit livelier as boys and girls orbit the plaza in opposite directions, exchanging small insults.

I start to go with the flow in the open-air market where I buy my produce. I tease the Indian market women by whining, *"Y mi llapiiiiita?"* They laugh full-bellied at my use of the Quechua word *llapita,* which refers to that extra veggie sellers give to bring themselves the luck of the return client. I'm constantly asked what country I'm from and always answer, *"Soy del pais de Nueva York."* This inevitably gets a laugh. Bolivians have a quick intuition for all sorts of humor; no one has ever replied, "Wait a minute . . . New York isn't a country." They get it.

I receive a message one day from a good friend from Brooklyn, Lisa. She's in Guyana and coming my way. I e-mail back that it may not be the wisest time to come to Bolivia, to which she responds, "Miss the revolution? What*ever*. I'll be in on the Saturday red-eye from Manaus."

252

A doctor, Lisa has been on a volunteer medical mission and arrives in Samaipata exhausted; there's dust in her curly brown hair, and her eyes look particularly pale. She's thirty-one and has been living a fiercely go-getterish life in the city for a long time. A Stanford grad from San Francisco, she's now chief resident at Bellevue's emergency room; performs in an elite modern-dance company; and reads every page of the *Times* each Sunday. "Once I start, I feel like I have to read every line or I'm missing something."

Lisa gets off to a rough start in Samaipata, quipping that "the fashions here are an unequivocal disaster, almost a sin," pointing out that she buys only from small designers and shuns anything mass-produced, which is often what Bolivians can afford. A Dutch friend of mine, Jacques, an economist who has opted out of the rat race to live in Samaipata and lead Amboró tours, says quite bluntly to Lisa, "When you first come into a different culture, your observations usually say more about you than they do about that culture."

I expect her to become defensive at this, but she instead says sincerely, "I've never thought of it like that." Her judgment dries up and is suspended for the rest of our ten days together. While I write in the mornings, Lisa meditates in my loft, cooks vegetarian lunches for us, and hikes through the hills to Inca ruins. One afternoon, we're leaving my house when a nearly blind old woman asks us, "Excuse me, can you point out the one for brooms?"

Though Lisa speaks Spanish, she's puzzled. Catching the woman's meaning, I take her hand and guide it along various bushes until her fingertips pinch the leaves of one. "*Gracias,*" she says, taking several fronds.

You don't buy a broom here, you make it. And then there are the herbs growing everywhere, Samaipateños harvesting them for ailments and dinner alike. Women chop baby eucalyptus from the trees outside my house, stuffing it in their bathrooms for fragrance. Wildflowers come not from a florist but are gathered out of the landscape and heaped atop the wheelbarrows of collected firewood. There is a town dump, but it sees little use since Samaipata's three thousand people use little packaging.

Even the food, so to speak, walks around the pueblo in deep baskets draped with white fabric over *cuñape* crumpets, juicy *salteña* meat pies, empanadas, nuts, and fruits of all sorts, nothing costing more than a quarter. Not just Bolivians, but the fairly Bolivianized thirty or forty expatriates who have settled in Samaipata—mostly Swiss, French, German, and Dutch—buy whatever walks by and in their laid-back clothing blend with the locals. Expats are fully included in the many festivals—to celebrate the town founding 387 years back, select Miss Samaipata, or honor mothers, teachers, and children.

From my balcony, breezes range the senses—I watch one begin on the far-off pines and cross the eucalyptus like a wave, its sound gathering until its slightly smoky scent enters my nostrils and massages my cheeks. Lisa loves to lie under the stars each night and once says, "I always forget there is so much energy in nature. It's deeper than urban energy, but harder to feel at first."

Living in Samaipata for what would turn out to be nine months in two separate stints brought me into the sensuous underbelly of Bolivia. There is no contradiction between the country's vast, quiet landscape and its furious protests. Road-blocking is the ruddy surface of a far deeper revolutionary act: being still. The space between the bars holds the jaguar; the space between the notes is the music. In an essential sense the Bolivian revolution is located between the flare-ups, the silence of nature quietly nourishing a nation.

Lisa and I hike into the Volcanoes section of Amboró Park, crossing a river in a narrow gully two dozen times and arriving several hours later in a ten-family hamlet. Entering a tangerine groove, I'm hit by a severe sense of déjà vu. The trees are close-packed and the ground is a block of shade and overripe and rotting fruit. A woman with a huge goiter on her neck stands in the doorway of a hut, and a man who is probably her husband calls out, "William! You're back!"

I'd passed through this grove and eaten tangerines with him for no more than twenty minutes, *three years* before. How many more farms and cities and parks had I been to since? This tangerine orchard had faded in my consciousness, but he remembers not just my name but exactly what we talked about. In places like Volcanoes people take on a greater importance because they are so rare against the isolated expanse. Lisa is recruited to doctor his wife; they retire into the hut—Lisa and I both assuming it's about the tangerine-sized goiter, but it's not. "She's much more worried about gas," Lisa says as we're leaving.

Lisa and I start listening to the river. "It's speaking," I whisper to her in the tent later, and she nods. Moonlight radiates on a dozen heavily jungled cones growing out of the landscape, casting one volcano-shaped shadow over us, and I begin thinking about something certain renegade linguists have long maintained: that our own language is fed by nature. We regularly speak of chattering brooks and howling winds, but these expressions go beyond metaphor. As David Abram writes, it is not by chance that "the terms we spontaneously use to describe the surging waters of the nearby river are words like 'rush,' 'splash,' 'gush,' 'wash.' For the sound that unites all these words is that which the water itself chants as it flows between the banks." What little we know about the Guarasug'wé suggests that Kusasu's ancestors were much like the Kaluli people of Papua New Guinea. Ethnomusicologist Steven Feld has recorded the Kalui singing with birds, insects, tree frogs, waterfalls, and rain. "And when the Kaluli sing with them," Feld writes, "they sing *like* them. Nature is music to the Kaluli ears. And Kaluli music is naturally part of the surrounding soundscape . . . In this rainforest musical ecology, the world really is a tuning fork."

Lisa heads back to Brooklyn, and I continue sleeping under the stars beside my Samaipata house, dragging a mummy bag under a Southern Cross anchored below the Milky Way. I begin doing a powerful meditation exercise that brings me into the present where Bolivians live, into the silence that is equally nature's voice and our own. With a full landscape around me, and not a human voice or tool to be heard, I imagine myself between two giant hot-air balloons, both inflated to bursting, to my left and right. One is my past; the other my future. My past is full of memories, mostly good, some hurtful; my future inflated with dreams, hopes, and possibilities. Slowly I let all the energy of both deflate, the air rushing into me, into the now. I feel large, light, and present. The balloons of past and future are dead, deflated sacks and the present is alive around me.

One day I'm on Samaipata's lush plaza, mesmerized by how the sun hits a raindrop. Lingering on the tip of a pine needle, the drop turns red, blue, aqua-green, and finally orange, an unseen metronome beating out the pulse of a prism. My trance is broken by an eight-year-old girl, Mariana, the daughter of the local woman who cuts my hair, and we get to talking. I ask the pigtailed Mariana about her dreams. Her response is a mallet on my tranquillity and the first suggestion of an enormous change about to enter Samaipata. She earnestly pipes out her dream: "World peace and no more *collyas*!"

CHAPTER 32

BOLIVIA BLURS. A gray area expands between the white-Indian and eastern *camba*–western *collya* divisions. Under the stress of a tanking economy and the impending "final battle," Bolivia fractures in a hundred places, worry lines on a nation's brow.

Apollonius exemplifies this gray area. I had suggested to him that we meet, and he mentioned a place he likes: the newly inaugurated New York Mall. It's Bolivia's first shopping mall, put up by a Santa Cruz developer; other developers from Chile have just completed Bolivia's very first cineplex, the Multicentro, along the second ring. Meanwhile, Santa Cruz millionaire Tomislav Kuljis has been expanding his Hypermaxi supermarket chain, which he hopes to transform into "the Wal-Mart of Bolivia." All of these changes have taken place over the past year.

Like the cineplex, the New York Mall is always empty. Both are undoubtedly subsidized for the first few years, with the developers hoping they'll catch on. I doubt it. There's just a smattering of the same folks you see along the Cristo strip— and my friend, the sultan.

I greet Apollonius and his daughters, who disappear into the mall. We find a seat in Bolivia's first and only food court, and Apollonius announces, "I closed the heart-of-palm factory." He tells me it's temporary; the world price has sagged. "But I've got other ideas. I want to start logging to provide jobs, if only *Salvador* would let me."

The bitter tale spills forth. Salvador insists that Apollonius do business the indigenous way—as a community. That means all two thousand Chiquitanos living on Kempff's border harvest a carefully controlled area each year and share the profits through AMAZONA. With Salvador and the chiefs standing firm on this, Apollonius-style capitalism is a nonstarter, but the sultan has switched tactics.

"I'm the new cacique of Porvenir!" he announces proudly. It sounds incongruous to hear the traditional term *cacique,* or chief, tossed about by the modern, New York Mall–frequenting Apollonius. Before I can consider the implications of this change—a merger of modernist thinking and political power in one of the two largest Indian Territory villages—Apollonius says, "We're going to bury Salvador in the next elections." He's got a slanted smile as he says this. The food court is completely empty; a beam of sunlight comes through the skylight, a break in the clouds overhead, and momentarily illuminates Apollonius's narrow face. He talks about how Bolivia needs to become more like Brazil. He's thrilled that New Men is to construct modern wood-framed homes for everyone—especially since he is the likely contractor. Construction is yet another business Apollonius has going.

"Salvador is out of touch—and almost out of power," he says. "We're not a bunch of barbarians."

"How would you describe yourself?"

Apollonius considers this, finally settling on a hesitant "I'm *camba.*"

But what exactly is a *camba*? It has come to mean people from the eastern states of Santa Cruz, Beni, and Pando, but in today's political environment the *camba* club is becoming more exclusive. The mustached *camba* elites outside of the Pro–Santa Cruz Committee might not welcome the short, Chiquitano Apollonius into their club. Nor would the Camba Nation separatists, headed up by eastern oligarchs. Guillermo Roy is as *camba* as it gets—but he's the very logger who gobbled up a big chunk of the Indian Territory, and certainly no friend of Apollonius's.

Other Bolivians are even more insecure about where they fit in the emerging landscape. I have an intriguing conversation with Samuel, a tenured agronomy professor at Santa Cruz's large public university and a rare example of Indian upward mobility. He's a friend's father, and we lunch together at his Santa Cruz home. At one point he lifts his shirt to show me some awful scars; Samuel had been a debt peon on an Amazon hacienda and was brutally whipped by his *patrón* as he hauled jugs of crude rubber. Assisted by Catholic-priest teachers, he scraped together sufficient education to escape to Cochabamba, where he attended university. He eventually won a scholarship to do further studies in Brazil, then attended Georgetown University in Washington, D.C.

Despite Samuel's incredible qualifications and thirty-three years of teaching, he can't retire: "Goni spent our pension funds." The ousted president shifted public-university funds to social security, politically calculating that the general senior vote exceeds that of liberal college teachers. I feel for Samuel. He's reached average life expectancy for men in Bolivia, sixty-four years, and will probably have to teach his backbreaking load of five classes right to the grave to support his family and pay for repairs on his 1970 VW Beetle and the upkeep of his modest seventh-ring home. Social security pays an insufficient one hundred dollars a month. But where does he turn? With Bolivia's public debt load eating up forty percent of fiscal expenditures, it is doubtful any president could bring his pension back, whether an Indian government or *camba automistas*. "Autonomy would just decentralize corruption," he tells me, looking completely spent. "We're trapped in so many vicious cycles. I don't know how we'll get out."

One observer dubbed Bolivia *el pueblo enfermo*—the sick people. It is a poor little rich country, cursed by the wealth of silver, gold, tin, magnesium, and petroleum under its soil.

Vaguely circular in shape, Bolivia is the apple of temptation, an object luring the greedy. If North America was originally settled by religiously persecuted yeomen farmers ready to work, South America—and nowhere more so than Bolivia—was founded by thieves. Buenos Aires used to be called Mar de Plata, but the sea of silver came from Potosí, Bolivia, the world's wealthiest city at the time. The open veins of Potosí capitalized Europe, but that city is today among the hemisphere's poorest. Bolivia was born of *engaño*, the fine art of the swindle.

Francis Fukuyama, author of *The End of History and the Last Man*, argues that the basis of the West's outward success is trust. Laws are developed and more or less followed; a handshake is, much more often than not, rock solid. But centuries of *engaño* have left Bolivia barren of trust. Apollonius, Samuel, and millions of other Bolivians have seen so much lying, cheating, and stealing that they've internalized the dysfunctionality. And this brings some observers to the most cynical, hopeless conclusion of all—a deep, dark well indeed. It is this: should the Indians finally come to power, they might turn out to be exactly as thieving as those who have robbed them for so long.

"We've got three demands," Salvador tells me over the phone. He's about to lead a fresh round of protests up-country in San Ignacio. He's got his speaking-to-the-media voice on, and he recites the demands in a rote manner. "First and foremost, nationalize Bolivia's petroleum. Second, no to demands for autonomy of the oil-rich states. And, three, a new national constitution, written by the people." I talk to other protest leaders, and also to their followers. Each repeats the same three demands in the same order. Though they claim to want to sell Bolivia's gas in a way that benefits everyone, the key question remains, Would the Indians, in power, be just as corrupt as the oligarchs?

Looking at the strongest Indian contender for the presidential sash, Evo Morales, one is tempted to say yes. Evo has not been caught stealing, but does certainly have a vainglorious streak. However, the real answer is that we don't know because there has never been an Indian government. What happens when you blend communal structures like the Aymara *allyu* and Guarani council into a social democracy? We have no idea. Would neighboring giant Brazil and global power brokers like the United States and IMF help or hamper the fledgling Indian government? But one thing suggests Evo's headstrong nature could be reined in: the worst insult among indigenous Bolivians is to call someone *egoista,* or selfish, and what, if not this, is the root of corruption?

But this all seems theoretical as Salvador at this very moment considers with other Indian leaders the if, how, and where of civil disobedience in the Grand Chiquitania. And it's not long before I get a disturbing piece of news: large hacienda owners are organizing fledgling militias that want to bust up any new round of protests. One of their targets is Salvador, and for the first time they are arming themselves.

CHAPTER 33

RIGHT ABOVE SAMAIPATA is a castle. That's what all the locals call the Tudor mansion, with its dozens of rooms and granite tower. Viewed from the town, its sweeping lawns and regal presence are a surreal cut-and-paste from the Middle Ages. The castle belongs to a Santa Cruz family of sugarcane plantation and petroleum wealth, but in my months living here I've yet to see light in the tower or smoke in its chimneys. Like aristocrats of old, these Bolivians cannot visit all their estates regularly. Beyond the castle are two parallel white pipelines operated by Transredes carrying natural gas to Atlantic ports in Argentina and Brazil, where it's shipped to homes and factories abroad.

Though in Bolivia the cost of producing and transporting a barrel of oil is just seven dollars, Bolivians must pay world market prices for their own oil: forty-nine dollars.

The vast landscapes of Amboró Park swallow up castles and pipelines alike as my taxi climbs the mountain from Samaipata up to La Yunga's fern forest. It's been over a year since I've been there, and I am curious to see what has become of our ecotourism efforts. I arrive to see trash covering La Yunga's once quaint little plaza, and the boom and whir of off-roading-vehicle motors grate on my eardrums. The Santa Cruz Four Wheeler club has arrived.

I speak with a few of the members before they motor back to the city and learn they hail from Santa Cruz's Miami-gazing upper echelons. Stuffed from the afternoon's pig roast, they rev up their fat-wheeled quads, trikes, and Land

Cruisers plastered with SKYJACKER and DETROIT LOCKER stickers. Granted, they're a tiny minority, and this type of tourism in La Yunga is unusual. But I still feel suffocated by all the smoke and noise and walk off alone into the fern forest. Some Bolivian Indians say that a part of their soul is taken along with a photo and do not allow pictures of their faces. But the four-wheelers snapped some anyway, despite being asked not to. And Fidel had to physically stop the motorcade from driving directly onto the millennium-old fern forests. As I collect trash from beneath the ferns, I recall my trip last year to Bonito, Brazil, and think, *I should have seen this coming.*

Gisela convinced me to go: "It's *the* model for ecotourism in South America."

The trip got off to a good start. I crossed the Bolivian border into Corumbá, and took an eight-hour luxury-bus ride to Bonito. Soon I was submerged in the Rio do Prada, clad in wet suit and snorkeling gear. Bloodred fish ventured within inches of my mask, flashing in a wavering green world. When I focused on my hand and the sleeve of my wet suit, I felt I was looking through air rather than water.

After an hour of floating in silence through this lucid aquatic world, all of the stress I'd been feeling seemed remote. Drifting away from the rest of the group, I explored crannies of the river. A blimplike fish nearly brushed my shoulder, while four or five other species swam just ahead—and all of a sudden it happened. A ten-foot snake slowly overtook me, swimming just a few feet to my right. I could see its unblinking eyes staring at me, its skin light-colored, splotched with black. I froze and then emerged gasping and yelling at the others, "*Serpiente!*"

They hadn't warned us about this—at least nothing I understood with my miserable Portuguese—so I assumed the worst: it was surely poisonous. Two of the young Rio de Janeiro women spotted the snake and surfaced, grabbing on to me and whimpering.

"That was an anaconda," our guide told me later. The story buzzed through our group and spilled into the Rio do Prada's tour groups ahead of us and behind. Before I knew it, the story was that I, the brave Hollywood hero, had fought off a giant anaconda poised to strangle the womenfolk.

To thank me for my supposed heroism, the Asian group invited me along in their Hummer to Cave Number Three. Thousands of stalactites dropped into a gigantic bowl that funneled into blue water. I stopped for a moment on the path down and became absorbed in the cave's peace, until a Motorola walkie-talkie went off on my companion's belt: "Where are you?" said one of the women.

"In the cave," he replied.

"We're in the cave too," she said. The others caught up to us and all four whipped out digital cameras and took identical photos. I walked by myself to the bottom and stared into that incredibly blue water until our guide said, "Okay, our eight minutes are up."

That night, I dined with the Japanese Brazilians, a couple of newlyweds from southern Brazil, and Diego, a photojournalist from Sâo Paulo whom I'd met on the bus to Bonito. I looked at my menu: crocodile burgers and "Brazilian wild boar" steaks. The small print assured "the Ecotourist" that these were "certified domesticated wild animals" grown on game farms for my eating pleasure and "never poached from wild forests."

"Brazil is so fucking first-world," said Diego, in Portuñol, a mixture of Portuguese and Spanish.

Some giggling, and then one of the newlyweds asked the Japanese Brazilians, "What tour did you do today?"

"Cave Number Three!" one of them said, in Portuguese.

"We did Number Twenty-four: rappelling from a cliff."

I began to see how "ecotourism" in Bonito worked. You

stayed at one of the town's thirty-two hotels and hired one of its twenty-six travel agencies to take you on packaged tours to one of the forty-one ecological attractions.

"Anaconda Fighter," one of the Japanese Brazilians said to me, "do you want to go to Number Sixteen with us tomorrow?"

Number Sixteen turned out to be Macaws in a Hole. After driving through forty-four kilometers of pastureland, we came to a fenced-in bit of forest on private land. Once we were inside, the gully and dozens of colorful macaws were spectacular, but it was an eco-illusion; the macaws were fed daily, and exactly beyond your sight line lay a sprawling clear-cut.

On the ride back I sank into the Hummer's leather shotgun seat, cooled by AC, and listened to some smooth bossa nova. The women in the back were singing along, and I asked my Japanese-Brazilian friend Naruto what he did in Sâo Paulo, and he said, "I import things from China." When I asked him what kind of things, he replied, "Anything at all."

Fazenda dude ranches and eight-minute cave hikes slipped by. Everything was flowing, from the singsong Portuguese and giggling, to the beautiful women, to the jazzy Sâo Paulo music. Everything, I realized, since I'd crossed from Bolivia into Brazil had been smooth, flowing, convenient—and dead. Each of the forty-one ecological attractions was reached by motoring through denuded cow pasture. I believed the menu's claim about the "domesticated wild animals" not being poached, because I'd not seen any wild forest since leaving Bolivia.

"Bolivians aren't like us," Naruto said later. "They don't want to work, so they don't have *this*." He grandly gestured at—what? Perhaps he was indicating the Hummer's luxurious interior; or maybe the four-lane highway cutting through cattle fields that once were forest; or did he mean the entire modernizing Brazilian nation?

* * *

Amid the four-wheeler rubbish strewn throughout La Yunga, some good news arises. "We've kicked out the *colonos*!" Ernestina exclaims, when I sit down over chicha with her and a few others. Helped by mini–Bill Clinton in city hall, the community has protected their landscape from new slash-and-burn migrants like the ones that overran FAN's private cloud forest. Their enthusiasm comes partly out of FAN's years of environmental education and from earth-friendly cultural norms. Most significantly, however, it now pays for the forest to stay. La Yunga has gained enough economic clout to eliminate go-betweens and begin selling their tours right in Samaipata. Noticing La Yunga's ecotourism boomlet, the city government has paid to grade the road up the mountain, installed a piped-water system, and even wired in phone service.

And as always ironies seep in. The profile of the average traveler to the fern forest hamlet is changing. Smaller in number now are the bong-hit hippies and scruffy biologists who used to blend into the forest like fern tendrils. They would eat local gruel with glee and camp for days or weeks at a time— just for the *connectivity* of the place, the undisturbed virgin jungles. The new tourists are more inclined toward "eco" in quotes, satisfied with something more like Brazil's eight-minute caves and tame macaws. FAN has unclogged this vein and the world's blood rushes in.

My mood is ambivalent as we wind back down the road from the cloud forest. No one in the taxi talks. We're nearly down when the driver stops to pick up another passenger. He's the chef for the local Transredes petroleum pipeline staff and asks to be dropped off at the firm's outstation near Samaipata. What a shock it is to enter a slice of first world. The modern buildings and intricate loops and angles of pipes, all surrounded by electric fencing, grows out of the standard rural Bolivian scenery of collapsing adobe, old clay roves, and anarchic foliage growth. We stop in front to let out the chef. A half dozen shinny vehicles are parked in white-lined spaces on the asphalt; workers in snowy white uniforms comply with the mandatory-hard-hats rule; signs of all sizes designate the what, where, and how of workspace behavior. But a moment later the chef has cleared the electric fence, and our taxi rolls back into Bolivia.

CHAPTER 34

M Y GERMAN NEIGHBOR in Samaipata is murdered.
The news blazes through the village. Dirk's body has just been discovered a mile outside town—stabbed several times, his neck snapped, and badly burned. Crying, one friend says, "I hope he was dead when they set him on fire." The town packs into the church on the plaza to mourn, and afterward the rumors begin to spread. It *must* have been someone from Santa Cruz. No one in Samaipata could have done this! And of all people Don Dirk, who's been teaching my kids for years, the kind man.

It is particularly eerie for me since Dirk lived right next door, his white house visible through the hedge. A vigorous seventy-year-old who lived alone with an exquisitely manicured miniature poodle, Dirk has for the last ten years divided his time between Oxford, England, where he was a teacher, and Samaipata. Dirk was well-loved here because he gave free English and German classes to Samaipata youth.

Looser tongues, however, take certain facts and hypothesize. The facts: Dirk was gay. He has been seen late at night with young men in their late teens and early twenties. He would disappear for days on end to Santa Cruz and always stayed at the same hotel there. The theory: this is a vengeance kill linked to the kiddie-porn underbelly of Santa Cruz. After all, Dirk was burned in the midsection and groin; clearly a message about what's done to perverts.

There's a saying: *Pueblo pequeño, infierno grande*—Small town, large hell—so I take all of this with a grain of salt, and fresh facts paint a different picture. It turns out that the killer was local, a twenty-year-old boy named Gustavo. His finger-prints are all over the house and Dirk's abandoned Jeep; wit-nesses testify to having seen them together. And all evidence indicates it was a robbery.

The U.S. Peace Corps evacuates the two American volun-teers in Samaipata. For the first time in this small town I expe-rience fear. I start locking my door; keep security lights on all night; and even consider taking a little Santa Cruz vacation. But I stay put, sleeping lightly and dreaming, strangely, that Dirk is the murderer instead of the slain.

And that's the complication. A consensus arises in the town that Dirk was not completely innocent. It is very out of the or-dinary here for a seventy-year-old—gay or straight—to be in-volved with a local twenty-year-old. His money undoubtedly attracted Gustavo. Dirk wasn't filthy rich but did drive his Jeep everywhere in a town where less than one percent of the people own vehicles. And his cousin Heine, who owns the larger bungalow complex that contained Dirk's house, has a net worth in the hundreds of millions of euros. Though not "the seventh richest man in Germany," as local legend has it, he does own factories and office buildings there. Heine has sheltered some of his cash tax-free in Bolivia in the form of dozens of houses in Santa Cruz and, as I come to find out, owns the entire valley behind my house.

Dirk's killer is never found. Some theorize that he escaped to Argentina. Others, disturbingly, begin murmuring that the police should end the investigation. "Dirk is dead, and there's no bringing him back. Besides, he was only a German."

"Those are just a bunch of *collyas*," I overhear a villager say, on Samaipata's plaza. "We need to get them off our highway."

A new buzz drowns out the gossip around Dirk. Three hun-dred farmers, many of them Quechua, have taken control of the only highway a few miles from Samaipata, right below the El Fuerte Inca temple. I find myself trapped, unable to head east to Santa Cruz nor west toward windswept La Paz, where tens of thousands of Aymara Indians are on the march.

I hire a Nissan bush taxi and head down to the roadblock. Our small car follows the shoulder, passing a hundred stalled buses and cargo trucks loaded with produce from the valleys—lettuce, tomatoes, squash, watermelon. Along the way my taxi driver curses the *collyas* up ahead for destroying the economy. We can finally go no farther into the impromptu parking lot, so I set out into the thick of the protest on foot. The *New York Times* has asked me to do an article on the Bolivia conflict, and I want to talk directly to the protesters.

The smell is the first thing to hit me. Body odor—there are neither showers nor even a stream in which to splash clean—blends with the scent of smoke and meat; women in polleras prepare food over open fires in the middle of the highway. Some of the protesters are lined up to receive a plastic bowl of quinoa soup with a single piece of stringy beef. Rainbow-checkered *huipalas,* or Indian unity flags, fly above men and women with the skin tone of the Indian majority: a dark brown that in the gathering dusk blends toward wine red. They are poor, all of them clad in tattered clothes, many covered with ponchos.

Another smell: fresh-cut foliage. They've not only dragged boulders onto the road, but have macheted down a dozen trees interspersed throughout the one-hundred-meter stretch separating the two lines of stopped vehicles. I glance above to see another thirty or forty Indians on a high embankment, machetes in hand. They are to let loose with rocks and crashing branches should the military intervene.

Perhaps rashly, I weave my way to a group of Indians who look to be the leaders and ask if I might speak with them, explaining it's for a foreign newspaper. "No time!" one of them snaps. "We're busy." Rather than standing around wondering whether this is sarcasm, which it undoubtedly is, I thank them and return to the edge of the crowd.

Glancing up at their rock-wielding comrades above, I question my wisdom at being here. Who among them can distinguish me from the foreign oilmen they'd like to oust? I stick to the outskirts and talk to those *being* blocked. But it's far from obvious who's who. The truck drivers and peasant travelers wear the same clothes and countenance as the protesters. Each time I find myself asking, "Blocking or blocked?" and they usually say, "Blocked!" before giving their forthright opinions, which are divided. About half are opposed, complaining about a day of work already lost. "The lettuce will be first to go," a dispirited farmer says, glancing nervously back at his cargo.

"How long will you wait?" I ask.

"I'll sleep here one more night, and then dump the lettuce and go back."

Most of the produce is being transported by hired drivers, who earn their two dollars a day no matter what. Many of them support the protesters. "They're fighting against the oligarchy," says one, "and for all Bolivians."

"Blocking or blocked?" I ask another group of four Quechuas spooning into a weak potato soup.

"Block*ing*!" one says.

I ask him why he's here, and the man robotically recites the same three demands Salvador did: nationalize gas, redo the constitution, and reject regional autonomy. When I press him a bit, he is unable to explain the nuances of each demand. Some observers use this as proof that these campesinos are hired guns. Otto Reich of the U.S. State Department recently said "everyone knows" that leftist Venezuelan president Hugo Chávez is funding Bolivia's Indian protesters.

This is not true. These men and women cannot explain how to rewrite a constitution because they've been neglected by their own government and are therefore illiterate. They have come not because of payments from a global communist conspiracy but because they are so poor it hurts. One of the men I talk to has only two molars left in the back of his mouth—tooth rot—though he's under twenty-five. Another stares at me through a single eye since the other is healed shut. His only eye doesn't leave my face; he's certainly never before seen a gringo. He and most of the other three hundred protesters here come from the deep countryside and are among the "extreme poor" earning less than a dollar a day.

I sense their anger toward me at first, not just in their abrasive answers but in their stiff postures. But as we continue chatting, I notice them loosening up, and the one-eyed man eventually passes a bag of coca leaves my way. As I thank him and stuff a few leaves in my mouth, they relax. "Why don't you come and block with us?" one asks, and the others agree, laughing. I tell them I have to get back to Samaipata. It's getting dark. On the taxi ride back to my house I wonder what it would have been like after dark, huddled on that mountain pass.

That roadblock stays up for three days and then suddenly comes down, even as the national protests continue into their second week. The campesinos I met on the highway retire to their villages, but within a day regroup with an expanded target. They plan not only to block the road again but also to take over the ultramodern Transredes petroleum plant I'd seen from my taxi.

News of the new blockade and pipeline takeover reaches the normally complacent Samaipata, and the church bells ring like never before. Loud and long they toll, and fifty villagers gather on the town square. Under the clanging bells one of the hotel owners rallies the troops, shouting out "No to roadblocks!" and "Autonomy now!" The group begins going door-to-door, pressuring, cajoling, and otherwise convincing other Samaipateños to join them. Around eighty people begin the march down from the old colonial part of town to "the gas station" or newer section of the town near the highway.

Samaipata is more than a niche ecology, at the nexus of Amazon, Andes, and Chaco—it's also a niche culture. With help from the fledgling European-established cafés, restaurants, tour services, and bungalows, people have found a somewhat prosperous way of life that they will defend from the *indios*. Referring to the people on the highway as *puro, t'ara, idiaco, cholango,* and *medio pelo,* they march down the hill until the enemy comes into sight.

Two small mobs: Samaipateños shouting "Autonomy!" and Indians crying out "A new constitution!" and "Nationalize Bolivia's gas!" They see each other for the first time and grab what they find around them—rocks, poles—and unsheathe machetes. The two groups stop for a moment, still several hundred meters apart, studying each other for weaknesses.

CHAPTER 35

T HE IMPENDING BATTLE of Samaipata is one detail
within a portrait of a radicalizing nation. Out in the
Chiquitano dry forests, on the road to the Paraguá Amazon,
Salvador leads another group of Indian roadblockers. In La
Paz, Evo says in a live CNN interview that the Indians have
added yet another demand: besides nationalizing petroleum,
President Mesa must step down to allow fresh elections. Mesa
responds that he will "serve his constitutional term through
2007" and "will not step down," adding that Bolivia is
"heading toward civil war."

The Bolivian news runs a rather ridiculous little piece of reportage every evening. It reminds me of one severe winter hur-
ricane during my Long Island childhood; my sister and I
listened to WBLI for a full hour until "Nassakeag Elementary"
was finally announced amid the endless list of school closings.
The reporter could simply have said, "All Long Island schools
are closed." Likewise, an oddly chipper Bolivian television an-
nouncer stands in front of a huge map covered with fiery flare-
ups indicating roadblock locations and says, "The following
highways are closed: La Paz–Oruro, Oruro–Cochabamba,
Cochabamba–Potosí, Potosí–Sucre, Cochabama–Santa Cruz,
Santa Cruz–Trinidad . . ." On and on through every single Bolivian highway, for a mind-boggling total of 109 roadblocks
covering all nine Bolivian states.

As a whole, global news coverage seems to sympathize with
the Indians. Sure, the *Wall Street Journal* downplays the events
and the *Economist* runs an article entitled MOB RULE IN

BOLIVIA. But the majority of U.S. and European media outlets call what is happening in Bolivia a unique example of "people power," even dipping a bit into the deeper waters of racism and marginalization.

But of more immediate concern is whether the movement will succeed or tip the country into anarchy. Across the border in Brazil, Sister Dorothy Stang, a well-known American nun now in her seventies, is repeatedly shot in the head and chest. She has long battled for the landless and to conserve rainforests in that country. Sister Dorothy was slain along with another environmental activist by gunmen tied to loggers and developers interested in moving deeper into the Amazon. Wisely, Brazil's populist president, Lula, immediately designates a large new reserve in the Brazilian Amazon in Sister Dorothy's honor, which helps reduce some of the rage. But such a high-profile killing in Bolivia could not so easily be diffused.

There's a phrase on everybody's lips: *Todo es posible*. Anything is possible. We don't know what will happen from one day to the next, including the very real possibility of a military putsch. Bolivia is the world's most coup-prone republic, and true to this part of its history, two left-leaning generals tell the press that President Mesa should "step aside and make room for a government of the people," a no-veiled reference to a leftist coup. But in the time it takes to eat a tasty Bolivian *salteña*, that idea is squashed by all strata of society, and the two generals are stuck in the broom closet. Coups are thankfully no longer an option; for two decades the country has run under the constitution, and everyone over thirty remembers that dictatorships are not fun.

However, Bolivian elites are itching for a leader who will "govern." Mesa, aware that more deaths would create deeper cycles of revenge and violence, has wisely announced he will not use force to break up roadblocks as his predecessor Goni did. Nevertheless, a restless oligarchy whispers of a coup from the right. Signals from the U.S. embassy suggest they would support someone like Santa Cruz millionaire Vaca Diez, who has promised to "govern" but only if he comes to power constitutionally; through a potential Mesa resignation, Vaca Diez, as Senate majority leader, would become president. Meanwhile, Mesa's position weakens by the day as he makes speech after ignored speech. All power lies with Evo, along with Jaime Solares and a few other populist leaders. That is, unless the military goes off on its own. *Todo es posible.*

I'm in Santa Cruz and seize a rare opportunity to meet with Salvador; he's briefly back to refresh supplies for the three hundred men and women protesters at his roadblock. We sit down at an outdoor buffet on the Plaza Blacutt, off the second ring. I look across the table at a changed Salvador. The erstwhile happy-go-lucky man with his featherlight bag now has worry etched into his brow, and some of the hugest black bags I've ever seen under someone's eyes.

"How are you?" I say. He's aged a decade on his actual thirty-eight years. His clothes are soiled and his hair matted against his scalp. Salvador's mouth is clamped shut, his cheeks stubbly leather pouches.

"My neighbor in Porvenir died two days ago of malaria," he says, looking away from me, his slumped figure profiled against the blue sky and greenery of the plaza's palm, paquío, tajibo, and almendrillo. "And my youngest child has it. Bad. He's sweating like crazy in bed now. I don't know if I should stay with the roadblock or head back to Porvenir."

Salvador's face is so tense that I feel a tear must simply burst out. In my mind, one does form and rushes down his face. A bundle of emotion unravels, and I suddenly understand something about why I'm back in Bolivia, and why for me Salvador's son must get better and his roadblock succeed.

* * *

It has always stayed with me: the antilittering television ad that ran constantly in the United States for a period in the late seventies. It had just a single image for the full thirty seconds: a solemn American Indian looks into the camera while a voice-over explains what whites have done to the ancient North American landscape. As the ad finishes, a single tear rushes down the Indian's face.

The ad was effective; roadside littering went down. Most people did not know that the spot was funded by a conservative business lobby *opposed* to recycling legislation. Environmentalists had at the time been using images of roadside trash as a rationale for "bottle bills" in many states, and the private-sector consortium ran the ad to convince people to stop throwing trash out the windows on their own, without additional government regulations. Ironically, the spot had the opposite effect of raising ecological consciousness and hastening along recycling laws. Being eight or nine years old at the time, I knew nothing of the politics behind that haunting Indian face. I just sat there mesmerized each time I saw it, waiting for the tear to drop.

The ad woke me up to the strange words all around Long Island. In our first town, Ronkonkoma, I attended Cayuga Pre-School; when we moved to Setauket, I transferred to Nassakeag Elementary. Both towns and schools carried Indian names but no Indians. My little sister, Amy, and I would search for arrowheads along the banks of the Nissequogue River; like the arrowheads we'd unearth, the exotic words all around us had lost their sharpness and function. They provided a historical dimension to the sameness of suburbia, but nobody seemed to know what they meant.

At our local beach, Amy and I would collect stones everyone called "Indian paint pots" and spit into the hollowed-out rocks, watching the ancient tincture come to life, thick and rich. We'd smear each other's face with brown and rust-red until we became warriors. I'd windsurf out into Long Island Sound in full war-paint, lowering my sail into the salt water when I was far enough out to hear nothing from the shore, gazing at the cliff-hanging mansions and wondering what Long Island used to be like.

During the seventies and eighties many wild spaces still existed near my home, interspersed with the subdivisions. There was a pine forest in front of Nassakeag Elementary, and Springer's Farm beside it. Amy and I traversed the cabbage rows into the forest to hunt for box turtles or arrowheads— there were still plenty of both. Recently though, as adults, we returned to Setauket to visit a close family friend on her deathbed. It was Christmas Eve, and we took the LIE out from the city to the appropriate exit, little surprised that our poky little Long Island town now had the edgier feel of Nassau. New box stores and mini-mansions had replaced pines and cabbages.

"Do you remember the sweat lodge?" Amy said. I nodded. A long-bearded organic farmer a couple of towns over led sweats and even put up a tepee once. We used to volunteer sometimes in his soup kitchen. "I wonder," Amy said, "if he still has that sweat lodge."

As we passed my old elementary school's pillared colonial front, a scene from Mr. Culcan's third-grade class arose in my memory. During math one day, a spirited chant began in the fourth-grade group next door, the words spilling into our classroom: "Andrew Jackson killed the Indians! Jackson killed the Indians! Jackson killed the Indians!" They sounded as if they were having a heck of a good time with their new teacher, Ms. Goldberg.

Mr. Culcan strode over to the door and shut it a little too loudly, muttering to himself about "liberal commies." When he got back to the board, he looked out at us, his class, as if surprised to see us gathered. We all stared back at him. As we waited for something to happen, the chant was muted but still quite audible through the wall. Mr. Culcan stood in front of an unsolved equation on the board, stroking his thick brown mustache (which everyone said he utilized to store boogers for later snacking purposes), considering what to do. Finally, he launched into a defense of former president Jackson that had something to do with Manifest Destiny. I don't remember much of Mr. Culcan's explanation, but how could I ever forget those piping voices we weren't supposed to hear? *Jackson killed the Indians! Jackson killed the Indians! Jackson killed the Indians!*

Later in life I would come across something Lieutenant James Calhoun wrote before the Wounded Knee massacre, while serving under George Armstrong Custer:

The hives of industry will take the place of dirty wigwams. Civilization will ere long reign supreme and throw heathen barbarism into oblivion. Seminaries of learning will raise their proud cupolas far above the canopy of Indian lodges, and Christian temples will elevate their lofty spires upward towards the azure sky while places of heathen mythology will sink to rise no more. This will be a period of true happiness.

The Christian churches do tower today above the occasional replica wigwam—but is this a period of true happiness?

Another childhood memory bubbled up when I looked into Salvador's distressed eyes: It is a freezing winter day on Long Island, a couple of weeks after the chanting in Ms. Goldberg's class. I'm walking up the hill to my home from Nassakeag. The road has been plowed and sanded, and honeycombed ice crunches under my boots. I'm chanting about Jackson and the Indians to the rhythm of my steps, as I've unconsciously come to do sometimes. Icicles hang from all the awnings, dripping into snowdrifts, beaming on this day with a prismatic light, like strange daggers, and I wonder what it would be like to push one into my thigh or forearm. And then I'm suddenly crying, like that Indian on television, except mine is not a single large tear but a stream of little ones falling onto ice. I've messed up the chant and have been telling myself rhythmically, like a heartbeat, *I killed the Indians, I killed the Indians, I killed the Indians.*

"You should go back to your children," I say to Salvador. "The roadblock could turn into a bloodbath."

He nods vaguely and looks out over Plaza Blacutt; he's well aware of the militia activity. "Where are the government health workers to help my son? Isn't it *our* government? The Indian majority must come to power," he says, before adding with an ironic half-smile, "It's about time."

"What will you do?" I'm focused on Salvador's face; the plaza's trees behind him sound like rich static and look like a fuzzy green screen. In his face I see the Indian from the littering ad; thousands along the Trail of Tears; and millions of others whose acres were removed by my own government through four hundred broken treaties. But when I look at Salvador, I see another chance. There is still a place, a country, where words like *Nassakeag* and *Cayuga, Nissequogue* and *Setauket,* hold meaning even today, rising from the lips of a two-thirds majority.

After a long moment Salvador stands up and tells me he's staying at the roadblock. I know it's possible I'll never see him again, and I know what I must say to him, something terribly foolish on the surface. For me this is about more than one Indian Territory, a novel global-warming experiment, or even the fate of a nation and what that means to the world. As absurd as it is, I need to tell Salvador I'm sorry.

But there's a check being paid, and a taxi swiftly hailed, and Salvador is talking about his "brothers at the roadblock" and how he must get back to them before any harm comes, and then he's gone.

CHAPTER 36

T HE ROCKS START flying in Samaipata.
One Indian goes down immediately with a concussion, and Samaipata's subgovernor takes a stone in the forehead, opening a bloody gash. Another Samaipateño takes one in the head and it "peels back his scalp like the skin of a mango," as someone describes it later. The Quechuas, outnumbered and sustaining more injuries, retreat into the hills in the direction of La Yunga's fern forest. The Samaipateños follow them, but feel a shower of stones hail down on them. One Indian takes a thwack in the head with a wooden pole and cries out. When the last of the would-be roadblockers disappear over the hill, a cheer goes up among the Samaipateños. The petroleum pipeline and road will remain open.

The villagers I speak with burst with pride. *Nothing* ever happens in Samaipata, and they'd gotten up and succeeded at something. One rather nerdy guy named Able, who gives weak, clammy handshakes, tells me he'd "served the home-land" (*hice la patria*) in routing "those *collyas*." But beneath a stripe of racism is a deeper vein preceding the tourism boom. The people in Samaipata are neither *cambas* nor *collyas,* but rather Samaipateños who cling to their status quo. Perhaps they see any protests as the beginning of a guerrilla force like the FARC, which controls half of Colombia, and the now routed Shining Path from neighboring Peru.

Bolivia's Aymaras and Quechuas are not the Shining Path; there have been no kidnappings or violent militant behavior. Bolivia's majority use nonviolent tactics—hunger strikes, marches, and economy-paralyzers such as shutting down pipelines and roads—and have responded with rocks and poles only when they've been attacked, as happened in Samaipata. More than anything, the folks in Samaipata see the roadblocks as, well, *weird*. It's not a baptism, wedding, funeral, or any of the other centuries-old traditions performed around here. Samaipateños have not heard of Gandhi, King, Mandela, or any of the other examples of civil disobedience that have changed unjust regimes, so they have little context to grasp the why of roadblocks.

Which makes this area, the southern flank of Amboró, exceptional in Bolivia. With the whole country shut down, the only road that has reopened is the one leading from Santa Cruz to my home in Samaipata. There had been two blockages, Samaipata and El Torno—and the latter fared even worse.

In El Torno, Santa Cruz Youth swept in with their white shields blazed with the green *cruzeño* cross, descending upon the two hundred farmers blocking El Torno, and "whipped them like dogs," a witness told me. The emaciated Quechuas, hungry from days at the blockade and general rural poverty, were easily beaten by the well-fed Youth. Another woman who was there said, "It was like beating a woman or a child. It was cowardly, because the Indians were hungry. They pegged them with rocks as they were running away."

The roadblocks enter their eighteenth day. Of the original 109 there are still 107, only El Torno and Samaipata opened. Rumors surface that if the country remains blocked one day more, there will be a militia-led massacre in Salvador's part of the Chiquitania.

Rather than return to Samaipata, I remain in Santa Cruz, because there is a decent chance my ex-girlfriend from La Paz, Anaí, will fly in from La Paz this evening if she can make it via back roads to the airport in El Alto. She recently returned home after stints in the States and Europe. She's started a Zen meditation center in La Paz and now directs a major Bolivian agency working on climate change. She tells me she wants to "ensure her country's growth pattern is less carbon intensive," adding that this involves spiritual work as well as political.

Daniel is also in town, and not for the first time since I've returned. He swoops in every month or so to get drunk. His wife, Gayle, e-mailed me to look after him a bit. "He gets depressed every time he goes to Bolivia." When I ask her why he keeps coming, she says she can't figure it out.

I'm to meet Daniel at the Gold Time karaoke. His choice. I can't say I'm looking forward to it and secretly hope Anaí will make it, thereby giving me a good excuse to bow out early. With time on my hands before Gold Time, I go for Chinese. The restaurant has an unfortunate name if you know English: Poo Ping. A water turtle in a fish tank greets you on the way in, and the place is decorated with the type of kitschy art found in Chinese restaurants everywhere. The sole customer, I order and ask the server, "What part of China are you from?" I say this slowly, carefully, in Spanish and receive a look of incomprehension in return. I ask the same question even slower.

"*Qué?!*" he asks sharply.

I triangulate, "How long have you lived in Bolivia?"

"*Cuatro años*"—four years—he says.

"And before you came here . . . four years ago . . . where in China did you live?"

"China," he says, and I realize what's going on. In his four years here no one has asked him this. Why on earth would anyone wonder where he was from in China? "Are you from Sichuan? Beijing?"

Now two other waiters have gathered around for the show, and the three of them talk excitedly in Chinese as the revelation builds. They laugh in controlled spurts as each proudly announces a province and city.

After eating, I stand outside the restaurant under the neon sign (COMIDA CHINA: POO PING) and look left and right. Where's Gold Time? I start walking along the third ring. The day is fading into dusk, and it's chilly. A *surazo* is blowing up from Antarctica, and anyway we're getting toward Bolivia's New Year's Day: June 21. It's not only the southern winter solstice and coldest day of the year, but also the day the Aymaran calendar flips from year 5512 to 5513 and indigenous Bolivians ritually remain awake until dawn, stretching out open palms to receive the first light of the rising sun. Despite the crisis, the usual crew of hundreds of city sanitation workers continue to scour the streets of trash for nine hours nightly, by hand, in exchange for two dollars from city hall. There are no public trash receptacles; people use the streets, which are emptied of litter each night.

Two doormen usher me into Gold Time's warmly lit entrance. Inside, against a casinoesque backdrop of Mercedes logos, beach scenes, and dreamy karaoke videos on large screens, sits a single customer, Daniel, lost in a book. He's squinting to read it while bringing a whiskey to his lips. Even from a distance I can see how skinny he's gotten, and when I approach him, it's harrowing—his beard sinks into two holes where his fleshy cheeks used to be.

He tosses the book to me and says, *"IQ 83."* That's the title on the cover. "It's science fiction crap, about these scientists who unleash a certain toxin that makes everyone on the planet's IQ slowly drop and level off at eighty-three. The scientists are the only ones immune, and they're struggling to reverse it."

He signals to one of the several waiters lingering by the bar. "It's also the story of Bolivia . . . Another whiskey, please." I glance at the drink menu and for some reason say, "Sex on the beach." Daniel gives me a look, and the disinterested waiter nods.

"So, how's Argentina?"

"Argentina is wonderful! I live on the beach. There's brine-enriched air . . . and the people are *intelligent*. Unlike here where IQs are quickly approaching eighty-three."

"So you don't like the roadblocks?"

"Of course they have to get their revenge for Goni's massacre. And everything else."

"So what exactly are you saying, Daniel?"

He drains his whiskey, record time, and signals for another. "What I'm saying is that I was the walrus, but now I'm John."

The conversation continues like this. We don't talk about his relationship with his wife and their child, or his cancer. But I know about these things from Gayle. The cancer has gotten worse and there's no going back. But their relationship has, somehow, improved. She's been nursing him, traveling less, convincing him to ease up on his "round-the-worlders."

Milli Vanilli's "Girl You Know It's True" comes on the karaoke screen. I could get up and take the mike, but I can't really sing, and, besides, singing Milli Vanilli is depressingly akin to mimicking an air guitarist. I finally say, "Gayle told me what you're doing with her company. I think it's great." Daniel paid big money to launch a new company that links Indian producers, including some of the ones with whom I work, with first-world consumers.

"Capitalism is under threat," Daniel says. "I'm doing it because I like capitalism, and I want it to survive."

"You're doing the right thing."

He stands with a slight swagger, slaps too much money on the table, and says he's heading back to Los Tajibos, Suite 101. And I don't need to thank him because he's "not doing what's right but what's necessary." Seeing him set to leave, both doormen have already swung the doors open into the dark street outside. Before turning to go, Daniel says, "It's like Beckett said: 'You're on earth, there's no cure for that.'" I watch Daniel goose-step past the doormen, raising his right hand in a high salute, and vanish.

I sit alone in Gold Time, draining a post–Poo Ping sex on the beach to the rhythms of Milli Vanilli. It is definitely time to go. I hail a taxi out front and ask the cabbie to just drive. I leave a message on Anaí's voice mail, asking her if she's coming. The driver says I'm his first ride in two hours; no one's out because there's no work and no money. He speaks wistfully about Salta, Argentina, where he lived for a while: "They have four public universities there. *Four.*

"And the government helps poor people. Here there's only one public university and it's all connections. *La corrupción.* There are no scholarships here. How am I going to pay tuition?

"I've got a kid. That was my big mistake. My girlfriend got pregnant when we were both eighteen. Now he's four. I work and just make enough to support him. I love him, but I want an education. I want a way out." He starts talking about an idea; he'll produce, fill, and sell fire extinguishers. "Nobody has them. The hardest part will be to convince people they need them."

He's silent for a while and finally says that Bolivia is divided into two groups: half who want to work and another half who want to block the others from working. This gets me chuckling, and he laughs too, and before long we're both in hysterics. And then after a while we're not laughing, and it's just the slow curve of the third ring ahead, and I ask him to take me home.

"You know I met a woman the other day in Samaipata," I say. "She named her kid MacGyver."

"MacGyver," he says, pronouncing it *MacGeever*. He knows about the American TV action hero who refuses to use guns, instead making do with whatever he has around him to achieve impossible goals. A lightbulb makes an excellent set of lockpicks; some duct tape and a dough scraper can ground a helicopter; a credit card can cause a traffic jam. Apt, after all, that MacGyver is so popular in the Bolivian imagination.

My cell phone rings. *Finally,* Anaí. "I'm stuck in La Paz, behind the roadblocks," she says, out of breath. "And have you heard? It just happened five minutes ago: President Mesa stepped down."

CHAPTER 37

WITH MESA'S RESIGNATION, the presidential sash is passed to Hormando Vaca Diez, the sixty-year-old, big-bellied head of the Senate. Though he seems jolly enough, Vaca Diez's scruffy head of hair and apparent fondness for ill-fitting suits is a studied neglect; the politician would like constituents to forget he's a powerful Santa Cruz *haciendado* and cattle baron.

It wasn't supposed to happen this way. The protesters thought they had made a deal: Mesa would resign, followed by Vaca Diez, and House leader Mario Cossío. The fourth in line, Supreme Court leader Eduardo Rodriguez, would then become interim president, constitutionally triggering early elections. But an unexpected fear has risen; there is no guarantee Vaca Diez will keep his word. At a press conference the cattle rancher postures presidential and is evasive about his plans. Mesa, feeling betrayed, goes public to demand Vaca Diez resign.

I cross the Santa Cruz plaza toward the café where I'm to meet Len. Bolivians are gathered in front of the cathedral, clutching "peace candles" and calling for Vaca Diez's resignation. My mind is stuck on what Anaí told me on the phone: she fears a military crackdown. She has not forgotten the strong-armed rule from her pre-1982 childhood: socialists and Indians were regularly found murdered, sometimes with broken bottles in their rectums. Throughout the Latin American region even mildly critical professors or health promoters "were disappeared." The juntas did what they wished with impunity.

Meanwhile, citizens surround the national congress in La Paz, forcing senators and congressmen to evacuate the capital via airplane for an emergency joint session in Sucre. Tensions rise. Indians have reportedly been cutting neckties off businessmen; Israel and France evacuate their nationals; and the U.S. Peace Corps pulls all Bolivia volunteers off their posts.

I climb the steps to the recently opened Café Lorca on the corner of the plaza. Its ambience blends old and new: the two-hundred-year-old colonial building with a courtyard is decorated with enormous puppets and abstract paintings of vaginas. Two men play violins while a few customers on sofas sip red wine. I order maracuja juice and take it out on the balcony, gazing down at the plaza's lush tree canopy and the hundreds of candles.

Len arrives, orders a drink, and comes out onto the balcony, but stops suddenly, looking slightly unsteady. He glances left and right, then takes a sip of his drink.

"What's the matter?"

"Temporary disorientation," he says. "But like a good Amazonian I centered myself on two distant points: the cathedral and that building over there."

We talk about Vaca Diez. If he stays put through military force, Bolivia could be added to two unfortunate lists—the World Bank's thirty "low income countries under stress" (Licus) and the British international development service's (DFID) forty-six "fragile states"—as it slides into a Haiti-esque anarchy. We worry too that Vaca Diez could unleash the army on the roadblocks, harming Salvador and others, and later exact revenge on Indians through further stonewalling or definitively curtailing their IT claims.

Len and I look down from the balcony. A hundred sausage-sized cacti eat away at a clay roof across the street; beside it, a papaya tree thrusts up through another crumbling affair, its sagging orange-yellow-colored fruits resting and rotting on the remaining *tejas*. Epiphytes burst from telephone wires and tajibos, a dozen colored flowerettes that blow in the cool *surazo* wind. "Bolivians are fatalistic," Len says. "Why do you think we build vegetable roofs and mud walls? The roofs get blown off in big winds, and the clay washed away in floods."

"Indians blocking the whole country for a month doesn't sound fatalistic," I say.

"It's because they don't fear death," he says, and I picture Salvador out in the dark Chiquitania right now, bonfires on the highway. "We're intimate with death because we are still so close to nature. Predator and prey; the way the jungle foliage penetrates even our biggest cities." He indicates the plants taking apart walls and roofs across the street; the sound of the violin duet streams out from inside.

Len shakes his head. "Those violins. There should be Quechuas hired to play walaychos in there." He talks about what he thinks is a new idea but sounds to me like something quite familiar. "If two people are going for the same job," he says, "we should give preference to the Indian. We must start to change."

"You mean affirmative action."

He touches his large eyeglasses and tries out the phrase in his mouth (*acción afirmativa*), and we lapse into silence, looking out over the plaza as the *surazo* moves in the palm trees, extinguishing candles.

The following afternoon I return to the plaza.

The overcast sky is striped with blue, not sure which way it will go, and the atmosphere of the crowd around me balances midway between vigil and festival. The country remains fully blocked, and the protests have intensified around Sucre, where an emergency joint session of congress is meeting to decide the nation's fate. Last night, the first protester was killed by the military, pushing tensions toward but fortunately not over the breaking point. An overwhelming sentiment says that Vaca Diez must step down to make room for Eduardo Rodriguez and fresh elections.

Civil war seemed a plausible scenario just this morning as Vaca Diez remained defiant. But additional hunger strikes and vigils like this one have bolstered the roadblocks, sending a yet stronger citizen message that the man must resign—and it now appears he will. Unofficial word has leaked out of Sucre that Vaca Diez will soon make the announcement.

More people swell the plaza, mostly families, producing a slightly Sunday feel, despite its being midweek and amid a major meltdown. The *cafezhino* guys are out with their thermoses, and I even spot a man in a starched white shirt selling animal-shaped balloons. Plenty of FAN's staff is here, including Gisela and some conservation-science staff, some participating in the vigil but others gathered out of a herd instinct: that desire to congregate in a crisis. There is some tentative hugging and backslapping, but no one is completely celebrating quite yet. Nor is anyone sloth-gazing, the three-toed critters having been relocated to the city zoo. Biologists had long complained that the sloths were on the brink of starvation since the trees lacked the nutrients they need. Sloth movements were recorded as low as three millimeters an hour, but it took several of the animals' plunging to their death on the plaza to get the city government to act.

Smithers walks by—holding hands with Raquela, a FAN accountant. I do a double take since I know Smithers is married. Noticing my reaction, he excuses himself from Raquela and approaches me.

"It's not what you think," Smithers says. "My wife and I separated last month and are getting a divorce. I'm in love with Raquela." He says that he'd married at nineteen and now has little in common with his provincial wife. More people stream into the Santa Cruz main square around us—as they do right now into a hundred other Bolivian plazas, awaiting the final news. I look back at Smithers, whose hair is no longer gelled firmly to his head. After his Argentina trip he became less embarrassed about being *indio*. He is still a modernizer, but, quirkily enough, it has now become "modern" to make your living as a neo-primitive jungle-oxygen rancher.

I ask him about his two-year-old son, and he explains he will share custody with his ex. "That's the hardest part," he says, as the sun briefly illuminates his slightly anxious expression. "Can I ask you a favor?"

Anything he wants, I tell him.

"I'm asking people to use my birth name, Cirilio. I don't like Smithers anymore."

"Okay . . . Cirilio."

Raquela comes over and joins us, taking Cirilio's hand, and he kisses her on the cheek. We all chat for a while, and then he asks me, "Do you think you'll ever settle down?"

I tell him my fellowship in Samaipata is almost up, and I have not yet made plans. What I don't tell him is about several conversations I've had with Anaí. The two of us have gone in very different directions emotionally since we split up in La Paz two years ago. She's more convinced than ever that the "oppressive coupledom" and kids would cramp her dedication to reducing poverty and healing the biosphere, whereas I have become ever more certain I'm ready to start a family—for many reasons, one of which has to do with Salvador. I told Anaí that he showed me how the intimate love of a wife and children doesn't get in the way of more universal ideals; quite to the contrary, Salvador's family is what fuels his commitment.

I could hear Anaí's slanted smile as she said over the phone, "But this goes totally against the way you've lived life up till now."

"Exactly," I replied, feeling suddenly hopeful. "Maybe that's exactly the point."

But now—on the swelling Santa Cruz plaza—I'm thinking about Salvador's child. Cirilio tells me his malaria has gotten worse, and that Salvador will head straight to Porvenir to be with him when the roadblocks come down.

Then Cirilio starts talking about a new threat to Kempff. He just got word over the radio from a troubled ranger: Brazilians, under the cover of all the social unrest in Bolivia, have quietly been invading the park through "marrying" Kusasu's granddaughters and the other nearly assimilated Guarasug'wé young women, settling with them in Bella Vista. Through these quasi-marriages they gain the special Guarasug'wé right to hunt and farm in the park. "They've already slashed and burned dozens of acres in the heart of Kempff and plan to go deeper."

As unforeseeable as this was, in retrospect it makes perfect economic sense; land prices across the border in Rondônia are sky-high, and this is a clever way for landless Brazilians to get free farms. Incongruously—in light of this terrible news about Kempff—Cirilio and Raquela begin to smile. A distant cheer spreads toward us like a breeze heralding rain. The sound crescendos, echoing off the stucco façades, and soon people are hugging, dancing, and igniting fireworks under the palms, tajibos, and almendrillos. Vaca Diez has stepped down and Eduardo Rodriguez is president of Bolivia.

CHAPTER 38

O NE SIDE IS green, the other brown. Looking down
from the plane, I see ecology on one side, economy on
the other, split by a river. This is the border between Bolivia
and Brazil.

I've already seen the satellite images revealing the stark green-
brown division between the two countries, but this is my first
flight over the divide, as I head to Piso Firme to meet Salvador.
To my left: *fazendas* and industrial soy fields, roads lined with
streetlights, and sport-fishing camps. To my right: Kempff's
teeming wilderness; verdant, shocking sheets of green. The pilot
banks the plane, following the river's contour, and I spot Bella
Vista, where two years ago I visited the Guarasug'wé. An enormous change has taken place in that short time—Brazil has bled
into Bolivia. Brazilians have indeed crossed over with machetes
and coffee seedlings and with military efficiency have clear-cut
old-growth forest within Kempff.

Salvador and I are not alone in the river. Moonlight smears
out across the water's surface from where we bathe, illuminat-
ing the occasional Amazon swimmer backstroking home. Below are the usual dangers—meter-long electric fish, stingrays,
caiman, and the omnipresent piranhas. The wind in the trees
above sounds like a fire, and all around us are jaguars. With
increased community awareness about hunting, the jaguar
population has spiked, and seventy percent of Kempff safari-
goers now spot the sleek cats.

Tomorrow at dawn Salvador will take a motorized canoe upriver to Guarasug'wé country to lead a mediation team dialoguing with the Brazilian "spouses." His goal, he told me this afternoon, is "to protect Kempff from these invaders." He had spent the last several days by his youngest son's bedside, as the small boy's sweaty body gradually cooled to 98.6. It was a close call, but his malaria is gone and the boy will live. When Salvador speaks about the revolution and what it has wrought, I know he is talking more than anything about what it has achieved for his family.

Bolivia has changed forever. The indigenous movements have ousted two presidents within twenty months. Remarkably, only one person was killed in twenty-two days of roadblocks, showing incredible restraint on the part of all Bolivians. President Rodriguez has announced a date for new national elections, and preparations for a constituent assembly to rewrite the constitution are under way. Salvador will represent his people at this assembly and also run for congress. He sees the successful revolt as meaning a near shoo-in for a legal Indian Territory within a year. And with the eco-timber business booming, Salvador feels they will have more clout to pressure the government for better malaria prevention and treatment, and other basic needs.

The Group of Eight (G8) meeting followed on the heels of Bolivia's much televised revolution, leading to an important announcement: Bolivia's entire debt to the IMF and the World Bank—roughly two billion dollars—will be forgiven. It's clean-slate time since the world's first Indian democracy may be close at hand. Coincidentally, Russia simultaneously became the 127th nation to ratify Kyoto, bringing the protocol into legal force, even without U.S. participation. The Amazon Project's corporate partners are buoyed by this news and will continue to support Kempff and add similar projects around the globe as the clock ticks toward 2008, when the first Kyoto targets must be met.

As I float beside Salvador, both of us now fully washed, our faces to the moon, I wonder at the difficult road ahead. A nation cannot flourish amid polarizing racial hatred. But should Salvador enter congress, I do not see him exacting revenge on former oppressors, because he will have achieved his goal: a territorial home and the hope that his children will live in a fairer, freer society. His voice—the voice of roadblocking—has given him and the Indians a hard-won respect. Though a few elites here, as in *Hamlet,* "exclaim against their own succession," most had to be made to feel the harsh blowback of their own prejudice. Now Guillermo Roy and others *must* reach across the chasm if they are to do business at all. This is how social change ultimately happens: enlightened values do not change behavior; the contours of self-interest are altered and new values rush into the vacuum.

When I finally roll out of my float, I'm startled to see Salvador right in front of me, not five feet away. His head tilts slightly to one side, and his large eyes reflect back some of the moonlight. In his rather wordy way, he thanks me for "all you have done to help the Chiquitano people," and then he wades a bit closer, crossing the final few feet between us, and lays a thick hand on my shoulder. Reflexively, I place my hand on his shoulder.

At dawn the next morning I watch his boat disappear around the river bend and can still feel the weight of his hand. Neither my own government, nor the vast majority of other governments in the hemisphere, have apologized to indigenous people for the genocide perpetrated against them. Perhaps that is part of why I've wanted to tell Salvador I am sorry, but now I know it would do nothing to atone for Jackson's Trail of Tears, the extinction crisis, or the artificial heating of the globe. The river dividing nature from civilization is within me. I must forgive myself, and in this moment I begin to do so.

Well-known futurists have published books entitled *The Ul-timate Resource, The Bottomless Well,* and *Hope for the Fu-ture,* positing that we are our own hope, the human mind the ultimate resource, and our ingenuity a bottomless well. The only brake to progress, these "cornucopians" proclaim with punch-the-air optimism, is a lack of imagination. While they are right that the human spirit is marvelous, they neglect the most important thing: our essential creaturehood. We live beneath a flowering tree supporting seven skies, on a planet large enough for wild places the size of nations. That which we allow to exist, to flourish freely according to its own rhythms, is superior to anything our little hands create.

A breeze ripples across the Paraguá River, scattering lime-green butterflies on the riverbank like blown leaves, sending goose bumps to the surface of my skin, and whispering something to me both mysterious and clear. The breeze plays in the fronds of assai trees, which inhale carbon dioxide and exhale oxygen; I too exhale, the wind carrying my breath upstream to where Salvador races away along a river dividing two possible futures. Salvador grows in size even as he becomes smaller; he is all the nearer with distance. In the delicate space between us lies the hope.

SOURCES

Information has mushroomed to the point where much of it is now *exformation*—data that enters but a few minds. Rather than mincing matters yet finer, I strove to fashion a holistic account of how global wealth, poverty, ecology, and power play out in one South American country. In doing so I have distilled liberally from a wide range of sources; I present some of the more significant ones here both to acknowledge my debt to the authors and suggest further reading:

Ecology
David Abram's *The Spell of the Sensuous* is one of those books you carry around in a backpack for weeks after finishing it, just to feel the afterglow. It lyrically blends linguistics and philosophy in a way that allows us to hear nature as oral peoples do. The late Edward Abbey's work, particularly his masterpiece *Desert Solitaire,* lives within me and percolates up in these pages. I hope Paul Hawken will forgive my grafting of his *Natural Capitalism* into the Bolivian Amazon. *Environmental Leadership in Developing Countries: Transnational Relations and Biodiversity Policy in Costa Rica and Bolivia* by Paul Steinberg provided a thorough analysis of the Bolivian environmental movement. And, as usual, some of Thoreau's *Walden* has inevitably slipped in.

Globalization
My thinking on U.S. foreign policy, the ecological crisis, and advertising have undoubtedly been influenced by Noam Chomsky, whose *Manufacturing Consent* (written with Edward S. Herman)

fulfills Kafka's imperative that a book be "an axe for the frozen sea inside us." The clear logic and good humor of Jagdish Bhagwati's *In Defense of Globalization* provided a sense of balance. And I am grateful for John Ralston Saul's *Harper's* piece "The Collapse of Globalism and the Rebirth of Nationalism" and John Gerard Ruggie's articles and talks on the "unbundling of territoriality."

Philosophy/Ethics

Bill McKibben's seminal 1989 book *The End of Nature* helped me and so many others become conscious of our responsibility vis-à-vis climate change. Joseph Campbell's *The Power of Myth* contextualized what would have been puzzling Amazonian lore. Vicki Robin's writings and activism at the Center for a New American Dream—along with that of others of the Slow Movement—hint at ways Westerners might live more harmoniously atop Pacha Mama, as does Eric Brende's *Better Off*, which relates his intriguing path from MIT scientist to St. Louis soapmaker and rickshaw driver.

International Development

Harvard professor Paul Farmer's work in global public health, as so vividly conveyed in Tracy Kidder's *Mountains Beyond Mountains*, inspired intense debates in Samaipata during the revision of this book. I credit Arturo Escobar's *Encountering Development* as my first exposure to a radical critique of the development industry. The writings and teachings of American University's Dr. Robin Broad continue to influence me.

Bolivia/Latin America

Anthropologist Kevin Healy's friendship and his colorful study of indigenous grassroots development in Bolivia, *Llamas, Weavings, and Organic Chocolate,* are part of what lured me into the Andes in the first place. I drew several facts and quotes from Jim Shultz's work at the Democracy Center and Juan Forero's Bolivia coverage in the *New York Times*. Jürgen Riester's decades of research on Bolivia's indigenous people was invaluable; Geoffrey O'Connor's *Amazon Journal* provided a parallel context in neighboring Brazil. For Bolivian history I leaned on Herbert S. Klein's *Bolivia: The Evolution of a Multi-Ethnic Society*. Finally, Lesley Gill's *Teetering on the Rim: Global Restructuring, Daily Life, and the Armed Retreat of the Bolivian State* enriched my understanding of Bolivian social movements.

ACKNOWLEDGMENTS

Thank you Faith Krinsky, Eric Morrisey, Pierre Ibisch, Alex Rogers, Jack Groves, Jacques Shillings, Cole Genge, Jenny Perez, Judy Quinn, Gisela Ulloa, Mike Tidwell, Ingrid Cortez, Karin Columba, Richard Vaca, and William Clark. Thank you to my mother, a fine editor; and to my father, Amy, and Andrew. The deft hand of my editor at Bloomsbury, Gillian Blake, helped guide the book through several drafts.

My gratitude once again to the Open Door Foundation for a second fellowship at the Artist's House in Samaipata, where much of this book was written.

Stan Crawford was my organic agriculture coach during a summer vineyard-sitting near Taos, New Mexico, in 1995; he has become both friend and writing mentor. His beautiful nonfiction (*Mayordomo*; *A Garlic Testament*) and fiction (e.g., *Petroleum Man*) have inspired me, as have his careful critiques of my work.

The very heart of this book comes from four years among Bolivia's people, including thousands of conversations and interviews and several rich and enduring friendships. To all of the people of the Bajo Paraguá Amazon I extend my deepest heartfelt thanks for welcoming me into *nosotros*.

A NOTE ON THE AUTHOR

WILLIAM POWERS has worked for over a decade in development aid in Latin America, Africa, Washington, D.C., and Native North America. His project in the Bolivian Amazon won a 2003 prize for environmental innovation from Harvard's John F. Kennedy School of Government. He is the author of the Liberia memoir *Blue Clay People*.

- What is the Kyoto Protocol & what does it have to do with Bolivia?

- What are the ecological & human benefits of the rainforests?

- What the there is a crisis in Indian Territory

- What examples are there of globalization in Indian Territory?